Contributions to Economics

The series *Contributions to Economics* provides an outlet for innovative research in all areas of economics. Books published in the series are primarily monographs and multiple author works that present new research results on a clearly defined topic, but contributed volumes and conference proceedings are also considered. All books are published in print and ebook and disseminated and promoted globally. The series and the volumes published in it are indexed by Scopus and ISI (selected volumes).

Eduardo da Motta e Albuquerque

Technological Revolutions and the Periphery

Understanding Global Development Through Regional Lenses

Springer

Eduardo da Motta e Albuquerque
Economics
Universidade Federal de Minas Gerais
Belo Horizonte, Minas Gerais, Brazil

ISSN 1431-1933 ISSN 2197-7178 (electronic)
Contributions to Economics
ISBN 978-3-031-43435-8 ISBN 978-3-031-43436-5 (eBook)
https://doi.org/10.1007/978-3-031-43436-5

This Springer imprint is published by the registered company Springer Nature Switzerland AG
The registered company address is: Gewerbestrasse 11, 6330 Cham, Switzerland

Paper in this product is recyclable.

This book is dedicated to Cláudia and Pedro.

Acknowledgments

The stimulating and collaborative intellectual environment at the Department of Economics and Cedeplar-UFMG is a key element driving the research that led to this book. My colleagues at UFMG are a permanent source of learning – many thanks to all.

Very special thanks to the students that have attended classes in various disciplines in undergraduate and graduate courses at Cedeplar and Face-UFMG since 2014 – *Revoluções tecnológicas e a periferia* (ECN 936), *Economia da Ciência e da Tecnologia* (ECN 978), *Microeconomia IV* (ECN 212), *Microeconomia Evolucionária* (ECN 010), *Sistemas complexos e teoria econômica* (ECN 956), *Variedades de Capitalismo e a Periferia* (ECN 063), *Revoluções tecnológicas e a dinâmica centro-periferia* (ECN 098), *Economia Política* (ECN 055), *História e Interpretação da Sociedade Contemporânea* (ECN 215), *Sistemas Econômicos Comparados* (ECN 265) and *Economia Política do Capitalismo Contemporâneo* (ECN 058). Their participation, questions and discussions are a source of learning, improvement and inspiration for the writing of this book.

I would like to thank my colleagues in two research groups that I participate at my university: Márcia Rapini, Leandro Silva, Ulisses Santos and Leonardo Ribeiro, from the Research Group on Economics of Science and Technology, and João Antônio de Paula, Hugo Eduardo Cerqueira, Leonardo de Deus and Alexandre Cunha, from the Research Group on Contemporary Political Economy.

I am grateful to the participants in an improvised workshop held at Cedeplar on 3 April 2023, an opportunity when I received critical comments on a draft version of this book – Pedro Loureiro (University of Cambridge), Leandro Silva, Leonardo Ribeiro and Leonardo de Deus (Cedeplar-UFMG), Laura Soares, Eduardo Sigaúque, Bruno Melo, Bruno Prates, Lídia Magyar and Estevam Peixoto (graduate students at Cedeplar-UFMG). I also benefited from Pedro Loureiro's written comments, results of a very thorough, critical and insightful reading of that draft.

I would like to thank Richard Nelson (Columbia University, New York) for the invitation to join the Catch-Up Project in 2005, a source of contact with scholars from some of the regions discussed in this book, and thanks to my colleagues in the research supported by the Catch-Up Project that became long-term collaborators and friends – Glenda Kruss (HSRC, Cape Town), Keun Lee (Seoul National University, Seoul), Gabriela Dutrénit (UAM, Mexico City) and KJ Joseph (GIFT, India). A special thanks to Wilson Suzigan (Unicamp), for his suggestions and conversations during the preparation of this book.

This book reflects the knowledge shared by both old and new friendships during my sabbatical year at the King's College, London, when I was collaborating with Alex Callinicos (King's College, London) and Valbona Muzaka (King's College, London, now at Uppsala Universitet), Ken Shadlen (LSE, London) and Pari Patel (SPRU, Brighton).

The more recent contacts with Carlos Bianchi (Universidad de la República, Montevideo) and Denis Melnik (Higher School of Economics, Moscow) were timely opportunities for discussions and learning, which helped to improve some portions of this book.

Academic and intellectual interactions with colleagues from Brazil helped to shape my views on many subjects of this book – among them, I would particularly like to thank Jorge Britto (UFF), Américo Bernardes (UFOP), Renato Garcia (Unicamp), Maria de Lourdes Mollo (UnB), Adalmir Marquetti (PUC-RS), Catari Chaves (PUC-MG), Marcelo Pinho (UFSCAR), Ana Cristina Fernandes (UFPE), Lia Hasenclever (UFRJ) and Rogério Gomes (Unesp).

Many thanks to Helena Mader (Customs Solutions), who did more than the English revision of many drafts, as her work contributed to shape many key parts of this presentation.

I would like to thank three anonymous reviewers from Springer Nature that read and commented the project of this book, contributing to its development from the beginning. Many thanks to Lorraine Klimowich – Springer Nature's editor of Economics – for her patience and incentives since April 2021.

Funding from CNPq (Grants 401054/2016-0, 307787/2018-4 and 307516/2022-9), from CAPES (BEX 1669/14-1) and from Fapemig (APQ-00685-16) have provided extremely valuable input – I am profoundly grateful for their support.

Errors are my responsibility.

Eduardo da Motta e Albuquerque
Belo Horizonte, Brazil
6 July 2023

Contents

Chapter 1
Introduction: The Peculiarities of the Propagation of Technological Revolutions Through the Periphery

This book has a very simple and clear objective: to include a new column in Freeman's scheme on long waves (Freeman, 1987, pp. 68–75). The periphery would be column number 18. This new column would summarize information on the impact of each technological revolution on the periphery.

Freeman (1987) is the first book that used the concept of national innovation system.[1] This book on Japan's catch-up investigates how countries behind the technological frontier can enter in new technologies: they need to build an institutional arrangement – national innovation system. How the technological frontier moved, opening new sectors, was explained using the framework of long waves. Freeman summarized these movements in a Table (pp. 68–75), with 17 columns and 5 lines – a synthesis of previous research and investigations from various fields of the economics of technology and industry.

The title of the Table: "a tentative sketch of some of the main characteristics of successive techno-economic paradigms". The 5 lines correspond to 5 long waves identified by Freeman – from the first - "industrial revolution" (p. 68) – to the fifth – "information and communication Kondratiev" (p. 71). The 17 columns, describing "the main characteristics" of each long wave are as follows: name, approximate periodization, description, main carrier branch, key factor industries, other sectors growing rapidly, limitations of previous techno-economic paradigms, organization of firms, technological leaders, other industrialized and industrializing countries, some features of national regimes of regulation, aspects of international regulatory regime, main features of the national systems of innovation, some features of tertiary sector development, and representative innovative entrepreneurs, political economists and philosophers (Freeman, 1987, pp. 68–75).

[1] For a history of the concept of innovation systems, see Lundvall (2007). Lundvall (2007, p. 873) shows the first written reference in Freeman (1982) and highlights Freeman (1987) as the book that "brought the modern version of the full concept of 'national system of innovation' into the literature" (p. 874).

E. da Motta e Albuquerque, *Technological Revolutions and the Periphery*,
Contributions to Economics, https://doi.org/10.1007/978-3-031-43436-5_1

This scheme offers readers a synthesis of that succession of long waves and is always a source of inspiration and ideas for further research.

Freeman's original synthetic scheme was later presented in other works: Freeman and Perez (1988, pp. 50–57), Freeman and Soete (1997, pp. 65–70), and in an abridged form in Freeman and Louçã (2001, p. 141).

Freeman's systematization of five long waves in his 1987 book is one of his important contributions to debates regarding long-term capitalist dynamics. His first known intervention in these debates is a chapter – *The Kondratiev long waves, technical change and unemployment* – in an OECD publication (Freeman, 1977). In 1981 Freeman edited a Special Issue of the journal *Futures*, later expanded and published in a book – *Long waves and the world economy* (Freeman, 1984) -, an excellent summary of the academic and intellectual revival of the interest on long waves of capitalist development. Those debates of the 1960s and 1970s pertain to a chapter of the history of economic thought that have as benchmarks Kondratiev's (1922, 1926a, b) initial elaboration on long cycles, Schumpeter's (1939) integration of Kondratiev in the theories of economic cycles, Mandel's (1972) efforts to reintegrate this long term view as a tool to grasp transformations in capitalist dynamics, and a broader revival of these issues in late 1970s and early 1980s. This has led to Freeman acting as both a participant (Freeman, 1977; Freeman et al., 1982) and an organizer (Freeman, 1981, 1984).

Freeman and Louçã (2001) masterfully presented an informed history of economic thought on long waves – see especially the first part of their book: History and Economics.

However, Freeman and Louçã (2001, p. 149) highlight that "we deal with only a few leading countries". This clarification can be read as an invitation for further investigations beyond the center of the capitalist system. Therefore, the objective of this book is to add a new column to Freeman's original scheme.

The inclusion of a column on the periphery demands an investigation that divides this new column into two tables with six lines and five columns – tables presented in Chap. 8 – Part III of this book –, summarizing research outcomes in Chaps. 3, 4, 5, 6 and 7 – Part II.

The investigation on the periphery must ramify into research about different regions because the periphery is heterogeneous now and the regions that form contemporary periphery were heterogeneous in the early 1770s. The early 1770s mark the starting point of Freeman's synthetic description of long waves (Freeman, 1987, p. 68). Perez (2010, p. 190) later rearranged that scheme defining the innovation that may have triggered each technological revolution as a big bang – in her summary the big bang behind the first technological revolution happened in 1771: Arkwright's mill. In 1771 the globe had diverse and heterogeneous economies and economic systems, and these were the systems that received the shock waves emanating from England.

Since an innovation that occurred in England propagated globally and impacted these different economic systems, it is necessary to contemplate them simultaneously in our analysis. Therefore, our choice to investigate five different countries/regions that correspond to contemporary periphery: India, China, Russia, Sub-Saharan Africa, and Latin America.[2]

The conjecture behind this choice is that each one of Perez' big bangs might not have had homogeneous impacts on the rest of the world – and these heterogeneous impacts in heterogeneous regions are a component of the global dynamics of capitalism. Therefore, we need to look to all these five regions simultaneously in order to investigate the logic of each big bang's propagation through the periphery, beyond the capitalist center. The unevenness of that propagation might be a structural feature, embedded in the system's inner logic, a feature that only can be grasped if we include these different and heterogeneous regions in our analysis.

The inclusion of contemporary periphery in Freeman's scheme brings up another question: unlike the cosmological big bang, Perez's big bangs have prior historical events. A look at the history preceding the Arkwright mill shows that by 1750 the Indian subcontinent was the "textile workshop" of the world (Darwin, 2007, p. 193) and a source of technological transfer to the West (Beckert, 2014, pp. 24–25). If we look to Freeman's column number 5, first long wave, of his original scheme – "key factors industries" (p. 68) –, pig iron is mentioned, below cotton: according to Needham (1954, p. 242), cast iron was invented in China and later traveled to the West.[3] There is a broader learning process that predates the earliest Western technological achievements: a long catch-up process that lasted until 1500, when the West completed the acquisition of knowledge available from the East (Mokyr, 1990, p. 55).[4]

The inclusion of a new column on the periphery in Freeman's scheme leads to new issues such as the intensity of previous learning of the emerging leading country – United Kingdom – from regions located in contemporary capitalist periphery. There are interconnections between the center and the periphery that might have a specific dynamic – a topic for investigation. In contemporary capitalism, Marques (2014) discusses a new phenomenon: the boomerang effect – contemporary periphery impacting the current reconfiguration of global capitalism, related to a post-www phase.

[2]This book does not deal with successful catch-up processes, as they organized the transition of countries at the periphery to the center of contemporary capitalism. South Korea and Taiwan are two of those cases that overcame underdevelopment. These processes have received deep analysis in well-known works: Amsden (1989), Wade (1990), Lee (2013, 2019).

[3]Mokyr (1990, p. 48) summarizes progress in metallurgical engineering in European Middle Age mentioning cast iron, and notes that "here, too, Europeans were preceded by the Chinese, who used cast iron". Mokyr questions Needham claim that the knowledge on cast iron was transmitted from the East, conjecturing that it is possible that "cast iron was invented independently in Europe" (p. 48).

[4]For Mokyr, in 900 Europe was a "technological backwater", in 1200 "the upstart imitator" (Mokyr, 1990, p. 57). The year 1500 could be a benchmark for Mokyr, as Europe "was soon to turn from borrower to lender (p. 55).

Interactions and interconnections between the center and the periphery may be part of the global dynamics of capitalism, and this dynamic can be investigated through the lens of the successive technological revolutions and their impact. Each technological revolution triggers structural changes that rearrange the global economy. A technological revolution at the center is a transformative event that will reverberate globally, affecting all economies.

Probably, what the industrial revolution – Perez' first big bang – did was transform global interactions between regions, with a new center assuming an active role as initial propagator of technical change (Furtado, 1987, p. 219). This is a structural phenomenon at the core of the capitalist dynamic, as it connects innovation and profits (Marx, 1867, chapter 12; Schumpeter, 1911, chapter 2; 1954, p. 646).

However, being a starting point of each successive technological revolution does not imply a unidirectional process – the process that transfers the technology to a peripheric region and the manner in which it is assimilated there may have a return effect on the economy at the center. These feedbacks between the center and the periphery may assume different shapes, different speeds, different intensities, yet are always present. Industrial capitalism emerges with a strong expansionary dynamic – Furtado's "first industrial nucleus" (1987, p. 217) -, and its first leading center needed other regions to implement the production of the first leading commodity – cotton textiles: England depended on cotton imports to expand the mechanized production of cotton textiles.

These feedbacks between the center and the periphery are part of the long process of the "making of global capitalism" (Panitch & Gindin, 2012) that has been investigated by various theoretical approaches. This book aims to investigate these feedbacks from the point of view of the propagation of technological revolutions impacting the periphery.

The starting point is the synthesis provided by Carlota Perez and her five big bangs (Perez, 2002, p. 11; 2010, p. 190), which helps in the organization of the investigation of a very complex and turbulent process.

Perez' synthesis provides a temporal dimension to this process, which should be combined with a geographical dimension, an integration necessary to understand the global nature of system's expansion.

Temporally, this investigation follows the processes triggered by the six big bangs: 1771, 1829, 1882, 1908, 1971, and 1991.[5] Geographically, it looks at their initial impacts on five regions: India, China, Russia, Sub-Saharan Africa, and Latin America.

[5] In this book a sixth big bang is included, triggered by the invention of the world wide web (www) in 1991, by Berners-Lee at the CERN (Berners-Lee & Fischetti, 2000). A preliminary discussion of this new technological revolution is found in a previous work (Albuquerque, 2019). An argument for this new technological revolution may be the proliferation of studies on "platform capitalism" (Srnieck, 2017), "surveillance capitalism" (Zuboff, 2019), "data economy" (World Bank, 2016, 2021), "digital economy" (UNCTAD, 2019).

How are these two dimensions combined in this book? The option made was to focus on each big bang – the temporal dimension – and investigate each of these five regions – the geographical dimension – looking for relevant historical events. The first historical event occurs in the year when the innovation that constitutes a big bang arrives at each region – an arrival date used for a systematization of time lags between the origin of the technology at the center and its initial assimilation at a specific peripheral region. The second historical milestone is the intensity of its initial diffusion through each region.

The resulting combination between these temporal and geographical dimensions is the content of what could be the new column in Freeman's scheme, which is in turn subdivided into five sub-columns. In fact, this new column on the periphery becomes a table with six lines (one for each big bang) and five columns (one for each region at the periphery) – a preliminary suggestion of how to include the periphery in Freeman's original synthesis.

This strategy of investigation organizes this book in three parts.

Part I – composed of Chap. 2 – presents the theoretical framework. There are three basic theoretical sources that organize it. The first source deals with the dynamic of technological revolutions emerging from the leading country: Nikolai Kondratiev is the main reference, with his pioneering works on long cycles, innovation, and the inclusion of new regions in an expanding global economy. The second source deals with the center-periphery divide reconfigured by the industrial revolution: Celso Furtado is a reference as a representative of a broader economic approach that investigates the specificities of economic dynamic in peripheric regions. The third source researches the nature of technological absorption of external knowledge, and the efforts that are necessary for those who are copying existing technologies. This process is not an easy one, of mere imitation: Wesley Cohen and David Levinthal are the references on a subject that shows how difficult it is to assimilate external knowledge within most developed countries – and they suggest that their concept of absorption capacity could be used to investigate knowledge transfer between different countries in different levels of development.

The theoretical interrelation between Kondratiev, Furtado, and Cohen and Levinthal suggests that the propagation of new technologies throughout the periphery is not a consequence only of expansionary forces emanating from the center, but also from assimilatory forces created at the periphery. The identification of these two forces introduces a question on how they are combined, considering how they do not operate in isolation. This combined operation of expansionary and assimilatory forces will be investigated in Part II.

Part II – composed of Chaps. 3, 4, 5, 6, and 7 – is organized according to each big bang. The chapters start with a synthetic description of the innovation which constitutes each big bang, and then investigate the arrival and initial spread of each big bang in each of the five countries/regions addressed. The operation of expansionary forces, on the one hand, and assimilatory forces, on the other hand, organizes the investigation of the arrival and initial spread of each big bang in our five regions. Each chapter in Part II contributes to the new column in Freeman's scheme preparing a line with information related to each big bang.

A research topic common to all chapters in Part II is the nature of the impact of each technological revolution on these five regions, with a look on the changes at the international division of labor.

As Chaps. 3, 4, 5, 6, and 7 summarize each big bang, their arrival and initial spread in our five regions, the historical narrative and data on these processes compose a broader scenario that helps our investigation. This scenario shows the heterogeneity of the diffusion of different technological revolutions through different regions, with evidence on the uneven processes involved. This unevenness would not be captured without the analysis integrating the temporal and the geographical dimensions. A turbulent process of diffusion, that is not symmetric nor linear, is built when we integrate these two dimensions. This integration unveils how the operation of expansionary forces change over time and also how assimilatory forces are transformed across the succession of technological revolutions.

All evidence systematized in Part II is the material to be analyzed in Part III.

Part III – composed of Chap. 8 – revisits the theoretical framework after the investigations in Part II. The main focus of Part III is how the expansionary forces triggered by each big bang interact with assimilatory forces created at the periphery. Chapters 3, 4, 5, 6, and 7 show that these two forces do not operate in isolation, and in addition to the transformation they undergo, they also change the forms of their interaction – of their interplay. Chapters 3, 4, 5, 6, and 7 discover that the interplay between expansionary and assimilatory forces is related to overlapping and superposition of different technological revolutions, a phenomenon that seems to be more intricated at the periphery than at the center.

The conclusion of this book revisits the issues presented in this introduction, discussing how the inclusion of this new column on the periphery in Freeman's original scheme might be helpful to understand contemporary political economy. This complex system is structured around a center and a very heterogeneous periphery – an uneven system, globally and locally, both at the center (Piketty, 2013) and at the periphery (Furtado, 1987). This very heterogeneous periphery has roots in the impact of each technological revolution, shaped by the interplay between expansionary and assimilatory forces. Over time, these different impacts reshaped societies and economies, leading to the current configuration of the global economy.

This analysis puts forward key elements of an agenda for international reforms. On the one hand, there is a wealth of scientific and technological resources accumulated globally – illustrated by an emerging global system of innovation -, and, on the other hand, the huge global challenges presented by global warming, emerging diseases and epidemics, accumulation of means of destruction through arms production, and unacceptable persistence of poverty.

Other forms of combination between expansionary and assimilatory forces might be initial steps for these necessary international reforms.

References

Albuquerque, E. M. (2019). Capitalismo pós-www: uma discussão introdutória sobre uma nova fase na economia global. *Cadernos do Desenvolvimento, 14*(24), 131–154.
Amsden, A. (1989). *Asia's next giant: South Korea and late industrialization*. Oxford University.
Beckert, S. (2014). *Empire of cotton: A global history*. Vintage Books.
Berners-Lee, T., & Fischetti, M. (2000). *Weaving the Web: The original design and ultimate destiny of the worldwide web by its inventor*. HarperBusiness.
Darwin, J. (2007). *After Tamerlane: The rise and fall of global empires, 1400–2000*. Cambridge University Press.
Freeman, C. (1977). The Kondratiev long waves, technical change and unemployment. In OECD (Ed.), *Structural determinants of employment and unemployment – Experts meeting, Paris, 7th–11th March 1977* (pp. 181–196). OECD.
Freeman, C. (1981). Introduction. *Futures, 13*(4), 239–245.
Freeman, C. (1982). Technological infrastructure and international competitiveness. *Industrial and Corporate Change, 13*(3), 541–569. (2004).
Freeman, C. (Ed.). (1984). *Long waves in the world economy*. Frances Pinter.
Freeman, C. (1987). *Technology policy and economic performance: Lessons from Japan*. Pinter Publishers.
Freeman, C., & Louçã, F. (2001). *As time goes by: From the industrial revolutions and to the information revolution*. Oxford University.
Freeman, C., & Perez, C. (1988). Structural crisis of adjustment: Business cycles and investment behaviour. In G. Dosi, C. Freeman, R. Nelson, et al. (Eds.), *Technical change and economic theory* (pp. 38–66). Pinter.
Freeman, C., & Soete, L. (1997). *The economics of industrial innovation*. Pinter.
Freeman, C., Clark, J., & Soete, L. (1982). *Unemployment and technical innovation*. Frances Pinter (Publishers).
Furtado, C. (1987). Underdevelopment: To conform or to reform. In G. Meier (Ed.), *Pioneers of development* (Second series) (pp. 203–227). Oxford University/World Bank.
Kondratiev, N. D. (1922). *The world economy and its conjunctures during and after the war*. International Kondratiev Foundation (2004).
Kondratiev, N. D. (1926a). Long cycles of economic conjuncture. In N. Makasheva, W. J. Samuels, & V. Barnett (Eds.), *The works of Nikolai D. Kondratiev* (Vol. 1, pp. 25–60). Pickering and Chato (1998).
Kondratiev, N. D. (1926b). The long waves in economic life. *Review of Economic Statistics, 17*(35), 105–115. (1935).
Lee, K. (2013). *Schumpeterian analysis of economic catch up: Knowledge, path-creation, and the middle-income trap*. Cambridge University Press.
Lee, K. (2019). *The art of economic catch-up: Barriers, detours and leapfroging*. Cambridge University Press.
Lundvall, B.-A. (2007). National innovation systems: From list to Freeman. In H. Hanusch & A. Pyka (Eds.), *Elgar companion to neo-Schumpeterian economics* (pp. 872–881). Edward Elgar.
Mandel, E. (1972). *O Capitalismo Tardio*. Abril Cultural (1982).
Marques, S. F. (2014). *Mudanças na Clivagem Centro-Periferia e o Efeito Bumerangue: o impacto da periferia na reconfiguração sistêmica do capitalismo no século XXI*. Cedeplar-UFMG. (Tese de Doutorado).
Marx, K. (1867). *Capital* (Vol. I). Penguin Books (1976).
Mokyr, J. (1990). *The lever of riches: Technological creativity and economic progress*. Oxford University Press.
Needham, J. (1954). *Science and civilization in China* (Vol. 1). Cambridge University Press.
Panitch, L., & Gindin, S. (2012). *The making of global capitalism: The political economy of American empire*. Verso.

Perez, C. (2002). *Technological revolutions and financial capital*. Edward Elgar.
Perez, C. (2010). Technological revolutions and techno-economic paradigms. *Cambridge Journal of Economics, 34*(1), 185–202.
Piketty, T. (2013). Capital in the twenty-first century. The Belknap Press of Harvard University Press (2014).
Schumpeter, J. A. (1911). *A teoria do desenvolvimento econômico*. Nova Cultural, 1985.
Schumpeter, J. A. (1939). *Business cycles: A theoretical, historical and statistical analysis of the capitalist process* (Vol. 1). McGraw-Hill Book Company, Inc.
Schumpeter, J. A. (1954). *History of economic analysis*. Allen & Unwin.
Srnicek, N. (2017). *Platform capitalism*. Polity Press.
UNCTAD. (2019). *Digital economy report 2019*. UNCTAD.
Wade, R. (1990). *Governing the market: Economy theory and the role of government in East Asian industrialization*. Princeton University.
World Bank. (2016). *Digital dividends: World development report 2016*. World Bank.
World Bank. (2021). *Data for better lives: World development report 2021*. World Bank.
Zuboff, S. (2019). *The age of surveillance capitalism*. PublicAffairs.

Part I
Theoretical Framework

Chapter 2
The Roots of System Expansion and the Role of Absorptive Capacity

2.1 The Roots of System Expansion

The industrial revolution is the starting point of a broad process, that began in one specific location of our planet – England – in the second half of the eighteenth century. Carlota Perez (2010, p. 190) characterizes Arkwright's mill in Cramford – 1771 – as a *big bang* initiating a technological revolution – the first, the industrial revolution, very clearly describing this strong expansionary drive that started in one single point, with one single change – a new process. This change, this *big bang*, triggered a chain of events that transformed England initially and simultaneously sparked changes across the whole world.

In 1750 the global population was 814 million and the United Kingdom (England, Scotland and Wales) had 7.5 million inhabitants – 0.92% of Earth's population (Statista, 2022; Anderson, 1990, p. 1). The process initiated in England would be an example and/or a reference for other peoples, 99% of Earth's population. Those peoples were organized in very different social and political arrangements, lived in societies with very different stages of development,[1] and had different information about what was happening in England.

This process, after 250 years, reshaped the whole world and what was limited, in 1771, to one single location now, in 2022, is global. Modern industrial capitalism expanded from one single point to the whole world – now there is the age of global capitalism.

[1]List (1841) is an illustration of this leading position, as he highlights how Great Britain had achieved a unique position in his time. List suggests that countries should pass through different "stages of development": "original barbarism, pastoral condition, agricultural condition, agricultural-manufacturing condition, and agricultural-manufacturing-commercial condition" (p. 143). Great Britain "alone at the present time has actually reached" that last stage (p. 93).

E. da Motta e Albuquerque, *Technological Revolutions and the Periphery*, Contributions to Economics, https://doi.org/10.1007/978-3-031-43436-5_2

If this system started in one place and now it is everywhere, involving the whole world, a key issue is to understand how this expansion took place, how this system over time spread to new regions and countries. This process of inclusion of new regions and countries resulted in a very unequal global economy, with a center-periphery divide and a very heterogeneous periphery. The contemporary shape of the global economy shows that this expansionary process is not a homogenizing and equalizing process, and is not based on the creation of replicas of the leading regions/countries.

What are the driving forces of this process? A tentative answer conjectures that, on the one hand, there are expansionary forces inherent to the technological change creating new processes and new products and, on the other hand, there might be forces related to other regions' and countries' capacity to absorb those new technologies and to develop them in their territories.

But those two basic forces might combine in very different forms: forces from the center, pulling expansion to new regions, forces from the periphery, pushing absorption to their regions. The combination between those two forces may have different gradients, resulting in different levels of diffusion of those new technologies.

The operation of those two basic driving forces (expansion and absorption) has to be articulated with two dimensions: space and time. At the spatial dimension, there is this movement from the center to the rest of the world – propagation of the *big bang*, perturbations at the global level that a new technology causes on geographic areas beyond the locale of the initial innovation. At a temporal level, as this new system continually generates new products and new processes, there will be other important innovations that will again shake the whole system, beginning at its dynamic center.

In sum, while the first *big bang* propagates throughout the rest of the world, a new innovation – either a new product or a new process – after some time will be generated at the center, and the process of diffusion will begin again. The synthesis suggested by Perez (2010, p. 190) organizes this succession of very important technological innovations in five phases, with five different *big bangs* (in 1771, 1829, 1875, 1908, and 1971). Each big bang represents a renewed start of the expansionary forces – the first side of our driving forces of change. Each *big bang* will spread from its initial point. But each successive *big bang* finds a different world, transformed by previous perturbations of important innovations. The transformation of the whole world takes place after the combined operation of expansionary and assimilatory forces. The outcome of those combined forces transforms economies and societies globally, and those transformed economies and societies will be the ones that will receive the new shock waves of technological change emerging from the center – with new absorptive capabilities.

For the periphery, this succession of important technological change at the center may be seen as an endless process: while the impact of the previous *big bang* is still reverberating at the periphery, a new *big bang* is triggered at the center. At the periphery, attempts to deal with the previous big bang are still in motion, while absorption efforts are still ongoing, and at the same time a new change emerges abroad. An incomplete absorption of technologies that are no longer the newest, may overlap with the start of efforts to absorb more recent technologies.

Over time, in a sequence of changes emerging from the center and impacting the whole world, the periphery of the system is transformed. And this periphery is an important part of contemporary capitalism, a truly global capitalism. Over time this periphery, as it is reshaped by those combined forces of expansion and assimilation, becomes a more decisive component of the overall dynamic of the system, as it grows and establishes new patterns of interaction with the center, even reaching a "boomerang effect" (Marques, 2014).

These overall changes can be named metamorphoses of capitalism (Furtado, 2002).

2.2 Three Dimensions for a Theoretical Framework

A theoretical framework to deal with this process and its combined driving forces should coordinate three different dimensions. The first integrates the technical changes at the center with the inclusion of new regions in the capitalist economy – Kondratiev (1926a) deals with those issues. The second focuses on what is the relationship between the industrial revolution (Perez' first *big bang*) and the reconfiguration of the center-periphery divide – Furtado (1987) provides a good introduction to the specificities of the periphery. The third deals with absorptive capabilities and their relationships with institutional building at the periphery – Cohen and Levinthal (1989, 1990) formulate the concept of absorptive capability and make room for its integration with the literature on innovation systems.

These authors and these three dimensions offer potential for a fruitful dialogue that may underpin a theoretical framework for this investigation.

2.2.1 Kondratiev: Technological Change and Inclusion of New Regions

From Russia, at the periphery of capitalism, Nikolai D. Kondratiev (1892–1938) investigates changes in capitalism, suggesting a periodization through his long cycles (1922, 1926a, b). Kondratiev's theoretical, institutional and empirical contributions to an understanding of capitalist dynamics in the long term are summarized and discussed by Freeman and Louçã (2001). Kondratiev's pioneering elaboration certainly contains limitations of that initial stage of research, in terms of availability of data and the short period of existence of his Moscow Conjuncture Institute. However, even with all these constraints, his contribution is key for any discussion of capitalism and its metamorphoses.

The sources of Kondratiev (1926a, 1928a) are very broad and updated, including Schumpeter (1911). Later, in his investigations and in his new book on business cycles, Schumpeter included Kondratiev's long cycle in the well-known three-cycle scheme, naming it Kondratiev cycles or waves (Schumpeter, 1939, pp. 161–174, pp. 212–219).

Kondratiev's periodization suggested that capitalism had gone through three different phases, long cycles, transformations that changed the system in many ways. For our research, what is relevant in this contribution is the dynamic framework that Kondratiev suggests, especially the determinants of those broad movements and changes in capitalism. There are four determinants of those changes: "1- changes in technology; 2- wars and revolutions; 3- the involvement of new territories in the orbit of the world economy; 4- fluctuations in gold mining" (Kondratiev, 1926a, p. 49).[2]

For our research, two of those determinants should be better evaluated: changes in technology and new territories – those two topics show how Kondratiev had theoretical questions that shape our tentative framework.

First, there is the role of new technologies at the origin of new phases in capitalism. In a summary of these lists, Kondratiev connects major technical inventions with changes and growth in capitalist dynamics, or connecting technical changes and new phases of capitalism: "[j]ust as the broad use of steam in the first half of the nineteenth century coincided with the start of a general increase in the tempo of economic life, so the broad use of electricity and chemical knowledge coincided with the start of a new period of increased tempo of economic growth" (p. 40).

A closer look at Kondratiev's interrelation between changes in technology and capitalist dynamics shows an approach that brings not one single technology, but a "series of technical inventions" (p. 39). In his interpretation, the start of each phase of capitalism – long cycle – would be connected to innovations distributed over different years. For the first phase – first cycle – "its rising tide wave begins at the height of the industrial revolution and the far-reaching changes in industrial behavior" (p. 39). The industrial revolution "was preceded and accompanied by a series of significant technical inventions... This period extended approximately from 1764 to 1795". For the second cycle, Kondratiev mentions a series of technical inventions that appeared between 1824 and 1848. There is a list of 19 technical inventions: among them "significant improvement of the steam engine", "the harvester reaping-machine", "invention of electromagnetic telegraphy", "the construction of the first wheeled steam engine", "the invention of the sewing machine", "the cable system" (p. 39). For the third phase, there is a list of 25 technical inventions – stressing their connection "with the rapid progress in natural science from the 1870s" (p. 40). Those inventions are distributed between 1875 and 1898. Among them "DC dynamo", "a machine for obtaining ammonia", "the drilling machine", "Thomas method for producing steel", "Siemen's electric locomotive", "petrol engine", "Westinghouse air-brake", AC and DC power transmission (p. 40).

---

[2]There is a debate on the nature of each of those four determinants. Kondratiev stresses how each of those determinants of capitalist dynamics are not "random and attendant" (p. 49) – the French translation of this is: "aléatoires ou exogènes" (1926b, p. 150). The random nature of those determinants was a subject important in the debates presented in Makasheva et al. (1998, pp. 24–158). The endogenous nature of technological change in capitalism for Kondratiev certainly had in Schumpeter's contribution an important source (Schumpeter, 1911, Chap. 2).

Kondratiev's description of technologies at the origin of each long cycle was reformulated by Perez (2002) in her suggestion of a "cosmological metaphor" – big bangs. Perez uses big bang as a metaphor for understanding the dynamics of technological revolution as a "point in time that explodes into an expanding universe of opportunities" (2002, p. 12). Big bangs are part of broader processes related to technological revolutions – among its movements, it expresses how the first innovation would trigger the chain of events that characterize one specific long wave and the related technological paradigm. Those different paradigms can be seen as systems, "[e]ach can be seen inaugurated by an important breakthrough acting as a big bang that opens a new universe of opportunity for profitable innovation" (Perez, 2010, p. 189). This relationship with profits – a key determinant of the capitalist dynamics – makes this "cosmological metaphor" go beyond a single explosion, leading Perez to broaden her definition: "for society to veer strongly in the direction of a new set of technologies, a highly visible 'attractor' needs to appear, symbolizing the whole new potential and capable of sparking the technological and business imagination of a cluster of pioneers" (2002, p. 11).

That attractor indicates also how cost-competitive the innovation is: "that event is defined here as the *big-bang* of the revolution" (2002, p. 11). As an illustration, Perez highlights the Intel microprocessor – November 1971: "it was the big bang of a new universe, that of all-pervasive computing and digital technologies" (2002, p. 3). That event, according to Freeman was "aptly designated by Carlota Perez as 'the big bang'" (Freeman, 2002, p. x). Perez' definition and use of *big bang* as an event at the start of a technological revolution is important for this theoretical framework because it stresses the expansionary forces connected to major innovations. As will be discussed in this chapter, this expansionary force is part of the explanation of how each technological revolution shapes and reshapes global economy. However, as Perez (2002, p. 12) comments, *big bang* is a metaphor.

As such, differences with the "cosmological" origin of this expression should be noted. First, even the first *big bang* in Perez's list (Arkwright's mill in Cramford – 1771) is a condensation of previous economic, scientific and technological history. As Beckert (2014, p. 50) describes, writing about events in the end of the seventeenth century and the first half of the eighteenth century, there is a long history of Europeans travelling to India "to understand and appropriate India technology" (p. 50). Between the processes involved, Beckert (2014, p. 50) links global trade networks and assimilation of technology: "[a]s European domination of global networks of cotton quickened, so too did the pace of European assimilation of Indian technology" (p. 50). Second, different from the cosmological concept, in economy there is more than one *big bang*, there is a succession of big bangs, summarized by Carlota Perez in five *big bangs* (2002, p. 11; 2010, p. 190). This succession of big bangs over time is important for our investigation on the periphery because the overlapping of those different explosions will create and recreate a phenomenon associated with the lag in their initial impact at the periphery, the specificities of the speed and scope of their propagation and how the previous big bang is related to the subsequent one. Third, contrary to the cosmological event, big bangs in the economy are not pure forces of expansion. Each big bang is associated with specific measures to contain its automatic expansion: in the first big bang, England took measures to block the emigration of skilled workers and entrepreneurs and block exports of machines (Jeremy, 1977); in contemporary capitalism, there is a strengthening of intellectual property rights (Mazzoleni & Nelson, 2007). Those blocking factors for the expansion of new technologies are one determinant of technological innovation, as appropriability conditions are seen as very important – see the findings of the Yale Survey on this topic (Levin et al., 1987). This role of appropriability to innovation is another way to show how absorptive capacity may be an important factor for the diffusion of technologies from the center.

However, there is one important similarity between the use of big bang in Carlota Perez' interpretation of technological revolutions and the cosmological big bang: immediately after the cosmological explosion, changes begin. Weinberg's book on the "first three minutes" of the universe illustrates this point: Weinberg's Chap. 6, for example, describes frame after frame the changes as the big bang irradiates forming the universe (Weinberg, 1993, pp. 102–109). This also happens with a technological revolution seen as a big bang – and this phenomenon is very important for our investigation: as the diffusion of new technologies takes time to reach the periphery, it undergoes transformation during that time interval. Therefore, the technology that will arrive at the periphery is different from the original technology that triggered the big bang. This similarity with the cosmological big bang can be theoretically supported by Rosenberg's reflections on the nature of technological revolutions: "history strongly suggests that technological revolutions are not completed overnight" (1996, p. 344). Rosenberg mentions an empirical regularity, a phenomenon common to new technologies: "new technologies typically come into the world in a very primitive condition. Their eventual uses turn upon an extended improvement process that vastly expands their practical applications" (1996, p. 338).

For our research, the idea of big bang as a metaphor is useful, because for the periphery the possibility of assimilation – imitation – begins with the outcome of a large fermentation behind each of the five key technologies selected by Carlota Perez (2002, 2010). These five big bangs, generated at the center, trigger perturbations that affect the rest of the economy and also start movements that will include new regions in the global economy. Therefore, this book deals with these key technologies that are products of long processes at the center that inaugurate the possibility of their assimilation by the periphery.

These lists of technical inventions at the origin of each long wave presented by Kondratiev (1926a, p. 39, p. 40) have a relatively long span, from 23 to 30 years. Both the list of different innovations and the lag between them and their industrial applications may suggest a dialogue with contemporary elaboration on "general purpose technologies" (GPTs) (Bresnahan & Trajtenberg, 1995; Rosenberg, 1998). Freeman and Louçã (2001, p. 155, p. 192, p. 231, pp. 272–273, and p. 307) list a set of technologies and inventions related to each big bang. A look at these different technical inventions that are related to each new phase, opens avenues for elaboration and dialogue between different theoretical approaches.

Revisiting Kondratiev's original elaboration of diverse technical inventions emerging in a temporally dispersed but closer period – leading one to ponder on how their overlapping and combination may create positive feedbacks in growth processes – helps to investigate the capitalist dynamics as more turbulent than an image of well-behaved overlapping cycles suggests.[3] Ribeiro et al. (2017) applied Fourier's techniques to data for the United States (1870–2010) and found indications of a more turbulent pattern, without a single long cycle of 50 years but rather a superposition of a myriad of different cycles of varying duration and frequency, with the more important being the 23-, 20-, 70-, and 35-year cycles (Ribeiro et al., 2017, pp. 296–297). The use of techniques derived from Fourier has some links to Kondratiev, as those techniques arrived at his Moscow Conjuncture Institute in the 1920s – but without the computing resources available today –, and the availability of data for a far bigger data series allows contemporary research to reevaluate the existing cycles of capitalist economies to investigate how they can be decomposed.

Focusing on a combination of different technologies instead of one single and independent innovation may be important in the investigation of how their combination generate perturbations and trigger chain of technological events that underlie capitalist dynamics. One speculation relates Kondratiev and Slutsky: Kondratiev hired Slutsky to work in his Moscow Conjuncture Institute and Slutsky's paper on random events producing economic cycles was closely followed by Kondratiev (Franco et al., 2022, pp. 14–15). Slutsky (1937) presents an exercise on how economic cycles can be composed from minor random events, and the superposition of these different and smaller changes could serve as a methodological exercise for a later application to investigations on how long cycles might be formed by those minor events and minor cycles – each of those "random events" might have been those "technical inventions" and their industrial applications at the start of each new phase.[4] These insights and theoretical explorations within the Moscow Conjuncture Institute and the nature of Kondratiev's research issues make their elaborations unprecedented in the field of complex systems: the persistence of innovations emanating from the center keeps the whole system out-of-equilibrium. The reverberations of technical change throughout central and peripherical regions impose a dynamic of ongoing changes, that trigger chains of events that in turn give rise to feedback in the region that had originally provoked all these changes. These

[3] Schumpeter (1939) and his three-cycle scheme of long waves of capitalist development can be an illustration of this well-behaved cyclical patterns (see his Chart 1, p. 213).

[4] Franco et al. (2022) presents a discussion on the exchanges between Kondratiev and Slutsky, mediated by an evaluation of how the contribution of J. B. Fourier reached the Moscow Conjuncture Institute in the 1920s. Fourier, in Franco et al. (2022), is a source of an open interpretation of cycles and waves, because it allows both the decomposition and composition of cycles. Slutsky's use of Fourier's technique brought to the Moscow Conjuncture Institute skills that enabled the collective work of that institute to investigate both sides of the methodologies necessary to deal with long term capitalist dynamics.

structural features of the processes investigated by Kondratiev combine very well with modern developments of complex systems in economics (Anderson, 1988; Arthur, 2013, 2021).

Disaggregating those different technologies at the beginning of each cycle makes it possible to think in terms of economic sectors. Kondratiev highlights this point, correlating these "advances in technology and technical inventions" with the "formation of new sectors of industry" (1926a, p. 39). These interrelations lend themselves to investigations at a sectoral level, and as will be discussed later, absorption processes from the periphery focusing on specific sectors or specific General Purpose Technologies (GPTs) (Lee & Malerba, 2017).[5]

Second, there is the issue of inclusion of new regions in the global economic system: Kondratiev's summary of determinants of capitalist dynamics might suggest connections between "changes in technology" and "the involvement of new territories".

One connection between them is that both are part of the basic dynamics of long cycles: a feature as important as changes in technology, for Kondratiev "[t]he start of long cycles usually coincides with the broadening of the orbit of the world economic relationships" (p. 41). Another connection might be established by the "potent effect on the course or capitalist dynamics" (p. 49) that changes in technology cause – a system with more resources, new productive capabilities, and needs can expand. These connections could explain why in his debates Kondratiev always stressed that the expansion of the world economy to new regions was not a random or exogeneous process.

The sequence of long cycles presented by Kondratiev can be read as an expansion process of that orbit of world economic relationships: in the first cycle he mentions those changes in industrial behavior "above all in England, but also to a lesser degree, in France and other countries" (p. 41). In this first cycle, Kondratiev stresses that "[f]rom the 1790s the first significant step towards the emergence of the USA on the world economy was observed, with consequent observation of a significant widening of its orbit" (p. 39). In the second cycle, "in the USA, England and France from 1830s to 1840s" there was a "rapid growth in railway and water transport" (p. 40). Australia is also mentioned due to its gold deposits (1847–1851). In the third cycle, a "major chance is the broad involvement of countries with a young culture (Australia, Argentina, Chile, Canada) in world economic relationships" (p. 41).

Kondratiev description shows that together with changes in technology there is a systematic expansion of the "orbit of world economy". For him, this expansion is related to forces emanating from the center: "under capitalism, new territories are historically only drawn into circulation in periods when countries of the old culture are acutely in need of new markets and raw materials. It is also completely clear that

[5]Those comments and elaboration on the combination of different innovations and the dialogue with GPTs may be inconsistent with the structure of this book, based on radical innovations behind Perez' big bangs. The option for structuring the book around the five (or six) big bangs aims to simplify the historical approach adopted herein, choosing important technologies for different phases of capitalism, and technologies that are consensually evaluated as GPTs.

the limits of this involvement are determined by these needs" (1926a, pp. 50–51). Furthermore, "by quickening the pace of economic dynamics of capitalist countries, makes it necessary and possible to exploit new countries and new markets and raw materials" (p. 51). As a new region is included, the whole system changes – a perturbation similar to that introduced by a new big bang.

This determinant of the long waves – inclusion of new regions – was a topic of intense debate, particularly in the discussions that took place at the Institute of Economics, in Moscow, in 1926 (Makasheva et al., 1998, pp. 24–254). This topic had been a source of criticism from Trotsky (1923) and in some way their previous debate reverberated at the Institute of Economics.[6] The main issue was whether or not the inclusion of new regions was a random or exogeneous process.

V. E. Bogdanov (1926, pp. 116–117) reviews Kondratiev's initial presentation and focuses on the issue of expansion to new regions. It is an interesting intervention, by a peculiar combination of determinants of that expansion. V. E. Bogdanov makes an important case for evaluating conditions that may limit that expansion: "the low level of development of the given country, the new market is not sufficiently large or because of the general poverty of the country's natural resources" (p. 117). For V. E. Bogdanov, two features may be considered: on the one hand, the "process of the achievement of capitalist supremacy in the whole world takes place unevenly, in jumps, with an alternation of epochs of intense expansion and epochs of long decline" (p. 117). On the other hand, "this unevenness and non-uniformity" should not be inferred "simply from an internal mechanism of capitalism, abstracting from the characteristics of extra-capitalistic environment" (p. 117). In his "concluding words", Kondratiev answers criticisms from Bogdanov (pp. 142–143), but does not incorporate those two fine comments.

Kondratiev influence on later economic theory goes beyond Schumpeter (1939): Freeman and Louçã (2001) prepared a book that is an excellent synthesis of his long-lasting impact. The contributions for research on long waves of capitalist development are very rich, and include other references to the expansive dynamic of the system. One reference could be Freeman's scheme of successive long waves (1987, pp. 68–75) that in its column #10 the leading countries – with Great Britain at the top in the first long wave, while over time the center widens to include Continental Europe and the United States in the second long wave, and Japan in the fourth long wave. Column #11 lists the emerging countries – the periphery also grows, as probably Freeman is listing the countries at the periphery that would be closest to

[6]R. Day (1976, p. 77) and Mustafin (2018, p. 8) mention a meeting that took place in 18 January 1926, both Kondratiev and Trotsky were present. According to R. Day, among other topics, Trotsky returned to the issue of long cycles and their causes, stressing that they are not consequences of the internal dynamic of the system, but of external causes such as "opening of new continents, colonies and markets for capitalist activity" (Day, 1976, p. 78). For a dialogue between Kondratiev and Trotsky on those issues and other references about those debates, see Albuquerque (2020). In that paper, I present my evaluation of that debate, highlighting Kondratiev's arguments on the economic preconditions for the inclusion of new regions in the capitalist system (Albuquerque, 2020, pp. 150–152).

the center, potential candidates to join the center of the system, as Japan was included as an emerging country in column #11 in the third long wave. It is not by chance that in this book Freeman discusses the long waves and presents the concept of innovation systems to understand the Japanese catch up during the 1950s and 1960s.

2.2.2 *Furtado: Technology Progress at the Periphery*

From Brazil, again in the periphery of capitalism, Celso Furtado (1920–2003) is part of a generation that is involved with the emergence of development economics (Meier & Seers, 1984; Meier, 1987) – a chapter of a history of economic thought could evidence greater awareness in the periphery of the preconditions for development, an important advance in absorptive capabilities.

Furtado benefited from the previous work of other "pioneers of development", as his works cites Prebisch, Lewis, Myrdal, Rosenstein-Rodan, Hirschman and others – see, for example, the references used in his *Teoria e Política de Desenvolvimento Econômico* (Furtado, 1986). These authors referenced by Furtado had worked in different regions of the non-developed world, including Asia, Latin America, Africa, South and Eastern Europe – the emerging economics of development had as subject and as point of view the periphery of global capitalism.

Furtado is an author that can introduce the topic of technical change from the viewpoint of the periphery.[7] There is a difference between the logic of technical progress at the center (developed) and the economies at the periphery (underdeveloped). On the one hand, at the center, economic growth is "mainly a matter of accumulating new scientific knowledge and advancing the technological application of such knowledge. The growth of underdeveloped economies, on the other hand, is a matter of assimilating techniques already extant" (1961, p. 61).[8]

Furtado's contribution for investigations of technological change from the viewpoint of the periphery begins with his interpretation of the industrial revolution and its impact on the global economy. Furtado highlights the "expansionary force of the first industrial nucleus" (1987, p. 217).

In his book *Accumulation and development: the logic of industrial civilization* (Furtado, 1978) the "emergence of industrial civilization" is discussed in two chapters. The industrial revolution is evaluated as a "genuine historical leap"

[7]Paula and Albuquerque (2020) present a discussion of the Furtado's formation and contributions. This subsection is based on the second part of that paper.

[8]This emphasis on assimilation and the importance of creativity for development at the periphery (Furtado, 1978, p. 131) introduce a dialogue with the next section, on the concept of absorptive capability.

(1978, p. 36). Its origins are discussed extensively, with a genealogy that includes two processes of "cultural creativity": "the bourgeois revolution and the scientific revolution" (1978, p. 163).[9]

Great Britain, the "first industrial nucleus", has a defining role in this new system. There is a "dynamic center", from where the technological progress irradiates: the "creation of the first industrial nucleus in Great Britain, of a relatively high technical level for the time, gave rise to a process of irradiation of modern technology on a world scale" (Furtado, 1986, p. 112). This powerful nucleus reshaped the global economy over time: "[t]he nucleus of modern industry was formed in Europe in the second half of the eighteenth century – the seed of an economic system that was to reach global dimensions" (1987, pp. 216–217).

But this process of "irradiation" is not a smooth or automatic process – those changes, stresses Furtado, "were far from uniform" (1987, p. 217). There are three movements caused by this "expansionary force of the first industrial nucleus": (1) the "expansion and increasing complexity of the original nucleus" (p. 217); (2) "occupation of temperate regions with low population density" (p. 217); (3) "expansion of commercial channels and the international division of labor" (1987, p. 218). Those three movements led to the formation – or reconfiguration – of a "center-periphery system" (p. 216).

The incorporation of the periphery in this new international division of labor was a process initiated at the center (1987, p. 219): "the international division of labor is the outcome of the efforts of the industrial nucleus to broaden channels of commerce or to create new ones. The initiative lay with the economy that was industrialized and generated technological progress" (p. 219).

This reshaping of the global economy, for Furtado, was consequence of "the expansionary force exerted by the center, which ordered the reallocation of resources and how they were used and imposed modernization. In this way the expansion of the industrial nucleus caused changes in the structural configuration of regions with which it came into contact" (p. 222).

In this new international division of labor, reshaped under the impact of these expansionary forces, at the center "technical progress permeates the forms of production without lags, at the same time that it modernizes the patterns of consumption" (1998, p. 62). In the periphery, "that penetration initially circumscribes the consumption patterns, and limit their effects to the modernization of the lifestyles of some segments of the population" (1998, p. 62).

The form of propagation of technological progress is at the root of underdevelopment. This divide is a structural phenomenon, therefore, concludes Furtado: "underdevelopment is nothing but a certain configuration of the economic structure,

[9]Furtado's discussion of the long-term roots of industrial revolution can be read here as processes that are behind the first *big bang*, as presented by Perez (2010): differently from the world of physics, the big bang that initiates the industrial revolution and modern capitalism – Furtado's "industrial civilization" – has a long previous history, a "centuries-long period that witnessed the birth of industrial civilization" (1978, p. 30). In the economy each *big bang* condenses previous history.

derived from the way in which technical progress was propagated on the international plane" (1998, p. 62).

The form of "propagation of technological progress" is at the root of underdevelopment as a structural phenomenon. On the one hand, in underdevelopment technological progress is exogenous, it takes place abroad: "[i]n the peripheral economies, changes in the system of production were induced from the outside" (Furtado, 1987, p. 222). On the other hand, the form under which the assimilation of technological progress takes place defines a key feature of underdevelopment: "inadequacy of technology", related to a "polarity of modernization and marginality" (1987, p. 223).

Underdevelopment is a "mechanism" (1998, p. 64), or, as Furtado puts forward, "underdevelopment is a historical trap" (1992, pp. 37–59).[10]

For Furtado a succession of technical innovations irradiating from the center reshapes the insertion of countries at the periphery. After his reflection on the impact of the industrial revolution, Furtado evaluates what he calls a "second phase of the Industrial Revolution" – "application to the transport sector of technology originally developed in connection with manufacturing industries" (1976, p. 43). Railways and mechanization of maritime transport "brought about radical changes in the conditions of international trade" (p. 43). In this new scenario, "between the Napoleonic Wars and the First World War" – "a new pattern in the world economy" (p. 44) – there was a rise in economic growth that included "those making use of their natural resources within the framework of geographical specialization" (p. 44). With the growth of capital goods industries at the center, there was "the creation of a network for transmitting technical progress as a subsidiary of the international division of labor" (p. 47).

A new round of innovations at the center, after the First World War, leads to changes in the composition of world trade, with important impacts on the periphery: Furtado mentions "[t]he relative decline in natural fibers and the rise in petroleum exports" (1976, p. 52), changes certainly related to advances in chemistry and the rise of combustion engines. In sum, Furtado contributes to understanding how changes at the center reverberate at the periphery, with new demands for natural resources and different insertion in the international division of labor.

Finally, Furtado (1978, p. 39) differentiates the origin of the industrial civilization and its diffusion: "the world-wide spread of industrial civilization is a significantly different historical process". Outside the "European context" (1978, p. 39) – the first two movements of the "first industrial nucleus" (1987, p. 217) –[11] Furtado introduces a discussion of different "routes" to "access the industrial civilization" (1978, p. 42).

[10] As discussed in Albuquerque (2007), this interpretation of underdevelopment as a trap can be integrated with concepts from the evolutionary economics such as lock-ins and path-dependence.

[11] Even in those two first movements, an active participation of the backward region vis-à-vis Great Britain took place. In the case of the United States, see Hamilton's Report on Manufactures (1791), in the case of Germany, see List (1841).

In *Accumulation and development: the logic of industrial civilization*, Furtado (1978) presents three different forms of access and speculates about a fourth type. These different forms of access show how the propagation of technological progress depends on the nature of initiatives taken outside the dynamic center of the capitalist economy. And these initiatives, triggering another chain of events from the periphery, reshape the whole economy.

The first form of access discussed by Furtado is the case of Japan (1978, pp. 40–41, pp. 58–60). This form is an example of "assimilating an entire system of material civilization" (p. 40), and required a political transformation in Japan, a process "under the leadership of an aristocratic faction which took control of the State and transformed it into an instrument for bringing about the required social and economic changes" (1978, p. 40). This new political arrangement was able to introduce new techniques "which had already been tried out in other countries and to which access could be gained on the international markets or through bilateral agreements" (p. 40). This route of access to the industrial civilization is an example of "the deliberate creation of comparative advantages in sectors enjoying an elastic foreign demand" (1987, pp. 224–225).[12]

The second route of access is exemplified by the policies in Russia,[13] especially after the political victory of Stalin's faction and the implementation of the "experience of 'building socialism in one country'" (1978, p. 41). This experience "took the form of a concerted effort to bring about the rapid spread of industrial civilization" (p. 41). In that experience "the State came to play a much more detailed role than in the Japanese experience" (p. 41).[14]

For Furtado both cases were determined by "the consciousness of backwardness in accumulation and the threat to external domination" (1978, p. 42). It is important to highlight here this "consciousness of backwardness" because this phenomenon is an important link to the discussion of absorptive capability.

The third route is "indirect access" (1978, pp. 42–44): "[t]he expanding markets of the industrializing European countries acted as a powerful suction valve, giving rise to an increased flow of international trade" (p. 42), an expansion in the 1840s "that took the form of an exchange between manufactured goods and raw materials" (p. 43).[15] This "indirect form of access to the industrial civilization is attributed to the

[12] A systematization of the literature on Japanese catch-up is organized in Albuquerque (2014). The Japanese case is evaluated as a successful and complete catch-up process, but without the capability to forge ahead.

[13] Furtado also mentions czarist Russia as an example of the "spread of industrial civilization" as a "result of the behavior of nations reacting to threats against their sovereignty or dominant geographical position" (1978, pp. 39–40).

[14] A discussion of the Russian experiment from 1917 to 1991 is available in Albuquerque (2005, 2018). In those texts the case of USSR is evaluated as a limited, an incomplete, catch-up process, related to middle-income trap.

[15] This powerful "suction valve" was strong enough to shape one region, Latin America, with three different types of economy, according to Furtado (1976, pp. 47–49): "economies exporting temperate agricultural commodities", "economies exporting tropical agricultural products", and "economies exporting mineral products".

"structural break between the 'center' and the 'periphery'" (p. 44). The role of industrialization in this access is a topic of Furtado's reflections on the evolution of his thoughts, as he wrote in a letter to Wilson Suzigan in 9 July 2002: "I started from the idea, in the early 1950s, that industrialization automatically led to development. It was only in the following decade that I realized that full access to high technology is a race of increasing difficulty." (Editorial *Revista Brasileira de Inovação*, 2020, v. 19, p. 2).[16]

Although there are those growing difficulties to access high technology, it is possible to overcome underdevelopment (1998, pp. 47–54), as the cases of South Korea and Taiwan demonstrate (1992, p. 51).

Writing under the impact of the Chinese "cultural revolution", Furtado discusses the Chinese case as a very peculiar, giving the size of the economy (1978, pp. 109–114). He eventually speculated if China could "escape the gravitational pull of industrial civilization" (p. 114). Changes in relation to China and its role in the global economy continued to be investigated by Furtado (1992, p. 49; 1998, p. 32; 2002, p. 28).

Furtado's work introduces technological progress from the viewpoint of the periphery, with a very broad view of this global system. His elaboration on metamorphoses of capitalism (2002) is a confirmation of this global view. Looking both to the center and the periphery Furtado is able to interpret the whole system. Metamorphoses of capitalism integrate both the center and the periphery. It is not possible to understand the periphery and technical change here without a comprehension of changes at the center, because structures at the periphery change as a result of "adaptive processes in face of structural evolution at the dominant centers" (Furtado, 1986, p. 185).

Furtado and Kondratiev have both a dynamic and complementary view and an example of other interrelations between them can be suggested. On the one hand, Furtado identifies the initiative in shaping of the international division of labor with the center during the industrial revolution. On the other hand, Kondratiev identifies a succession of technological revolutions. A complementary view between them suggests that during each technological revolution the initiative in the reshaping of the international division of labor returns to the center – to the leading region. A final interrelation between these approaches is highlighted by Perez and Soete (1988): technological revolutions open windows of opportunity for backward countries to catch up.

---

[16] Furtado's view, in the 1950s, on the role of industrialization might be shared by Kondratiev in the 1920s. This suggestion of a point in common in their elaborations comes from an essay prepared by Kondratiev in 1928 – "Industry and agriculture and their interrelations" (1928b, pp. 195–216). In this essay, he writes: "Each country in a particular period in history has a specific degree of industrialization" (p. 195). Here he suggests a division of countries associated with its "degree of industrializations", according to "the proportion of industrial production in the overall production of its national economy" (p. 195): less than 1/3: "an agrarian country"; between 1/3 and 2/3: "dual agrarian/industrial", greater than 2/3: "an industrial country" (p. 195). Later, Kondratiev identifies the USSR as "an agrarian/industrial country" (p. 195). Degree of industrialization seems to be the key indicator also for Kondratiev at that time. Apparently, for Furtado in the 1950s and for Kondratiev in 1928, industrialization would be enough to solve the problem of economic backwardness.

2.2.3 Cohen and Levinthal: Absorptive Capacity

From the contemporary United States' academic world, Wesley Cohen and Daniel Levinthal put forward an important concept for our theoretical framework: absorptive capacity (Cohen & Levinthal, 1989, 1990).[17] Their concept, although elaborated to deal with innovative activities of leading firms of the leading innovation system – the United States' innovation system – is a concept essential for understanding learning and catch up – either complete or interrupted – at the periphery. The concept of absorptive capacity organizes the investigation of assimilation of technologies and knowledge from relatively backward regions, countries or firms. As discussed in the two previous sections, assimilation is a key process for the propagation of technologies from the center to the periphery.

This concept could be included as one important contribution of evolutionary economics to economic theory. As Cohen and Levinthal (1989, 579) explain, they used data from the Yale Survey (Levin et al. 1987, pp. 788–793), an investigation that is part of a collective effort to investigate the United States' innovation system. Indications of the importance active efforts and investments for learning from leading firms are already among the main results discussed by Levin et al. (1987, p. 806): "independent R&D" was ranked as the most effective method of learning in that survey. That finding confirms the theoretical elaboration from Rosenberg (1976, pp. 75–77), a reference for rethinking imitation processes as active and depending on investment for knowledge acquisition.

Absorption may be read as a synonymous with learning (1989, p. 569). But it is a special case of learning, as Cohen and Levinthal (1989, p. 570) differentiate processes of learning-by-doing, in which a firm "becomes more practiced, and hence, more efficient at doing what it is already doing", from learning related to absorptive capacity, in which "a firm may acquire outside knowledge that will permit to do something quite different" (p. 570).

Internal R&D contributes to the ability of a firm to "identify, assimilate and exploit knowledge from the environment" (p. 569). Given the dependence of "industrial innovation upon extra-mural knowledge, absorptive capacity represents an important part of a firm's ability to create new knowledge" (p. 570). Those two processes are so connected that they are in the title of their paper: "innovation and learning: the two faces of R&D".

Investments from firms contribute to the growth of "a stock of prior knowledge that constitutes the firm's absorptive capacity" and internal R&D is part of this "knowledge base" (p. 570).

A summary of the concept of absorptive capacity may put forward that it is a knowledge base necessary to "recognize, assimilate and exploit information" (p. 593) or to "identify, assimilate and exploit knowledge" (p. 569).[18] Therefore, this concept highlights that there is something before assimilation: a prior knowledge

---

[17] This subsection is based on Albuquerque (2022).

[18] For a definition of absorptive capacity see Cohen and Levinthal (1989, p. 128).

base is necessary to recognize and identify external knowledge, available knowledge. This step is very important for the propagation of new technologies discussed in the previous two sections. But to integrate the concept of absorptive capacity in our theoretical framework, we need to move from the level of firms – at leading countries – to the level of regions and/or countries.

Cohen and Levinthal make room for this move, as they observe that "sources of external knowledge are often crucial to the innovation process, whatever the organizational level at which the innovation unit is defined" (1990, p. 128). As examples of other levels, they list industries, organizations and countries (p. 128). Those comments open the door for an integration of the concept of absorptive capacity with innovation systems at the periphery, as innovation systems are institutional arrangements that are at another "organizational level" – they include firms, universities, research institutes interacting at local, regional and/or sectoral levels. Their "model structure" presents an eq. (1989, p. 571) that may connect each variable to an institution of a modern national innovation system (see Appendix, topic A.1).

Cohen and Levinthal (1990, p. 128) themselves, at least implicitly, made this connection between absorptive capacity and innovation systems as they mention that "the example of Japan illustrates the point saliently at national level". This reference allows for a theoretical transition from an elaboration within a country to an elaboration that deals with knowledge flows and learning from different countries. Wright (1999) may be useful to this transition, within the elaboration on innovation systems, as he discusses if "a nation can learn".

Another example that Cohen and Levinthal (1989, p. 569, footnote #1) present that broadens the interpretation of absorptive capacity is related to "international transfer of agricultural technology", mentioned to deal with a "different context": the research of Evenson and Kislev (1973). From that research, Cohen and Levinthal note that "international transfer of agricultural technology depends, in part, upon recipients' own research efforts" (1989, p. 569).

This example from Cohen and Levinthal (1989, p. 569) is very useful for our theoretical framework, because Evenson and Kislev (1973) are investigating technologies associated with the Green Revolution, technologies that are not under the monopoly of intellectual property – a Peace Nobel Prize, in 1970, was awarded to Norman Borlaug. This example is very instructive because it deals with technologies that were public, available for diffusion with no artificial monopolies attached to them – Evenson and Kislev (1973) show that even these public technologies do not spread automatically: their diffusion puts forward a question of "optimal research effort and the mixture of indigenous research and borrowing of knowledge" (1973, p. 1310).

Connecting local investments in knowledge and its transfer, Evenson and Kislev (1973, p. 1324) show that a "major component of research contribution is through the acceleration of the transfer of knowledge". They highlight that "[l]ittle knowledge is borrowed if no indigenous research takes place" (1973, p. 1324). Later, making an explicit case for "other organizational level", Evenson and Gollin (2003, p. 759) point the complementarity between international research centers and national systems of agricultural research, as "diffusion patterns reflect the importance of location-specific breeding" – a "second-stage research" developed locally for better adaptation of seeds to specific local conditions (2003, p. 759).

The institutional bases of these diffusion processes are empirically investigated by Evenson (2005). His database shows that in 12 countries the technologies of Green Revolution had spread in a very limited way – less than 2% of adoption of those modern varieties (p. 365).[19] In those countries, notes Evenson (2005, p. 368) "[n]one had universities to train agricultural scientists".

This finding from Evenson connects basic references for our theoretical framework: the concept of absorptive capability with key institutions of innovation systems – universities and research institutes (Nelson, 1993). This connection is another way to introduce innovation systems in this discussion, suggesting that innovation systems, especially at the periphery, are institutions that incorporate absorption capacity.[20]

Firms are another key institution of innovation systems. Firms at peripheral countries will also try to exploit outside knowledge, from foreign sources – therefore it is not difficult to apply the concept of absorptive capacity to firms located in different countries. This is an additional reason to integrate innovation systems and absorptive capacity.

Although the concept of absorptive capacity had not yet been formulated, its connection with innovation systems can be grasped since the works that pioneered the concept of innovation system – Freeman (1982) discusses the case of nineteenth century German catch up and the contribution of List (1841),[21] and Freeman (1987) investigates the Japanese catch up after the Second World War. Since national innovation systems and their institutions depend on political initiatives, a connection with analysis of political institutions seems to be necessary to understand preconditions for absorptive capacity. Analyzing the spread of mechanize textile technologies, Beckert (2014, p. 156) highlights that "the map of modern states corresponds almost perfectly to the map of the regions that saw early cotton industrialization".

In both cases, learning was an essential part of those processes, and in both cases institutions for this process of learning with more advanced countries were created. In the case of Germany, Freeman points how List understood "the mental capital and productive powers of the nation" depended on "the capacity to assimilate and use all the discoveries, inventions and improvements which had been made in any part of the world and improve them" (Freeman, 1982, p. 558). There were three channels for acquisition of English technology: emigration of British inventors, "German inventors and entrepreneurs working in England", and "development of an education and

[19] Those 12 countries are: Afghanistan, Angola, Burundi, Central Africa Republic, Congo, Gambia, Guinea-Bissau, Mauritania, Mongolia, Niger, Somalia and Yemen (Evenson, 2005, p. 365).

[20] Additionally, Evenson's discussion of technological progress within agriculture contributes to rethink schemes of development – as that suggested by Kondratiev (1928b, p. 195): agrarian countries should incorporate technical changes from abroad to keep their production. Another way to note that changes at the center – new techniques of food production – impacts the periphery.

[21] Freeman (1995) suggests that List (1841), with his proposals for German catch up, puts forward what latter was conceptualized as national innovation systems.

training system" (p. 558).[22] In the case of Japan, almost a century later, R&D had a very important role, as one section of Freeman's chapter on innovation system shows: "strategy for research and development at enterprise level in relation to imported technology and 'reverse engineering'" (Freeman, 1987, p. 39) – R&D at firm level was part of the strategy to acquire foreign technology.[23]

In those two pioneering papers, Freeman makes a clear connection between the need of relatively backward countries to learn with more advanced ones, assimilate their knowledge, and the formation of institutions to support that assimilation – innovation systems are these institutional arrangements.

The literature of innovation systems, especially when dealing with countries that implemented catch-up processes, is rich in examples of how absorptive capacity was built. The case studies presented in Nelson (1993) can be read as a collection of examples of formation of absorptive capacity.

Mowery and Rosenberg (1993), in their review of "the US system before 1945" (p. 31), comment the "ability of the United States to exploit foreign sources of knowledge (importing machinery, blueprints, and skilled tinkerers from Europe and elsewhere)" (p. 31). In that section there is a reference to a previous study of Rosenberg (1972), a book that summarizes the United States transition from "America as borrower" (1972, chapter 4)[24] to "America as initiator" (1972, chapter 5). Mowery and Rosenberg (p. 36) also stress how important US scientists before 1940 "completed their studies at European universities" (p. 36).

Keck (1993) presents the "historical origins in the nineteenth century" of the German NSI, with a reference to F. List, a "leading protagonist of industrial development" (1993, p. 116).[25] Keck shows how "[i]n the first third of the nineteenth century Germany turned to foreign countries, mainly to Britain, but also to Belgium, for new machinery and for skilled workers to bring advanced technology to its

[22] List's (1841) propositions and Freeman's (1982) analysis qualify Furtado's (1987) interpretation of the initial expansion of "industrial civilization" to the European continent: that process was dependent on internal efforts to assimilate technologies from abroad, from the leading country – England in that case.

[23] A comparison of those two cases – Germany, end of the nineteenth century, Japan, second half of the twentieth century – may introduce a broader discussion on the changes of mechanisms necessary to import foreign technologies. As succeeding technological revolutions, over time, impact the rest of the world, the institutions to assimilate them also change – that is why internal R&D is mentioned only for the case of Japan in those two texts from Freeman.

[24] In Rosenberg's chapter on "America as a borrower", he explains the process: "In large measure, her economic development in this period involved the transfer and exploitation of British techniques. But this does not mean that the transfer process and its internal diffusion through American economy was either simple or effortless" (1972, p. 60).

[25] List's influence is very important for our investigation, as Maria Bach (2021) describes how he was discussed by authors involved in the emergence of an Indian Economics, in the end of the nineteenth century. However, Maria Bach presents some limits of List's elaboration, as he "denied the possibility of Asian progress" (2021, p. 492). For this aspect of List's elaboration, related to a broader elaboration on his vision on industrialization possibilities of nations outside "the temperate zone", see Boianovsky (2013, p. 649).

industries" (p. 116). Keck's relates Germany's backwardness to the important role of the government in development, highlighting the "government-financed system for education and research in technology, science and business" (p. 117).

Odagiri and Goto (1993) describe the government policies in Meiji Japan, "to import advanced foreign technology and to catch up with Western countries economically and militarily" (p. 79). For them, Meiji Japan used diverse methods to absorb science and technology from abroad: written information, people, goods and capital (p. 79). In this chapter, they summarize the development of three industries since the Meiji era: iron and steel, electrical and communication equipment, and automobiles (pp. 89–101). These chapters, especially the chapter on iron and steel, are excellent illustrations of the role of learning and experiments to imitate existing technologies – an example of how imitation involves the continuity of innovative process. For the catch up after the Second World War, Odagiri and Goto (1993, p. 111) confirm the positive relationship between local R&D expenditures and imported technology described by Freeman (1987, pp. 39–45).

For the cases of South Korea (Kim, 1993) and Taiwan (Hou & Gee, 1993), the policies to learn from more developed countries described in those chapters probably included learning from all previous catch-up processes, given their broad structure. Kim (1993, p. 358) defines "technological capabilities" as the most important factor for development – "[t]echnological capability enables one to assimilate, use, adapt, change or create technology" (1993, p. 358). The "acquisition of technological capabilities" is a process with different macro- and micro-factors, that involve different things as "procurement of turnkey plants" (p. 360), reverse engineering of "imports of foreign capital goods" (p. 361), government priorities for "'strategic industries' for import substitution and export promotion" (p. 362) and building of science and technology infrastructure, with the establishment of the Korea Institute of Science and Technology (KIST), in 1966 (p. 364). In the case of Taiwan, new modes of learning are mentioned, as "overseas mergers" (Hou & Gee, 1993, p. 403–404), a way for "acquiring needed technology" (p. 404).

In sum, Nelson (1993) may be read as a collection on illustrations on how innovation systems in different times and different countries use a mosaic of tools, policies and strategies, from the firm level to government policies, to create and develop absorptive capacities to support technological development, processes that involved a transition from imitation to innovation in all countries that are now part of the center of capitalist global economy.

Returning to the original elaboration of Cohen and Levinthal (1989, 1990) after these short references of Nelson's book on national innovation systems, it may be suggested that the concept of absorptive capacity is well connected to one key role of innovation systems, that use both universities and firms to learn from external knowledge coming from abroad. This dialogue between absorptive capacity and innovation systems broadens the application of Cohen and Levinthal's concept and enables its inclusion in our theoretical framework. Since it is a concept important, at one extreme, to understand innovation in leading sectors of leading countries – the case of United States' firms discussed using the data from the Yale Survey – and at another extreme, to understand how agricultural techniques are transferred to least developed countries – the case shown by Evenson (2005) – our theoretical framework can incorporate it as an explicative element for the propagation of new technologies at all levels of development.

Cohen and Levinthal's elaboration also can deal with dynamic changes in absorptive capacity. There are changes in the technologies to be assimilated and changes in the organization capacity to absorb external knowledge.

For the nature of the knowledge to be assimilated, Cohen and Levinthal (1989) includes in their model a variable "ease of learning", which "depends upon the characteristics of the underlying technological and scientific knowledge upon which the innovation depends in a given industry" (1989, p. 570) (see Appendix).

For the nature of the organization that tries to assimilate knowledge, they stress that "firm's capacity to absorb externally generated knowledge depends on its R&D effort" (p. 571)

Those two characteristics may be broadened to include other types of knowledge, beyond what is the target for firms. Their comments on international transfer of agricultural research are an illustration of this possibility: on the one hand, there is technological and scientific knowledge produced in leading research institutions as public knowledge, on the other hand, there are not firms but agricultural research institutes. This broadening of those two variables – ease of learning and internal R&D efforts – makes room for a utilization of the concept of absorptive capacity in innovation systems and for changes over time in both variables. Resuming a dialogue with Perez' *big bangs*, certainly each succeeding *big bang* is related to technologies that differ in their scientific content and in their complexity. Those different *big bangs* will propagate differently on a global scale, given different stages of innovation systems' formation at the periphery: between the first *big bang* and the sixth *big bang*, the presence of firms and universities at the periphery changed, with larger absorptive capacity built. The combination of those two features of absorptive capacity is a component of how different technologies propagate throughout the world.[26]

2.3 A Tentative Theoretical Framework: A Combined Dynamics of Expansion and Assimilation

A tentative integration of the contributions of Kondratiev, Furtado and Cohen and Levinthal starts with a recapitulation of their most important points.

From Kondratiev, this theoretical framework learns how technological revolutions trigger major cyclical movements in the capitalist economy, how they are integrated with expansionary forces that incorporates new regions into the global

[26] In Appendix, topic A.2, there is a tentative adaptation of Cohen and Levinthal's model to learning between different national systems of innovation.

economy – searching for new markets and new sources of raw materials – and how this expansion depends on the resources, economic needs and strength at the leading capitalist regions.

From Furtado, the contribution is on how the industrial revolution – and other important technological changes – expands the economies at the center and reconfigures the global economy with a center-periphery divide. In this reconfiguration the initiative is with the center, that irradiates expansionary forces arriving at and impacting the periphery, that gain new roles with the changing international division of labor. Late developing regions and the periphery are loci of assimilation of technology, a process that uncovers the nature of technological progress at the periphery.

From Cohen and Levinthal, the formalization of the concept of absorptive capacity elaborates all dimensions necessary for the assimilation of technologies at the periphery – identification, assimilation and exploration of external knowledge. Their reference to the works of Evenson makes room for its application beyond industries and to regions and countries at different levels of development. The variables in their model allow a theoretical integration of absorptive capacity with the concept of innovation systems.

These three contributions – technological revolutions at the center, the nature of technological progress at the periphery, and absorptive capacity – must be integrated to compose a dynamic that underlies this book's research: a dynamic that combines expansionary and assimilatory forces.

Expansionary forces from the center have many forms, with impacts that may be direct or indirect. In some situations, there is the direct impact of the destructive side of the process of creative destruction: the impact of existing goods produced in improved technical condition – this is the case of the first technological revolution, the British industrial revolution. These direct impacts – note, we are not dealing with an automatic process of spread of the new technology, but of its effects – reconfigure economies, reshape traditional producers of existing goods and trigger a chain of events that transforms the impacted economy, first, and later the leading economy – by the reverberation of the reactions to this first impact.

Expansionary forces have also indirect – or not immediate effects – through the rise of incomes in the leading country, a consequence of the productivity gains from the technological revolution, that will later create a new or growing demand for consumer goods – agricultural products, mineral products – or natural resources that are input for the new product or process. This demand will reorganize the international division of labor, with new or reinforced roles of regions in the provision of these goods. This new role of regions at the periphery will provide resources that may be reinvested later in new opportunities opened by these domestic changes. Over time – the time delay here is very important – small nuclei of industrial investment may arise at the periphery, changing its structure and initiating a local and own economic dynamic – a transition to peripheric forms of capitalism. This long and time-consuming chain of economic events is necessary for a process of assimilation of the technology that started the whole process. But since it took time to accumulate all conditions for an initial process of technological assimilation, the original technology – related to the big bang of a specific technological revolution – has improved, changed, and eventually might have incorporated features of a subsequent technological revolution.

Expansionary forces, therefore, may assume different forms, from sales of goods processed by new machines to the creation of subsidiaries of transnational corporations – but all of them impact and change the affected economy forever. In sum, the nature and the path of the chain of events created by the perturbation, mediated or not, consequent to each big bang depends on the nature of the technological revolution.

Assimilatory forces in the periphery are the main source of propagation and irradiation of big bangs. The concept of absorptive capacity shows how real assimilation depends on diverse factors, conditions and institutions. The interrelation between absorptive capacity, development at the periphery and innovation systems stresses how important are both its microeconomics foundations and its relationship with political institutions. Absorptive capacity can be read as microeconomic concept, an elaboration related to the imitation side of Schumpeter's classic innovative process – as Rosenberg puts forward, imitation is not an effortless process and is a continuation of the innovation. Absorptive capacity depends on institutions – firms, universities, public research institutes – that are building blocks of innovation systems. Innovation systems, in turn, depend on political conditions and organizations.[27]

The key point of this theoretical framework is the combined operation of expansionary and assimilatory forces, arising from different geographical locations: expansion from the center, assimilation by the periphery. This combination is not homogeneous in time nor in space: different technological revolutions would have different expansionary forces – would propagate in different forms, with different speeds, with different blocking factors, demanding different absorptive capacities – and they would impact different societies and different socio-economic formations, with different assimilation skills, shaped inter alia by previous reconfigurations triggered by previous technological revolutions. This means that the combinations between the forces of expansion and assimilation change over time – combined processes with different combinations.

The combined operation of those two forces has a delayed dynamic. It takes time for the big bang to reach the periphery, it takes time for the creation of the necessary conditions for the assimilatory forces to operate.

[27] In Appendix, topic A.2, there are two variables that may depend heavily on political conditions. First, the variable NSI: national innovation system is dependent on domestic initiatives, thus institutional changes as political independence has implication for its formation and evolution. Second, the variable α: a country awareness of technological revolutions happening abroad -, a variable that depends on international relations between different regions, that include even the capacity to very simple initiatives such as foreign travels and visits to know what is happening abroad.

Different combinations between expansionary and assimilatory forces generate different outcomes. One outcome may be a country (or region or firm) that builds a high level of absorptive capacity and achieves a full assimilation of a given technology or set of technologies: this process is a successful catch up. Another outcome may be a country (or region or firm) that does not build any significant absorptive capacity and therefore is unable to assimilate a given technology: this process is a persistent lagging behind.

"Underdevelopment as a historical trap" (Furtado, 1992) has a peculiar combination between expansionary and assimilatory forces. Interpreted as a structural phenomenon, on the one hand it allows a country to be inserted in the international division of labor in a predominantly passive way. This passive insertion can be related to late and limited industrialization – a pattern of industrialization that increases the structural heterogeneity within the peripheric economy. On the other hand, this phenomenon contains internal factors that block the complete dissemination of technological revolutions – limited size of local markets, derived from income concentration and related consequences on education and health. Underdevelopment, in Furtado's view, shows an oscillation between periods of limited catch up followed by periods of lagging behind. This oscillation, over time, generates the dynamic that traps a country at an income level – therefore the low-income trap and the middle-income trap.[28]

This overall dynamic can be summarized as having a *big bang* as a starting point, each having specific characteristics related to the nature of the technology and the ways and routes of its expansion. Each new technology is related to geographical inclusion of new regions in the global economy. The change brought by the first *big bang* – the industrial revolution – reshaped the global economy with a reconfiguration of the center-periphery divide. This divide defines two different dynamics that put forth specific challenges to the countries that are impacted by technological revolutions coming from the center. For the periphery, assimilation of technologies is a key issue and it is consequence of absorptive capacities built in those regions. The level of absorptive capacity is dependent on institution building, which by its turn depends upon political conditions to build innovation systems.

As the initial big bang did not find a void global economy, but rather very different societies, with different pre-capitalist economies with diverse levels of manufacturing production and different political organization, a global differentiation process started. The first *big bang* had an uneven impact, also depending on the knowledge of the peripheral region of the events at the center – it is not possible to absorb technologies that you do not identify or recognize. In the end, all regions of the world were able – or forced – to recognize the industrial revolution. This level of recognition may be seen as the initial factor to shape the regions' absorptive capability. The outcome of the form of the impact and level and speed of assimilation of the first *big bang* was the starting point for a subsequent process triggered by a

[28]For the middle-income trap in Brazil interpreted as this oscillation of periods of catching up and falling behind over time, see Albuquerque (2019).

second *big bang* – with repercussions on different societies reshaped by the first process. After the first *big bang*, at least in five other moments this process was triggered again. The current outcome of these big bangs and their impact is a global economy based on a very heterogeneous periphery.

The sequence of five (or six) technological revolutions – a simplification and a stylization of a more turbulent dynamic involving overlapping and interactions between many more GPTs irradiating from the center – transforms again and again the global economy, making it impossible to have any repetition of previous events. This superposition and overlapping might be more complicated at the periphery, given the different previous levels of development of backward economies and different processes of assimilation.

The resulting out-of-equilibrium economy has all the features of complex systems, as there are more technologies – more products, more processes – more agents – firms, universities, banks, governments – more regions with more complicated structures, more networks, larger markets, more feedback mechanisms operating and self-reinforcing interactions, more possibilities of crises and transformations derived from their impact and overcoming. As "more is different", those processes are signals and evidence of complex systems (Anderson, 1972) – a theoretical framework that this book, whenever possible, will try to apply.

The next chapters focus on perturbations triggered by different big bangs, to help us to understand in more concrete and illustrated way this combined and uneven dynamic of expansion and assimilation. The chapters in Part II follow the order of the big bangs selected by Perez, a simplification that helps to organize the investigations of this book, making it possible to follow each isolated technology, its arrival at different regions and how it spread there.

Appendix: Notes on Absorptive Capacity and National Innovation Systems

This Appendix presents Cohen and Levinthal's original formulation and a tentative suggestion on how to adapt it to investigate absorption between countries. Only the equations more directly related to the theoretical framework presented in this chapter are shown.

A.1. Cohen and Levinthal's Original Elaboration

In their article Cohen and Levinthal (1989, p. 571) prepared an equation to summarize their elaboration – their Eq. (2.1), presented below:

$$z_i = M_i + \gamma_i \left(\theta \sum_{j \neq i} M_j + T \right) \tag{2.1}$$

Where:

- z_i: "additions to firm i's stock of scientific and technological knowledge" (p. 571);
- M_i: "firm's investment in R&D" (p. 571);
- γ_i: "firm's capacity to absorb externally generated knowledge" that "depends on its R&D efforts", with values between 0 and 1 (p. 571);
- θ: "the degree to which the research effort of one firm may spill over to a pool of knowledge potentially available to all other firms" (p. 571);
- T: "the level of extra-industry knowledge" (p. 571).

Completing the explanation of their equation, Cohen and Levinthal (1989, pp. 571–572) introduce a new variable (β) that affect the firm's absorptive capacity, in Eq. (2.2):

$$\gamma_i \equiv \gamma(M_i, \beta) \tag{2.2}$$

Where:

- β: a variable that "reflects the characteristics of outside knowledge", which "would include the complexity of knowledge to be assimilated" (p. 572).

Later in their elaboration, this variable (β) is associated with the "ease of learning" (Cohen & Levinthal, 1989, p. 574).

A.2 An Exploratory Adaptation for Flows Between Countries

A tentative adaptation of the basic equation of absorptive capacity to help investigations of flows between countries is presented below. This exploratory adaptation is presented as a tool, to be potentially used in Parts II and III of this book. The original contribution of Cohen and Levinthal, as discussed in Part I, is a key component of the theoretical framework presented in this chapter, and it may be extended to include countries and/or regions – as they suggest (Cohen & Levinthal, 1989, p. 569; 1990, p. 128). The mediation for this extension is a dialogue with the literature on innovation systems.

The adapted scheme is as follows, in three equations – (2.3), (2.4) and (2.5):

$$z_{NSIi} = \left(\sum M_i + T_i\right) + \alpha\gamma_{NSI_i}\left(\theta\sum_{j\neq i} NSI_j\right) \tag{2.3}$$

$$\gamma_{NSI_i} \equiv \gamma\left(\sum M_i + T_i, \beta_n, GAP\right) \tag{2.4}$$

$$GAP_{(t)} \equiv NSI_{L(t-1)} - NSI_{P(t-1)} \tag{2.5}$$

Where:

- z_{NSIi}: additions to country i innovation system's stock of scientific and technological knowledge;
- NSI_i: stock of scientific and technological knowledge accumulated by country i innovation system
- α: a variable to measure the country i innovation system's awareness on technological revolutions emerging abroad;
- γ_{NSI_i}: the country i innovation system's capacity to absorb knowledge generated abroad;
- β_n: as defined by Cohen and Levinthal (1989, p. 592) – see Eq. 2.2, above – but now adapted to include n – the number of each technological revolution.
- $GAP_{(t)}$: the technological gap between one peripheric country (P, in Eq. 2.5) and the leading country (L, in Eq. 2.5)

The additions in Cohen and Levinthal original formulation suggested in Eqs. 2.3, 2.4 and 2.5 are based on two changes of viewpoints. The first is to broaden the elaboration to think in terms of countries – using national systems of innovation as a reference, a concept that includes firms and universities as key institutions. The second is to include succeeding technological revolutions.

The investments in science and technology in NSI_i involve investments and previous knowledge accumulated by firms (M) and by extra-industrial sources (T), that may include universities and research institutions (Cohen & Levinthal, 1989, p. 573). One country's NSI will learn with other countries NSIs – therefore the $i \neq j$ in the second summatory of Eq. 2.3. This learning will depend on the country i innovation system's absorption capacity (as in the case of firms in the original formulation of Cohen and Levinthal) and also from a new variable α – a way to measure a previous condition for any absorptive capacity: to be aware of the existence of a given or new technology. While this variable is equal to zero, no chance of an absorption process to begin.

The absorption capacity of innovation systems in an economy that generates successive technological revolutions is impacted by two dynamic variables. The first is related to the complexity of technologies, which may vary according to each technological revolution: one empirical regularity in the comparison of these different technological revolutions is the growing dependence of technologies in relation to science – a regularity that demands a new item to describe differences in this feature of the nature of each technology: changes over time. This feature might be translated in a conjecture that over time – following successive technological revolutions – the variable β increases (thus, $\beta_{(n)} > \beta_{(n-1)}$). The second new variable – GAP – captures intertemporal changes between stocks of scientific and technological knowledge of countries: the size of this GAP may facilitate (if small), difficult (if big) or even block (if very large) the absorptive capacities of peripheric countries.

These tentative adaptations in Cohen and Levinthal's original elaboration are only a tool to help the investigation in Part II and the reflections on the theoretical framework that Part III presents.

References

Albuquerque, E. M. (2005). Lições da tragédia: limites e contradições do progresso tecnológico na União Soviética. In J. A. Paula (Ed.), *Adeus ao desenvolvimento: a opção do governo Lula* (pp. 253–273). Autêntica Editora.

Albuquerque, E. M. (2007). Inadequacy of technology and innovation systems at the periphery. *Cambridge Journal of Economics, 31*, 669–690.

Albuquerque, E. M. (2014). Catch up completo e forging ahead bloqueado: notas sobre o processo de desenvolvimento japonês. *História Econômica & História de Empresas, 17*, 535–565.

Albuquerque, E. M. (2018). Natureza da transição e tipo de capitalismo: notas sobre o fim da economia de comando na URSS e a emergência de um capitalismo dirigido pelo estado. *História Econômica & História de Empresas, 21*, 203–232.

Albuquerque, E. M. (2019). Brazil and the middle-income trap: Its historical roots. *Seoul Journal of Economics, 32*, 23–62.

Albuquerque, E. M. (2020). Uneven and combined development as a methodological tool: A dynamic approach after a dialogue between Kondratiev and Trotsky. *Revista da Sociedade Brasileira de Economia Política, 57*, 143–173.

Albuquerque, E. M. (2022). Aprendizado tecnológico: capacidade de absorção, conhecimento e processos de catching up. *Análise Econômica* (forthcoming).

Anderson, P. W. (1972). More is different: Broken symmetry and the nature of the hierarchical structure in science. *Science, 177*(4047), 393–396.

Anderson, P. W. (1988). A physicist looks at economics: An overview of the workshop. In P. W. Anderson, K. J. Arrow, & D. Pines (Eds.), *The economy as an evolving complex system* (pp. 265–274). CRC Press.

Anderson, M. (1990). The social implications of demographic change. In F. Thompson (ed.) The Cambridge Social History of Britain, 1750–1950. Cambridge: Cambridge University Press, (pp. 1–70). https://doi.org/10.1017/CHOL9780521257893.002

Arthur, B. (2013). *Complexity and the economy*. Oxford University Press.

Arthur, B. (2021). Foundations of complexity economics. *Nature Reviews Physics, 3*, 136–145.

Bach, M. (2021). A win-win model of economic development: How Indian economics redefined universal development from and at the margins, 1870–1905. *Journal of the History of Economic Thought, 43*(4), 483–505.

Beckert, S. (2014). *Empire of cotton: A global history*. Vintage Books.

Bogdanov, V. E. (1926). Discussion of the reports to the meetings on 6 and 13 February 1926. In N. Makasheva, W. J. Samuels, & V. Barnett (Eds.), *The works of Nikolai D. Kondratiev* (pp. 114–118). Pickering and Chato.

Boianovsky, M. (2013). Friedrich List and the economic fate of tropical countries. *History of Political Economy, 45*(4), 647–691.

Bresnahan, T., & Trajtenberg, M. (1995). General purpose technologies: 'Engines of growth'? *Journal of Econometrics, 65*(1), 83–108.

Cohen, W., & Levinthal, D. (1989). Innovation and learning: The two faces of R&D. *The Economic Journal, 99*(397), 569–596.

Cohen, W., & Levinthal, D. (1990). Absorptive capacity: A new perspective on learning and innovation. *Administrative Science Quarterly, 35*, 128–152.

Day, R. (1976). The theory of long cycle: Kondratiev, Trotsky, Mandel. *New Left Review, 99*, 67–82.

Evenson, R. E., & Gollin, D. (2003). Assessing the impact of the green revolution, 1960 to 2000. *Science, 300*(2), 758–762.

Evenson, R. E., & Kislev, Y. (1973). Research and productivity in wheat and maize. *Journal of Political Economy, 81*(6), 1309–1329.

Evenson, R. E. (2005). The green revolution and the gene revolution in Pakistan: Policy implications. *The Pakistan Development Review, 44*(4), 359–386.

Franco, M. P. V., Ribeiro, L. C., & Albuquerque, E. M. (2022). Beyond random causes: Harmonic analysis of business cycles at the Moscow Conjuncture Institute. *Journal of the History of Economic Thought, 44*(3), 456–476. https://doi.org/10.1017/S1053837221000092

Freeman, C. (1982) Technological infrastructure and international competitiveness. Industrial and Corporate Change, v. 13, n, 3, pp. 541–569. (2004).

Freeman, C. (1995). The "National System of innovation" in historical perspective. *Cambridge Journal of Economics, 19*(1), 5–24.

Freeman, C. (2002). Preface. In *Perez* (pp. ix–xii). Edward Elgar.

Freeman, C. (1987). *Technology policy and economic performance: Lessons from Japan*. Pinter Publishers.

Freeman, C., & Louçã, F. (2001). *As time goes by: From the industrial revolutions and to the information revolution*. Oxford University.

Furtado, C. (1961). *Development and underdevelopment*. University of California Press. (1964).

Furtado, C. (1976). *Economic development of Latin America* (2nd ed.). Cambridge University Press.

Furtado, C. (1978). *Accumulation and development: The logic of industrial civilization*. Martin Robertson. (1983). https://archive.org/details/accumulationdeve0000furt/

Furtado, C. (1986). *Teoria e política do desenvolvimento econômico* (2ª edição). Nova Cultural.

Furtado, C. (1987). In G. Meier (Ed.), *Pioneers of development Underdevelopment: To conform or to reform* (Second Series) (pp. 203–227). Oxford University/World Bank.

Furtado, C. (1992). *Brasil: a construção interrompida*. Paz e Terra.

Furtado, C. (1998). *Global capitalism*. Fondo de Cultura Económica. (1999) Available at: http://webshells.com/spantrans/furtado.html

Furtado, C (2002) Metamorfoses do Capitalismo. In: D'aguiar, Rosa F. (Org.) Essencial Celso Furtado. : Penguin/Companhia das Letras, pp. 450–457 (2013).

Hamilton, A. (1791). *Report on manufactures*. Senate. (1913).

Hou, C. M., & Gee, S. (1993). National systems supporting advance in industry: The case of Taiwan. In R. R. Nelson (Ed.), *National innovation systems: A comparative analysis* (pp. 384–413). Oxford University.

Jeremy, D. I. (1977). Damming the flood: British government efforts to check the outflow of technicians and machinery, 1780–1843. *The Business History Review, 51*(1), 1–34.

Keck, O. (1993). The national system for technical innovation in Germany. In R. R. Nelson (Ed.), *National innovation systems: A comparative analysis* (pp. 115–157). Oxford University.

Kim, L. (1993). National system of industrial innovation: Dynamics of capability building in Korea. In R. R. Nelson (Ed.), *National innovation systems: A comparative analysis* (pp. 357–383). Oxford University.

Kondratiev, N. D. (1922). The world economy and its conjunctures during and after the war. *Moscow: International Kondratiev Foundation, 2004*, 1922.

Kondratiev, N. D. (1926a). Long cycles of economic conjuncture. In N. Makasheva, W. J. Samuels, & V. Barnett (Eds.), *The works of Nikolai D. Kondratiev* (Vol. 1, pp. 25–60). Pickering and Chato. (1998).

Kondratiev, N. D. (1926b). Les grand cycles de la conjuncture. In *Les grands cycles de la conjoncture* (pp. 109–168). Economica. Édition presenté par Louis Fontvielle (1992).

Kondratiev, N. D. (1928a). La dynamique des prix des produits industriels et agricoles. In *Les grands cycles de la conjoncture* (pp. 377–492). Economica. Édition presenté par Louis Fontvielle (1992).

Kondratiev, N. D. (1928b). Industry and agriculture and their interrelations. In N. Makasheva, W. J. Samuels, & V. Barnett (Eds.), *The works of Nikolai D. Kondratiev* (Vol. 3, pp. 195–218). Pickering and Chato. (1998).

Lee, K., & Malerba, F. (2017). Catch-up cycles and changes in industrial leadership: Windows of opportunity and responses of firms and countries in the evolution of sectoral systems. *Research Policy, 46*, 338–351.

Levin, R., Klevorick, A., Nelson, R., & Winter, S. (1987). Appropriating the returns from industrial research and development. *Brookings Papers on Economic Activity, 3*, 783–832.
List, F. (1841). *Sistema nacional de economia política*. Abril Cultural. (1983).
Makasheva, N., Samuels, W., & Barnett, V. (1998). *The works of Nikolai D. Kondratiev*. Pickering and Chato.
Marques, S. F. (2014). *Mudanças na Clivagem Centro-Periferia e o Efeito Bumerangue: o impacto da periferia na reconfiguração sistêmica do capitalismo no século XXI*. Cedeplar-UFMG. (Tese de Doutorado).
Mazzoleni, R., & Nelson, R. (2007). Public research institutions and economic catch-up. *Research Policy, 36*(10), 1512–1528.
Meier, G. (1987). *Pioneers in development* (Second series). Oxford University/World Bank.
Meier, G., & Seers, D. (1984). *Pioneers in development*. Oxford University/World Bank.
Mowery, D. C., & Rosenberg, N. (1993). The U.S. national innovation system. In R. R. Nelson (Ed.), *National innovation systems: A comparative analysis* (pp. 29–75). Oxford University.
Mustafin, A. (2018). *Kondratiev long cycles: New information about discussions in the USSR in the 1920s*. National Research University/Higher School of Economics (WP BRP/168/HUM/2018).
Nelson, R. R. (1993). *National innovation systems: A comparative analysis*. Oxford University.
Odagiri, H., & Goto, A. (1993). The Japanese system of innovation: Past, present and future. In R. Nelson (Ed.), *National innovation systems: A comparative analysis* (pp. 76–114). Oxford University.
Paula, J. A., & Albuquerque, E. M. (2020). A formação do pensamento de Celso Furtado, o imperativo tecnológico e as metamorfoses do capitalismo. *Revista Brasileira de Inovação, 19*, e0200027.
Perez, C. (2002). *Technological revolutions and financial capital*. Edward Elgar.
Perez, C. (2010). Technological revolutions and techno-economic paradigms. *Cambridge Journal of Economics, 34*(1), 185–202.
Perez, C., & Soete, L. (1988). Catching up in technology: Entry barriers and windows of opportunity. In G. Dosi, C. Freeman, R. Nelson, et al. (Eds.), *Technical change and economic theory* (pp. 458–479). Pinter.
Ribeiro, L. C., Deus, L. G., Loureiro, P. M., & Albuquerque, E. M. (2017). Profits and fractal properties: Notes on Marx, countertendencies and simulation models. *Review of Political Economy, 29*(2), 282–306. https://doi.org/10.1080/09538259.2016.1265823
Rosenberg, N. (1972). *Technology and American economic growth*. M. E. Sharpe.
Rosenberg, N. (1976). *Perspectives of technology*. Cambridge University Press.
Rosenberg, N. (1996). Uncertainty and technical change. In R. Landau, T. Taylor, & G. Wright (Eds.), *The mosaic of economic growth* (pp. 334–353). Stanford University.
Rosenberg, N. (1998) Chemical engineering as a General Purpose Technology. In: Helpman, E. General Purpose Technologies and economic growth. Cambridge, Mass./London: The MIT Press, pp. 167–192.
Schumpeter, J. A. (1911). *A teoria do desenvolvimento econômico* (p. 1985). Nova Cultural.
Schumpeter, J. A. (1939). *Business cycles: A theoretical, historical and statistical analysis of the capitalist process* (Vol. 1). McGraw-Hill Book Company, Inc.
Slutsky, E. E. (1937). The summation of random causes as the source of cyclic processes. *Econometrica, 5*(2), 105–146.
Statista. (2022). *Population of the world 10,000 BCE-2100*. https://www.statista.com/statistics/1006502/global-population-ten-thousand-bc-to-2050/
Trotsky, L. (1923). *The curve of capitalist development*. Available at https://www.marxists.org/archive/trotsky/1923/04/capdevel.htm
Weinberg, S. (1993). *The first three minutes*: A modern view of the origin of the universe. Updated edition. Basic Books.
Wright, G. (1999) Can a nation learn? American technology as a network phenomenon. Stanford: Stanford University (captured at http://www-econ.stanford.edu/faculty/workp/, Oct. 20, 2021).

Part II
Technological Revolutions and Their Impacts on the Periphery

Chapter 3
The Initial Impacts of the Industrial Revolution: An "Astonishing Reversal" – 1771–1850

3.1 Introduction

Arkwright's mill in 1771 is, for Carlota Perez (2010, p. 190), the big bang of the first technological revolution.[1] Arkwright's invention was the cotton mill, a new machine that transformed the production method of an existing and important commodity – cotton textile. This is a peculiarity of the first technological revolution: a change in a commodity that was produced, by artisanal and handicraft methods, in many different regions.

This first technological revolution had a direct impact on the world as it reverberated in all previous cotton textile producing regions.[2] The history of cotton manufacture has roots in ancient times: Diamond (2017, pp. 120–121) describes the domestication of cotton and later cultivation of cotton as a fiber crop as a process that spread through different regions in the Old World, such as India, West Africa/Sahel, Andes/Amazonia and Mesoamerica (see also, Beckert, 2017, pp. 12–13).

---

[1] Kondratiev (1926, p. 39) presents three features of this first industrial revolution: (1) it "affected almost all the main industrial sectors: spinning and weaving, the chemical industry, the metallurgic industry and so on", it "also affected techniques of communication"; (2) a set of innovations were at the starting point of this phase, and there was a time lag between them – it "was preceded and accompanied by a series of significant technical inventions", lasting "from 1764 to 1795" -; (3) a lag between the invention and its practical application, as "significant inventions began in mid 1760s", while its "broad practical application . . . . occurred after the 1770s in the 1780s and later" (p. 39).

[2] This may be a difference with the other technological revolutions: only this first impacted a product already produced – cotton textiles. The subsequent technological revolutions were based on new products – steam-engines, electricity, automobiles, computers. These new products replaced other forms of transport, of energy production, of information processing, but they did not displace their previous producers – later stages of each technological revolution impacted regions that began to produce these new technologies but did not follow the sequence of "improvements after improvements", as suggested by Rosenberg (1996). Another specificity of this first technological revolution is the inauguration of a "natural trajectory", as suggested by Nelson and Winter (1977, p. 58): "increasing mechanization of operations that have been done by hand".

E. da Motta e Albuquerque, *Technological Revolutions and the Periphery*, Contributions to Economics, https://doi.org/10.1007/978-3-031-43436-5_3

These early roots may explain why cotton textiles were manufactured in different regions located in India, China, West Africa and Japan before the Industrial Revolution (Beckert, 2014, pp. 18–22). The initial spread of cotton manufacturing techniques from India and China to Europe is a process dated from the tenth century (Beckert, 2014, pp. 22–23).

Until the eighteenth century, India was the "textile workshop of the world" (Darwin, 2007, p. 193). Regions in India, China and Japan were "neck to neck" with regions in Europe in the eve of the Industrial Revolution (Pomeranz, 2000, pp. 7–8).

The global dissemination of diverse forms of cotton manufacturing – handcraft production -, under the leadership of India and China, puts forward a global scenario that will be impacted by the big bang initiated by Arkwright's mill. This big bang triggered changes that led to an "astonishing reversal" (Darwin, 2007, p. 196): the British rise as a cotton textiles producer and exporter and the transformation of India into an importer of British textiles. For this "astonishing reversal", Darwin (2007) presents a long list of changes involving state action, military interventions, colonization and other forms of political power – thus, this big bang is part of a much broader transformation, the technological side of these changes. There is a relationship between this technological change, its spread and the rise of British hegemony (Darwin, 2007, 2009; Arrighi, 1994).

The innovation introduced by Arkwright – the cotton mill, "a novel institution" (Beckert, 2014, p. 68) – triggered simultaneous changes in diverse dimensions. The simultaneity of these changes must be highlighted, as each of them was necessary for the others.

First, the productive changes brought by the invention of the cotton mill and by subsequent improvements affected the demand for a "key factor" in that phase: cotton.[3] These productive changes are combined with an immense growth in the production of cotton textiles, growth that has a backward linkage, the immense demand for cotton. Initially, this rising demand was matched by an increase of cotton production under slavery – an example of uneven and combined development: modern capitalism in the making supported by slave conditions. This combination of old and new modes of production is a feature of the broad impacts of the first technological revolution on the periphery. For Africa, especially for West Africa, the increase in the slave trade was its initial impact (Inikori, 2002) – with long-lasting effects (Michalopoulos & Papaioannou, 2020).

Second, the mechanization of cotton spinning triggered a long sequence of subsequent innovations in the cotton mill.[4] There is a long history of innovations introduced after 1771 that includes the transition from water to steam as a driving

[3]Cotton, the "key factor" in Freeman's scheme of long waves (Freeman, 1987, p. 68) – the column number 5.

[4]Beckert (2014, pp. 65–67) lists innovations from 1733 to 1785, the increase in productivity and the fall of prices. Freeman and Louçã (2001, p. 155) present data on labor productivity, from "Indian hand spinners" (eighteenth century) to "Roberts's automatic mule" (1825) – from 50,000 to 135 operative hours to process 100 pounds of cotton.

force and, later, the transition from steam to electricity – overlapping of the first technological revolution with the second and the third. These changes in the nature of the cotton mill are important for our research because there is a late diffusion to the periphery, therefore there is time enough for new changes in that technology before its arrival in Russia, China, India, Africa and Latin America. Related to those changes there are incentives and knowledge to sustain the emergence of a specialized new sector to produce textile machinery – a step forward in the division of labor that pushed the productivity of the cotton industry in Britain, with further improvements in the volume of production and cost reduction. Those improvements consolidated the global competitive advantage of British cotton textiles. This competitive advantage is the economic source behind that "astonishing reversal".

Third, the global diffusion of this new form of production – the cotton mill – to regions beyond United Kingdom took a very specific form – Beckert (2014, pp. 139–141) describes it as a puzzle –, a late and uneven spread through different regions of the world. This spread began impacting societies at different levels of economic development and political organization – from its "initial nucleus", as Celso Furtado (1987, p. 217) called England, the shock waves from this first big bang hit societies in pre-capitalist stages. These shock waves triggered initial steps towards the transformation of those societies into different forms of capitalism – peripheric capitalism.

These simultaneous and integrated changes organize this chapter.

3.2 An Impact Mediated by Cotton Production: Slavery

One of the consequences of the technical changes related to the beginning of the industrial revolution was the rise in the demand for cotton – the key raw material of this initial phase of capitalism. Marx, in his analysis of the industrial revolution, presents what could be interpreted as a general model of technological revolutions, as a change in one point of the productive structure reverberates in all other sectors – "the transformation of the mode of production in one sphere of industry necessitates a similar transformation in other spheres" (Marx, 1867, p. 505).[5] This type of forward and backward effects is discussed in a similar line of thought and applied to the cotton textile industry by Farnie (1979, pp. 27–32).

In terms of its impact on the production of the raw material, Marx makes a short reference: "So too, on the other hand, the revolution in cotton-spinning called forth the invention of the gin, for separating the seeds from the cotton fibre, it was only by means of this invention that the production of cotton became possible on the enormous scale at present required" (p. 505).

[5]This passage from Marx (1867, pp. 505–506) as a model for other technological revolutions is presented in Albuquerque (2021, pp. 55–58).

These backward linkage effects were much broader, however. The rise in the demand for cotton was fast and new pressures on the cotton production were present. The answer to these pressures came from strengthening older modes of production: slavery. Beckert (2014, chapter 5) presents a comprehensive picture of this process. First, knowledge flows regarding the cultivation of cotton – from the West Indies and from the Mediterranean. Second, an initial perception of this rising demand: "in 1786, American planters also began to notice the rising prices for cotton engendered by the rapid expansion of mechanized cotton textile production in the United Kingdom" (p. 101). Eli Whitney's invention in 1793, "a new kind of cotton gin", mentioned by Marx, contributed to the spread of cotton production in the south of the United States (pp. 102–103). The growth of cotton production in the United States is reflected in the statistics of cotton imports by Great Britain: from zero by 1786, United States' exports reached the 50 percent by the end of the eighteenth century and almost 70 percent by 1850 (Beckert, 2014, p. 121). A relationship between slavery and cotton production is summarized by Beckert (2014, p. 103): "[a]ll the way to the Civil War, cotton and slavery would expand in lockstep, as Great Britain and the United States had become the twin hubs of the emerging empire of cotton". Initially slavery contributed to the "industrial takeoff" and later to its expansion (Beckert, 2014, p. 11 7). An illustration of the importance of uneven and combined development as an expression of capitalist global expansion, as in "the wake of the Industrial Revolution, slavery had become central to the Western world's new political economy" (Beckert, 2014, p. 133).

The growth of cotton production in the South of the United States was supported by the barbaric slave trade in the Atlantic, with the concomitant growth in the "supply of African slave labor to the Americas" (Inikori, 2002, chapter 5). A long lasting trade, from the 1750s to the 1850s, the "African trade", "was based on the exportation of one commodity, African slaves, for service on American plantations, growing tropical produce for sale in western Europe" (Fage, 2002, p. 247). Inikori (2002, p. 237) presents estimates that between 1701 and 1807 (the year of British abolition of slavery) 10,967 ships "exported a total of 3,319,756 slaves from Africa and landed in the Americas 2,931,012". These totals are for slaves transported by ships clearing from ports in England – see Inikori (2002, Table 5.1, p. 238). Inikori's research to evaluate the contribution of Africans to the industrial revolution is very important, and he explores other implications and impacts of the slave trade, on sectors like shipbuilding, finance etc.

Long-lasting consequences of the slave trade are important for our research, as the "Atlantic slave trade retarded the development of commodity production in Western Africa" (Inikori, 2002, p. 481). Hopkins (2020, p. 19) and Michalopoulos & Papaioannou (2020) stress the relationship between slave trade and underpopulation in African regions, and the relationship between population density and technological progress has been elaborated by Boserup (1981, pp. 144–157) – "sparse population as an obstacle to industrialization".[6]

Beyond the important issue of modern production emerging based on slavery production of its key factor, cotton, this section introduces the contribution of cheap cotton for another global impact of this first technological revolution: cheap textiles displacing India's position. Tomlinson (2013, p. 88) evaluating this impact stresses that the textile production from Lancashire was dependent on "cheap raw cotton exports from the American South and the introduction of mechanized spinning technology" (p. 88). And those cheap exports were based on slavery.

The Civil War – 1861–1865 – in the United States ended slavery, impacting the whole world: "a war reverberates around the world" (Beckert, 2014, chapter 9). During the Civil War the sources of cotton were transformed, with another impact on India, that expanded its role as exporter of that raw material: in 1860 it contributed with 16 percent of British demand, in 1862 with 70 percent – representing an increase of 50 percent in cotton production in India (Beckert, 2014, p. 255). The impact of the Civil War, for Beckert (2014, p. 377), was determinant for "a new global periphery".

3.3 An "Astonishing Reversal"

The characterization of the global impact of the first technological revolution as an "astonishing reversal" (Darwin, 2007, p. 196) helps the understanding of two sides of this process. On the one hand, before 1771 there was a global spread of cotton textile production – handicraft production -, with India and China as leading producers. On the other hand, after a long learning process a technological revolution reshaped the world of textile production and relocated its leading region.

3.3.1 Textile Production Before 1771

The arrival of cotton textile manufacturing in Britain seems to be around 1601 (Beckert, 2014, p. 39). In Europe, there was a slow growth of cotton manufacturing during the sixteenth and seventeenth centuries, probably restrained by the "difficulty of accessing cotton" (Beckert, 2014, p. 40). Cotton arrived in Europe, as "a result of the spread of Islam", in the tenth century (p. 22).

A map prepared by Beckert (2014, pp. 12–13) – "Worlds of cotton: the first 5,000 years" – shows the weakness of Europe as a textile producing region. Beckert (2014,

[6]Boserup (1981, p. 157) may be a source for intertemporal spill-overs of this phenomenon, as she highlights that "[w]hen African colonies became independent, the sparse population was split among more than forty countries".

pp. 7–10) presents evidence of how cotton growing and manufacturing had long histories in regions like the Indus Valley, Africa and the Americas.

A special place in this history is held by today's India, Pakistan, and Bangladesh: "[f]rom the earliest time until well into the nineteenth century – that is, for several millennia – the people of the Indian subcontinent were the world's leading cotton manufacturers" (p. 7). For a long time, therefore, Asia was the "center of technological innovation" (p. 21): roller gin, the bow, the spinning wheel and new kinds of looms, "all originated in Asia" (Beckert, 2014, p. 21). The domestication of cotton was a process implemented in different regions, "through centuries", that "drastically altered the physical properties of cotton" (p. 21).

Those historical roots explain the position of India as the "textile workshop of the world" in the eighteenth century (Darwin, 2007, p. 193).

Politically, the Indian subcontinent between 1500 and 1750 was divided among diverse political units – in contrast with China, which was a unified empire. Metcalf and Metcalf (2002) review the political organization of the Indian subcontinent between 1500 (see their Map 1, pp. 10–11) and 1798 (see their Map 2, pp. 68–69), describing its changing political structures and their divisions. Political division and fragmentation of the Indian subcontinent were sources of opportunities for Western powers to trade and build an increasing political presence in the region, which culminated with the region's transformation into a British colony.

The textile industry in pre-colonial India is described by Chaudhuri (1990), investigating "the regional location of textile industries in different parts of Asia" until 1750 (p. 309) – "a combination of favourable natural resources and the cumulative effect created by a hereditary concentration of craft skills". Chaudhuri (1990, p. 307) finds "four significant industrial regions of India specializing in the manufacture of cotton fabrics": "Punjab. Gujarat, the Coromandel coast, and Bengal" (see his Map 17: "India: main textile weaving areas 1600–1750", p. 311). Evaluating the "technology in textile industries", Chaudhuri (p. 313) explains the "most significant technological development": "[t]he introduction of the single- or multi-spindle wheel which supplemented hand spinning with the spindle and distaff and the gradual development of the treadle-looms and the drawlooms". Once introduced and assimilated, textile industries remained in a "steady state" until the arrival of Western technologies in mid nineteenth century (p. 313).

Chaudhuri (1990, p. 318) mentions a distinction between the production for local markets and for distant markets. The hierarchy of the caste system was interconnected with the organization of textile production, that involved many stages: each piece of textile needed the work of "farmers growing cotton, harvesters, those who ginned the cotton fibre, carders, spinners, weavers, bleachers, printers, painters, glazers and repairers" (p. 319).

The *Cambridge Economic History of India* in its first volume presents descriptions of the importance of textile industries in three different regions, for the period between 1200 and 1750. In Mughal India, Raychaudhuri (1982, pp. 269–270) comments that "[t]he country's leading manufacture, cotton textiles, was produced probably in every part of the country both for local consumption and distant markets. The bewildering variety of cotton fabrics mentioned in the contemporary sources

-150 names occur in the first ten years of the English factory records – can be divided into a number of overlapping categories according to the criteria of classification used". In Maharashtra and the Deccan, for Fukazawa (1982, p. 310) "[t]he most important of the urban industries were cotton- and silk-weaving. Throughout the seventeenth century Aurangabad, for instance, was famous for white cotton cloth and silk-stuff, and Burhanpur for fine white and printed cloth, which was exported in quantities by Persian and Armenian merchants to Persia, Arabia and Turkey". In South India, Alaev (1982, p. 318) shows that "[u]rban crafts were developed in India from the ancient period and distinguished by the high quality of goods". During the seventeenth century, trade with Europe intensified: "[t]extile industry now had more possibilities for expansion. The concentration of textile workers in the sea-ports of the Coromandel Coast was enhanced" (1982, pp. 319).

The *Cambridge Economic History of India* in its second volume deals with the period starting in 1750, therefore identifying the initial consequences of the British presence. For Raychaudhuri (1983, p. 7), "[c]otton textiles, the major manufacturing industry, flourished despite the negative consequences of the Company's monopoly till the loss of its export markets in the nineteenth century. In the mid-eighteenth century, Bengal is estimated to have had a million weavers" (p. 7). The importance of manual skills was the main asset, as there was "indifference to technological progress in sharp contrast to the extraordinary sophistication of manual skills. By the end of the seventeenth century, the Indian weaver could reproduce on his rudimentary looms 'the nicest and most beautiful patterns' imported from Europe" (Raychaudhuri, 1983, p. 19). Still it was a predominantly rural activity, "[t]he growth of the domestic and export markets stimulated the tendency towards localization, especially in textile manufactures and in coastal territories like Bengal, Coromandel and Guajarat, around the inland emporia and the centers of export trade. In the 1750s in Bengal, Orme found hardly a single village near the main roads and large towns where every inhabitant was not engaged in the manufacture of textiles" (Raychaudhuri, 1983, p. 22). A pattern of regional specialization may be shown, even in relation with exports, as Raychaudhuri (1983, p. 26) describes it: "[o]f the three main regions concerned with the export trade in India, Guajarat had concentrated on coarse textiles for consumption in the Asian and African markets; finer fabrics, including those in demand in Europe, were major exports of Coromandel and Bengal".

The importance of Indian exports of textiles was captured by foreign trade statistics presented by Chaudhuri (1983, p. 806): in the period between 1757 and 1813, the trade was "based on an exchange of fine textiles, foodstuffs, and other raw materials for precious metals and certain manufactured products" (p. 806). These data are in line with statistics presented by Beckert: (2014, pp. 45–46): in 1727, 30 million yards of exported from India; during the 1790s, 80 million annually.

In China, during late Ming, "[i]n almost every province, family farms not only planted cotton but organized cotton spinning, weaving, calendaring, and dying for the market place" (Myers & Wang, 2002, p. 617). For Myers and Wang (2002, p. 619) "cotton cloth products constituted the second most important commodity (after foodgrains) to circulate on the Ch'ing market economy". Myers and Wang

(2002, pp. 619–620) describe the market relationships that existed between farmers, brokers, village spinners and weavers, handicraft producers of special cloth products, processors of refined cloth. In the customary economy, there was also cotton spun and wove by households for their use or for local exchange (2002, p. 620). In Kiangnan, an exporting region, some villages in the South specialized in "producing socks, shirtings and footwear" (p. 618). The handicraft industry, including in the cotton cloth industry, was so strong that it was preserved until the twentieth century. In mid-nineteenth century, "the most important household handicraft in rural China was the spinning and weaving of cotton" (Feuerwerker, 1980, p. 17), a position preserved until 1911 (p. 16). Historical evidence of the importance of that production is presented by Feuerwerker (1980, p. 18): "[u]ntil 1831, England purchased more 'nankeens' (cloth manufactured in Nanking and other places in lower Yangtze region) each year than she sold British-manufactured cloth to China".

Africa had also long-lasting historical roots in cotton textiles. Beckert (2014, pp. 9–10) highlights Africa as one of the 3 poles with "the domestication, spinning and weaving of cotton". In West Africa, during the pre-colonial era, there was a manufacturing sector that "closely resembled those of pre-industrial societies in other parts of the world" (Hopkins, 2020, p. 93). Clothing was the most important of these manufactures, specially cotton cloth – "[c]otton, a long-established crop in West Africa, was manufactured at a very early date", probably spread by the Islam after the eighth century (Hopkins, p. 93). Hopkins mentions different regions such as Western Sudan, Timbuctu, and Kano, in different times, as regions producing textiles. Other centers produced cloth of different types (p. 94). Krieger (2009, p. 108) presents a map of "centers of cotton textiles production in West Africa, c. 1000–1500". For East Africa, Clarence-Smith (2014, pp. 265–270) describes textiles being produced in different times in different regions like Madagascar (p. 265), Darfur (p. 266), Mogadishu, Highland Ethiopia (p. 267) and in the 'Swahili World' (pp. 267–268). A specific type of textile – *machira* – was produced in East Africa, a production that even survived "deliberate Portuguese attempts to suffocate it" in the eighteenth century (p. 269). *Machira* was produced in the northern bank of the Zambesi, a production that "penetrated deep into the southern plateau and across the Limpopo" (Marks & Gray, 1975, p. 388). In Central Africa during the seventeenth century, "a large volume of cloth was produced", according to Thornton (1992, p. 12).

In Russia, Beckert (2014, p. 142) provides a hint of pre-industrial revolution textile manufacturing, as "[i]n Russia, the cotton manufacturing industry emerged from eighteenth-century linen and woolen manufacturing". This previous manufacturing experience has two different origins. One is the "small beginnings" of textile production "in Astrakhan in the 16th century under the auspices of Eastern traders" (Thompstone, 1984, p. 45). The other is the consequence of modernization and westernization efforts from Peter the Great, that ruled Russia between 1696 and 1725 and implemented commercial and industrial policies, according to

Ananich (2006).[7] These policies had military motivations (war with Sweden), requiring the development of industry in a "short period of time": "Peter I went down in history as one of the founders of active government entrepreneurship" (Ananich, 2006, p. 395). There was then a "sharp jump in the development of manufacturing" (p. 395). Daniel (1995, pp. 7–8) focuses in textiles among those policies: "[w]hen he established the new linen industry, Peter wanted to provide sailcloth for the navy, to reduce imports of broad linen, to raise demand to flax and hemp produced at home, and to make linen sailcloth for export" (p. 7). These initiatives resulted in a "promising beginning" for textile manufacturing by 1725 (Daniel, 1995, p. 8). During Catherine II's kingdom (1762–1796) there was a second stimulus to manufacturing and westernization – Russia increased its links with Western Europe, especially by iron-mining and exports: "[a]t the end of the eighteenth century, this development became very noticeable. Western European states gladly purchased inexpensive Russian raw materials. Russia in return imported cotton, wool, silk and colonial goods including tea, coffee, sugar and wines" (Ananich, 2006, p. 397).

This very synthetic list of textile-producing regions before 1771 is a reference for the evaluation of the global impact of the industrial revolution.

3.3.2 Indian Textiles, Markets in Europe and Technology Transfer from the East

The textile manufacture outside Europe was a source for a long process of Western learning from the East.[8] Beckert (2014, pp. 24–25) describes how still during the twelfth century the European textile industry through the Islamic world appropriated technologies that had originated in India and China. Entrepreneurs from Northern Italy were early agents of this absorption of foreign knowledge.

At the same time, imports from India created markets in Europe for cotton textiles – "beautiful chintzes and muslins attracted the attention of a growing class of Europeans who had the money to purchase them and the desire to flaunt their social status by wearing them". Indian textiles became more fashionable (Beckert, 2014, p. 35).

This huge process of market creation in Europe (Lemire, 2009) triggered two interconnected processes. The first was the rise of cotton as a "global commodity" – one key contribution of Beckert's analysis. This process involved the emergence of a

[7]Translating to the language of absorptive capacity, Peter knew that something was happening at the West. According to Falkus (1972, p. 24), "[r]eturning from his European visit in 1698, Peter brought hundreds of foreign technicians and skilled artisans". According to Daniel (1995, p. 5), "his visit to Paris in 1717, encouraged him to develop policies to help private entrepreneurs".

[8]Riello (2013), especially its Part II – "Learning and connecting: making cottons global, circa 1500–1750" – presents a broad review of this long learning process from Indian techniques and textiles.

complex commercial web, globe-spanning system (Beckert, p. 36) – a commercial web that would be retransformed many times in the future, following other changes in the cotton production and distribution. The second was a systematic process of learning with the East, a process of technology transfer especially from India, a process strengthened by the European increasing control of global trade between 1678 and 1807 – Beckert lists various examples of reports, observations, local investigations to learn how to copy Indian manufacture techniques, to learn how Indians artisans produced muslin and chintz (Beckert, 2014, pp. 49–51).

These two processes had one specific consequence as they stimulated an import substitution industrialization in England (Inikori, 2002, p. 150). Since at least the second half of the eighteenth century, "replacing Indian cloth imports with domestically manufactured cloth became an important, albeit difficult-to-realize priority" (Beckert, 2014, p. 47).

After Europe learned how to manufacture cotton textiles, the global history was transformed by a new process to produce them – the mechanization of textile production.[9]

3.3.3 Consequences of Mechanization of Textiles on Previous Producing Regions

The process initiated in 1771 effectively constituted an import substitution industrialization, with British textiles replacing Indian imports by 1800 (Darwin, 2007, p. 196). Between 1771 and 1850, the British mechanization of cotton textiles produced larger volumes and cheaper products, two preconditions for a huge global impact.

India was surpassed by British exports of calicos by 1800, by 1817 Indian weavers were buying British yarn, and "by the 1820s India had become a net importer of cottons" (Darwin, 2007, p. 196). With the continuity of technological improvements of British techniques in cotton textiles, by 1835 "cotton goods made up more than half of British exports to India, and India had become Britain's second largest market for cotton manufacturers" (Darwin, 2007, p. 196). This is the "astonishing reversal" in Darwin's analysis.

These changes in India are analyzed by other authors. Chaudhuri (1983) analyses the foreign trade of colonial India, dividing it in four different phases. During the second period – 1813 to 1850 – "India was gradually transformed from being an exporter of manufactured products – largely textiles – into a supplier of primary commodities, importing finished consumer goods and certain intermediate industrial goods as well in return" (Chaudhuri, 1983, p. 806).

[9] The industrial revolution is a well investigated topic. Inikori (2002, Chapter 3) organizes a broad review of the "historiography of the first industrial revolution". Freeman and Louçã (2001, Chapter 5) present a review of the "British industrial revolution".

There is a debate on Indian deindustrialization after British rise in cotton textiles. Pomeranz (2000, pp. 294–295) summarizes this debate evaluating that "it does seem fairly well established that the number of full-time weavers and spinners (especially those based in towns) decreased significantly beginning in the late eighteenth century" (p. 294). Farnie (2004, pp. 415–417) presents data on the survival of hand-loom weavers, that were 2.669 million in 1901 (p. 416).

Tomlinson (2013), analyzing "deindustrialization and the fate of handicrafts", stresses how changes in the global exports were connected to "local persistence of handicraft production": "[t]he history of Indian industry across the nineteenth century has often been analysed in terms of deindustrialisation, with British rule seen as destroying handicraft industries and ruining their workforce by commercializing agriculture, promoting imports of manufactured consumer goods, and inhibiting India's established exports of cloth" (p. 83). According to Tomlinson, "All the main issues in the 'deindustrialisation' debate are ambiguous and difficult to test. While the proportion of the labour-force employed in manufacturing certainly did not rise over the course of the nineteenth century, it is hard to estimate how far it fell since the employment figures cannot be corrected to allow for underemployment and for those following multiple occupations. One careful estimate for textiles has suggested that between 1800 and 1850, over the subcontinent as a whole, the loss of export markets was balanced by a growth in domestic demand, with only a small fall in employment in manufacturing; but that from 1850 to 1880 between two and six million cotton weaving and spinning jobs were lost, enough to have given full-time employment to between 1 and 2 percent of the population" (p. 85).

For Tomlinson (2013, pp. 87–88), "[c]otton cloth was probably the biggest manufacturing sector of eighteenth century's India, and certainly the most important export commodity". At that time, India was the larger global exporter of calico, but between 1780 and 1830 that position was lost. Among the causes, Tomlinson lists British tariffs, the Napoleonic wars and the production from Lancashire (p. 88). Facing this new scenario, after 1815, "the handicraft cotton textile industry managed to survive inside Indian market throughout the nineteenth century" (p. 89). Handicraft production would "succumb to the more intense competition from Indian mills after 1870" (p. 89) – but, Indian cotton mills were the product of another British import in India: textile machinery. Beckert (2014, pp. 328–329) mentions a "tsunami of deindustrialization", in the "last third of the nineteenth century" – a process related to a movement of "former weavers to agricultural labor" (p. 329) – the Civil War in the United States is important for this process, given the rise of the demand of cotton in other regions.

In China, the arrival of British cotton textiles took more time. There was a first attempt in 1793 to establish trade relation with China (Darwin, 2007, p. 201). The way to China was paved by deep changes as the consolidation of British power in the Indian sub-continent – "Indian soldiers were used to force open the ports of China" (p. 266) -, geopolitical change in Europe after the Napoleonic wars and the Congress of Vienna (1814) (pp. 227–228), and the emergence of steam engine to revolutionize transports.[10] In 1842 the British return, "from Eastern India and its South East Asia outposts" – to open Chinese ports in 1842 (Darwin, 2007, p. 222) – a case "where military power was used in the interest of trade" (Darwin, 2009, p. 40).

Before the Opium Wars, a key change: "[o]nce foreign merchants had come just for Chinese goods. Now, Western manufacturers were beginning to look for Chinese markets" (Wakeman, 1978, p. 174). Grove (2004, p. 436) indicates 1827 as the "year that Manchester textiles were first sold for a profit in China". After the Opium Wars, "foreign imports of cotton yarn and cloth began to increase significantly after the 1858–60 treaties opened additional treaty ports, including three on the Yangtze" (Feuerwerker, 1980, p. 19). Later, new sources of mechanized textiles: in the 1870s, cheaper yarn from Indian spinning mills, and in the 1890s, Japanese products (Feuerwerker, 1980, p. 21). Also in China, the persistence of handicraft production is a phenomenon. On the one hand, "the principal markets for imported machine-spun yarn were those regions where cotton growing and handicrafts were least developed". On the other hand, "the most obvious consequence of the increasing inflow of foreign yarn was thus a geographical dispersion of the handicraft weaving industry which in the first half of the nineteenth century had been concentrated in the major cotton-growing provinces" (p. 22). Even later, as "the adoption of machine-made yarn, moreover, strengthened the handicraft weaving industry as a whole" (p. 22). The form of economic organization of those imports in the Chinese case led to a formation of a specialized sector – *compradors* – that later were "the original investors in Chinese-owned shipping, financial and manufacturing firms in Shangai" (p. 57).

In general, de combined effects of British industrial revolution on previous leaders of manufacture exports – India and China – may be grasped by statistics presented by Allen (2017, p. 323): in his graph on the "distribution of world manufacturing", in 1750 the share of United Kingdom was negligible vis-à-vis China and India. In 1880, United Kingdom's share alone was greater than China and India together. Allen (2017, p. 322) integrates the changes in Britain with their effects on global employment: "As jobs proliferated in the British cotton mills, massive technological unemployment spread across Africa and Asia".

In Africa also there is the phenomenon of survival of handicraft production of textiles: "where cotton textile-production was well-established (that is, mainly in West Africa) it had maintained its position, since the factory-made imports, though cheaper than the traditional product, were on the whole less desirable" (Wrigley, 1986, p. 122). In East Africa this survival is also a long-lasting phenomenon, as there was "the persistence of artisanal textiles in the era of Independence" (Clarence-Smith, 2014, p. 284) – attempts to combine modern and artisanal forms of production would be part of the policies for late industrialization in the post-Independence period (Clarence-Smith, 2014, pp. 284–286).

[10] As British industrialized cotton textiles arrived in China transported by steam boats, there is a superposition between the first and the second technological revolutions.

Inikori (2002, p. 395) describes other type of impact, derived from new demand from Britain and Europe for primary products available in Africa. Between 1650 and 1850, there were "two sets of commodities produced in Western Africa and imported into England": "gold and raw materials for the finishing processes in textile industries" (Inikori, pp. 395–396). These raw materials were "redwoods, gum and palm oil (used as a lubricant for the expanding machines and by the wool-combers in Yorkshire and soap boilers)". The abolition of slave trade (1807) transformed "Western Africa into a quantitatively important producer of raw materials for the United Kingdom" – and palm oil was a leading product, as "in 1842 over 20,000 tons were imported" (p. 403).

In Latin America the initial impact was on the demand for primary products (Furtado, 1976, pp. 45–47). On the one hand, there was an increase in the demand for mineral products, a consequence of the growth of production of metal products. On the other hand, the income growth in Europe and consequent changes in consumers' behavior led to bigger and/or new demand for agricultural products. The increase in the demand for primary products led to an initial accumulation of wealth, to imports of British and European industrialized products, creating local markets that could later be supplied by local production. This mediated initial impact of the industrial revolution took time to accumulate the necessary resources and knowledge to start the local production of industrialized textiles – time enough for a second big bang to happen in the United Kingdom.

3.4 The Puzzle of the Spread of Cotton Industrialization

Beckert (2014, p. 141) puts forward the puzzle: "Why did it take ten or more years to travel a few hundred miles to continental Europe, twenty or more years to cross the Atlantic to the US, fifty or more to reach Mexico and Egypt, and a hundred or more to reach India, Japan, China, Argentine and most of Africa?"

This puzzle, for Beckert, can be solved looking to two previous processes, interrelating technology and political developments: history of textile manufacturing and formation of national states.

From the technology dimension, there is "a prior history of textile manufacturing" (p. 142). Beckert observes that it didn't matter what type of textiles – wool, flax, cotton -, regions that had previous manufacturing experiences later hosted cotton manufacturing: examples of this first process are Ghent, Puebla, Russia, New England, Alsace, Switzerland (p. 142). This turns the puzzle even more puzzling – Sect. 3.3 shows the importance and dissemination of cotton manufacturing in India and China.

From the political dimension, there is the interaction between political organization and absorptive capacity, as Beckert (2014, p. 156) matches the "map of modern states" with the "map of regions that saw early cotton industrialization" (p. 156).[11]

These two processes help to decipher that puzzle. On the one hand, if a map of political organization helps to understand early diffusion of cotton industrialization, the colonial status during the early stages of the industrial revolution – between 1771 and 1807 – of the Indian subcontinent, Latin America and Africa, and the of the weakness and crises within the Chinese imperial state may be part of the explanation of the late arrival of cotton industrialization in these regions. On the other hand, given that late arrival, the nature of the technology that spread to these regions was transformed by developments that took place in the United Kingdom until the early decades of the nineteenth century: the rise of a specialized textile machine-making industry.

These two processes are related and their interconnection define the form of propagation of textile manufacturing – the rise of a new industrial sector in the United Kingdom shaped the form of the late spread of cotton industrialization to these five regions: diffusion through imports of textile-making machinery.

3.4.1 Political Organization of Peripheric Regions

If the map of modern states corresponds to the early cotton industrialization outside the United Kingdom, as Beckert (2014, p. 156) suggests, then an investigation of political transformations of peripheric regions may help to understand the nature of the later spread of cotton industrialization.

The issue here is what were the political organizations that existed in the eve of the industrial revolution and how they changed until its later phases. Table 3.1 highlights predominant political organizations in each of the five regions in 1750 and in 1850.

The political dimension, summarized in the first column of Table 3.1, may be connected with a first component of the absorptive capacity: the capacity for identification of the new knowledge created abroad, in this case, initial perception on what was happening in England. The level of political organization might be a precondition for this very basic component of absorptive capacity. This perception is, in Cohen and Levinthal's terms, the ability to "recognize" (1989, p. 593) or to

[11] This process may be articulated with Furtado's elaboration on the first movements of the expansion of the initial industrial nucleus of the industrial revolution (Furtado, 1987, p. 217) and with Landes' elaboration on continental Europe emulation of the British industrial revolution, as he stresses the contribution of the states in France and Germany (Landes, 1969, p. 151), where "... the government provided technical advice and assistance, awarded subventions to inventors and bestowed gifts of machinery, allowed rebates and exemptions of duties on imports of industrial equipment" (p. 151). Landes also mentions government support for the cost of travels even to the United States – visits to learn (Landes, 1969, p. 151).

Table 3.1 Political organization in the Indian subcontinent, China, Russia, Sub-Saharan Africa, and Latin America (1750 and 1850)

Region	1750	1850
India	Diverse local kingdoms and princely states. Localized British colonial presence. Caste system	British colony. Caste system
China	Ching's imperial state. Tributary mode of production	Defeat in the Opium War, Treaty-port cities
Russia	Forced modernization under Peter, the Great. Tributary mode of production/serfdom	Serfdom. Modernization and westernization efforts under Catherine, the Great
Africa	Slave mode of production, fragmented and uneven political organization. Colonial presence. Slave trade	Broader colonial presence. End of external slave trade
Latin America	Spanish and Portuguese (with slavery) colonies	Independent (Brazil with slavery) and fragmented states

Source: For 1750 – India, China and Russia (Banaji, 2010); Africa (Lovejoy, 2012), Latin America (Furtado, 1976). For 1850, author's elaboration based on the literature reviewed in this chapter

"identify" (1989, p. 569) new knowledge. This first step is a precondition for the other steps – "to assimilate and exploit knowledge" (p. 569, p, 593).[12]

Illustrations of this identification capacity are the contrasting cases of, on the one hand, the newly independent United States and Czarist Russia, and, on the other hand, imperial China.

The United States may be an example of a region that knew that something important was taking place at England. Hamilton's Report on Manufactures published in 1791 puts this forward very clearly: "[t]he Cotton Mill invented in England, within the last twenty years, is a signal illustration of the general proposition, which has been just advanced. In consequence of it, all the different processes for spinning Cotton are performed by means of Machines, which are put in motion by water, and attended chiefly by women and Children; [and by a smaller] number of [persons, in the whole, than are] requisite in the ordinary mode of spinning" (Hamilton, 1791, p. 12).

Russia, an imperial state with military initiatives to modernize the country, followed what was happening in West Europe since Peter's modernization push in the eighteenth century. Russia in the early 1700s sent young people "to learn the secrets of Western industrial processes" (Falkus, 1972, p. 24). These early movements might have contributed to later identify initial steps of the industrial revolution. Initiatives to access and diffuse knowledge are illustrated by Thompstone (1984, p. 46): "In 1798 mechanical spinning had been put on a permanent basis in Russia with the establishment by the government of a model spinning and weaving plant, the Alexandrovsk State Textile Mill. This plant, according to Khromov, played an important role in the spreading of improved production methods in

[12]This is the variable α (Eq. 2.3 of Appendix 1, Chap. 2).

Russia's growing cotton textile industry" – Beckert (2014, p. 139) mentions the Russian Treasury supporting initiatives "to start a cotton spinning mill" in 1793. The Russian Academy of Sciences was founded in 1725, under an initiative from the Czar (Graham, 1993, pp. 18–20).

The case of China would be a case of "not-knowing-that-you-don't-know". Fairbank (1978) identifies the military defeats during the Opium Wars, in the 1840s and 1860s, as eye-opening events for the Ching's imperial state delayed perception that it should look to the West – those defeats triggered a chain of political events that led to the self-strengthening movement within China, in the second half of the nineteenth century – a movement with the explicit goal to absorb Western technology (Kuo & Liu, 1978).

As Table 3.1 shows, India, Africa and Latin America had the handicap of a colonial condition in the beginning of the industrial revolution.

In the Indian case, the perception of the impacts on the subcontinent of the British industrial revolution had as one route the emergence of an Indian Economics, from 1870s, as Maria Bach (2021) suggests. Her suggestion is based on a review of the works of Naoroji, Ranade and Dutt, that connect the colonial status of India and the structural changes driven by British cotton textiles. According to Maria Bach (2021), their works defined the nature and impact of British colonial power in India – "the imperial promotion of free trade led to deindustrialization" (p. 492) – and explored policy prescriptions, looking for "an appropriate development plan" (p. 499). Bach stresses the use of List by those pioneers of Indian Economics (p. 499). These works organized a preliminary understanding of the impacts of the industrial revolution in India: Dutt (1906, pp. 101–102), for instance, uses data and reports from the British Parliament to identify 1814 as the year of an important change, as India became a net importer of British textile goods (Dutt, 1906, p. 101). The emergence of Indian Economics was part of a broader process that would change the political organization in the subcontinent: the formation of the Indian National Congress in 1885 (Darwin, 2009, p. 193), as Naoroji, Ranade and Dutt were part of the first generation of the new political organization – Tripathi and Tripathi (2014, p. 23) mention the three as "moderates", and Wilson (2016, p. 526) stresses the role of Naojori. The foundation of the Indian National Congress (INC) is a step forward in the political organization of India because it introduced a new actor – an important political actor – in the definition of policies for the colony, and also because it started a political history underpinning the Indian independence. This new political actor is a source of the formulation development plans: in 1939 the INC forms a "National Planning Committee" with the task of "devising a broad economic plan for future Indian Development" (Chibber, 2003, p. 86). Only then did clear broader initiatives to absorb foreign knowledge take place in India. Therefore, until 1939–1947, the absorption of foreign knowledge was related to movements defined by the center – colonial policies – or by consequences of these movements within the Indian economy – many times, unintended consequences.

In Africa, the intrusion of colonial powers, the fragmentation of local societies and their initial levels of political organization and centralization (Michalopoulos & Papaioannou, 2020), and the predominance of the slave mode of production

(Lovejoy, 2012) were forces that operated against the initial development of absorptive capacities. Furthermore, as discussed in Sect. 3.3, Africa suffered from a drainage of population through the slave trade, also a process in the opposite direction of the formation of absorptive capacity.

In Latin America, in the nineteenth century the colonies were governed by peripheric European states like Spain and Portugal, countries that suffered the consequences of the British industrial revolution and lagged behind it. These two kingdoms economically at the periphery of an industrializing Europe, imposed restrictions to the development of local manufactures as part of the colonial system. Independence in most of Latin America took place between 1808 and 1825 (Escosura, 2006, p. 463). After Independence, in the former Spanish colonies there were political processes leading to fragmentation (Escosura, pp. 480–481) – that may have impacted the conditions of active policies from within those newly independent countries. In the former Portuguese colony, the preservation of slavery is a blocking factor for national market formation and growth. Fragmentation and slavery are processes that weaken local forces to learn with more developed regions.

In sum, there is a politically conditioned capacity of regions to "recognize" or "identify" knowledge available abroad. The level of political organization achieved may be one important determinant of this initial step of the formation of absorptive capacity. Political change may be a precondition for a society to pay attention to important changes elsewhere.

Table 3.1 shows that during the initial phases of industrial revolution the formation of modern states in those regions did not take place. Therefore, as Celso Furtado (1987, p. 219) puts forward, during this period the initiative to reconfigure the global system stemmed from the center. The combination of colonial presence and the stage of state formation in these five regions explain their limited and uneven – different timings – ability to evolve towards absorptive capacity. This may be one important reason for the delayed spread of cotton industrialization in these regions, a delay that witnessed new changes within the United Kingdom: the rise of a new industrial sector, a textile machine making industry. This rise took place between 1771 and 1850, defining which textile-making technology would arrive at these peripheric regions.

3.4.2 A Specialized Sector for Textile Machine Making

A novel entity, the cotton mill (Beckert, 2014, p. 68), initiated in 1771 a history of sequential improvements and changes. Between 1771 and 1850 – the time frame of Table 3.1 – many improvements and new innovations transformed the cotton mill.

James Watt's steam engine – patented in 1794 – is an invention at the root of the next technological revolution. The connection between the mechanization of textiles – and its continuous improvement with new and better machines – and steam power – a new technology that was burgeoning at that time – has various steps. In 1790, "steam power, in the shape of Boulton and Watt engine, was first applied to an Arkwright mill, in Nottingham" (Cookson, 2018, p. 33). In 1825, the self-acting mule was patented: according to Malm (2016, p. 66), it was "the first truly automatic machine, but also the first invention of the cotton industry to be geared, from its birth, to the steam engine as a prime mover".

The rise of steam power and its connection to the mechanization of textiles began to change the structure of cotton industry in the United Kingdom. Malm (2016) describes the transition of cotton production from hydraulic power to steam power as a process that had a turning point only in 1830, when "steam had caught up with water" (2016, p. 79).[13] Later, after another technological revolution derived from the invention and commercialization of electricity, new changes in the textile manufacturing: Devine Jr (1983, p. 355) explains that "by the early 1890s... mechanical drive was first electrified in industries such as clothing and textile manufacturing". Textiles manufacturing, therefore, being a starting point for the first technological revolution, later incorporated technologies derived from other radical innovations. For an investigation on the spread of textile industrialization, these incorporations matter because they would define which machine would be absorbed in a latecomer economy. In Brazil, for instance, electricity in textiles was first installed in the early 1890s, in Juiz de Fora, Minas Gerais -[14] the diffusion of electrical textile machinery in Brazil later transformed the industry and its geographical location (Suzigan, 1986, pp. 155–156). Saxonhouse and Wright (2010, p. 551) find that "most of large Mexican mills were electrified by 1905". In the case of Congo, the first textile factory installed, in 1925, was driven by electricity after 1927 (Clarence-Smith, 2014, p. 276).

Those improvements of textile machinery and the connections with steam power were developments that took place within the formation of a new branch of production: a machine-making industry. Cookson (2018) presents the initial steps of this new industry. Saul (1967, p. 112) lists the leading producers of textile machinery in 1914, the largest being Platt Brothers, Oldham, "founded in 1821". This firm is part of a long history narrated by Cookson (2018) that starts from individual engineers and machine makers like Arkwright, presents regions with machine making business like Keighley and Leeds and shows in a chapter intitled "Reaching Maturity" how this new industry began to move towards international markets.

This drive of the United Kingdom textile machinery industry towards foreign markets can be seen through the changes in the restrictions on emigration and machines exports. Cookson (2018) describes two moments: the first, Acts from 1719 to 1786, restricting movements of skilled people and machines, engines and equipment (p. 186, p. 213–214); the second, from 1824 to 1843, parliamentary investigations, committees and decisions ending those bans (pp. 252–256). In

[13]In the US, a report from 1833 cited by Rosenberg and Trajtenberg (2004, pp. 68–69) described "a manufacture scene that was powered almost entirely by water". In 1869, according to Rosenberg (1972, pp. 63–64) steam power was the source of power for half of the manufacture in the United States.

[14]Wilson Suzigan, personal communication with the author (15 August 2022).

1846 there was the repeal of the corn laws, an economic change related to these events.

These changes, structural changes, may be an expression of the consolidation of a machine-making industrial sector in the United Kingdom. Farnie (1990, p. 151) argues that these changes express an internal differentiation of global interest between two sectors: "[m]achine makers served the needs of their foreign clients so well that they separated their interests from those of the Lancashire cotton industry". (Farnie, 1990, p. 151). This separation is also highlighted by Cookson (2018, p. 252), as for him discussions in the British parliament on export ban "exposed a stark difference between customers for machinery and those who made it. It came down to economic self-interest". Saxonhouse and Wright (2010, p. 542), discussing the laws prohibiting the exports of machinery, observe that machinery firms promoted a campaign to repeal them. Later, machinery firms "took full advantage of their new opportunities when repeal finally came: exports of British machinery and millwork doubled between 1842 and 1846". This structural change had global implications, as Saxonhouse and Wright (2010, p. 542) conclude: "the year of 1843 thus stands as a watershed in the history of international technology diffusion".

Farnie (1990, p. 150) shows the importance of British textile machinery industry and its different roles before and after that structural change: "Firstly, it had provided the Lancashire cotton industry with cheap and efficient machinery. Secondly, it had equipped with even more efficient machinery the foreign competitors of Lancashire". The global relevance of this industry is such, that "for a century from 1843 to 1942 (British) textile machinery supplied the most valued portion of the exports of machinery" (p. 151). Until 1924 Britain alone exported more than half of the world exports of textile machinery (Farnie, 1990, p. 167). These two different roles of British textile machinery industry show a change in the nature of expansionary forces, as the imports of textiles by backward countries in the long run made room for later import substitution processes. Import substitution processes were supported by changes at the center through the development of this capital goods sector in the United Kingdom – a sector that had different interests than those of the cotton industry (Farnie, 1990, p. 151, p. 153).

3.5 Cotton Industrialization Through Machinery Imports

The consolidation of a textile machinery industry changes the main form of propagation of cotton manufacturing, from technological transfer through movements of people – emigration, travels, international visits – to transfer through the movements of the machines.

Before the structural change presented in the previous section, in late eighteenth century, skilled immigrants were the channel of technological transfer, as Samuel Slater and its move to America exemplifies: the first Arkwright-style machinery arrived in America "replicating the machines from memory in 1790–1791"

Table 3.2 Year of installation of the first cotton textile modern factory in the Indian subcontinent, China, Russia, Sub-Saharan Africa, and Latin America

Region	Year
India	1856
China	1889
Russia	1793
Sub-Saharan Africa	1925 (Congo)
Latin America	1834 (Brazil)

Source: author's elaboration based on Tomlinson (2013, p. 91) – for India -, Yangzong (1994, p. 61) – for China -, Beckert (2014, p. 139) – for Russia -, Clarence-Smith (2014, p. 276) – for Africa, Suzigan (1986, p. 401) – for Brazil

(Cookson, 2018, p. 217). Other examples of this form of technological transfer are shown by Cookson: in 1812, in the US, more than 1300 Britons were "registered as alien immigrants in US textile trades" (p. 217). These movements of skilled people may be connected to what Celso Furtado evaluated as an "expansion of the first industrial nucleus" (1987, p. 217). Export bans and travel restrictions, although not so effective,[15] were related to an initial and immature phase of the textile machinery industry in the United Kingdom.

After that structural change – the repeal of export bans, in 1823 those restrictions begin to change and in 1843 those export bans were ended – there is a predominance of a new form of technological transfer of textile industrialization to our five regions. Therefore, mapping these imports of textile machinery is to follow the spread of cotton industrialization.[16]

That structural change in the United Kingdom – the rise of a specialized machine-making industry and its outward push – is part of the process. But, there is a second question: who will import the textile machinery in these five regions – and with which resources? Machinery imports suppose a dynamic, active and informed entrepreneur at the periphery – an agent with the first condition of absorptive capacity: the previous identification or recognition of a technology available abroad – and with ability to raise the necessary resources to fund the venture.

Table 3.2 summarizes a review of the literature on the initial mechanization of cotton textiles in our five regions. This line of data collection was pioneered in Brazil by Suzigan (1986), a book with a very detailed investigation of exports of British machinery to Brazil until the First World War – the arrival date for Brazil comes from his book (Suzigan, 1986, Apêndice 3), and the data on the diffusion of cotton industrialization presented in Table 3.3 follow his analysis using the number of spindles installed in different countries (Suzigan, 1986, p. 157).

[15] For the limitations of British governments policies to contain the unwanted technological transfer, see Jeremy (1977).

[16] In his summary of the "Anglo-Indian textile trade", Farnie (2004, p. 396) identifies the role of textile machinery, as it defines a phase with India as "an importer of textile machinery to equip its own new cotton mills" (p. 396). This phase followed a previous one that had India as "an importer of cotton piece-goods and cotton yarn" (p. 396). India would become the "largest export market for British machinery in the years 1856–7" (p. 403).

Table 3.3 Year of installation of the first cotton textile modern factory and the number of spindles installed in 1909, in the Indian subcontinent, China, Russia, Latin America and Sub-Saharan Africa

Region	Year	Spindles (1909)
India	1856	5,800,000
China	1889	800,000
Russia	1793	8,076,000
Sub-Saharan Africa	1925 (Congo)	49,000 (1950)
Latin America	1834 (Brazil)	1,000,000

Source: Year: see Table 3.2. Spindles: author's elaboration, US Bureau of Census (1909, p. 24) – data for Zaire in 1950, Mitchell (1998, p. 438)

OBS: United Kingdom in 1909: 53,312,000 spindles; United States in 1909: 28,018,000 spindles; "All other countries": 215,000 spindles; World total: 133,377,000 spindles (US Bureau of Census, 1909, p. 24)

3.5.1 *India: Different Interactions with Handcraft Production*

In India, the first mechanized cotton mill was inaugurated in Bombay in 1856, "the first steam-powered cotton mill in Asia" (Tomlinson, 2013, p. 91). This first initiative is well documented (Jeremy, 2004, p. 101; Farnie, 2004, pp. 400–405). Headrick (1988, p. 361) describes it: the "first successful venture" with cotton mills in India involved a contact between an Indian merchant, Davar, and a British machine-making firm, Platt Brothers and Company (Oldham). According to Saul (1967, p. 112), Platt Brothers, founded in 1821, had "its staff of engineers in India" (p. 127). In India, the process of textile industrialization involved Indian entrepreneurs "who imported English machinery and hired English expatriates" (p. 361). The initiative from India – the agent of transfer of foreign technology, was a consequence of a long learning process within India, involving Indians with information and knowledge on key aspects of cotton textiles. Indian merchants involved in the export trade had knowledge on raw materials, Indian markets for textiles, and the protection offered by transport costs, therefore, it was easy for them to "recognize the commercial possibilities of local factory production of cotton yarn and cloth" (Morris, 1983, p. 574). This starting point of Indian cotton mechanization includes knowledge of the British machine-makers and ability to raise the necessary funds.[17] The Indian production of mechanized cotton textiles initially had a relationship with the

[17] The first commercial success of the Tata group was with cotton textiles (Morris, 1983, p. 588). Headrick (1988, pp. 363–365) presents J. N. Tata involvement with textile manufactures, and his initial connection with the Platt Brothers as suppliers of equipment (p. 364). From that beginning Tata diversified to other sectors – for iron and steel, see Morris (1983, pp. 588–592). Tata's business group will be part of the preparations of plans for an independent India (Chibber, 2003, p. 95) – another connection between movements in the end of the nineteenth century and plans for independent India. For Indian "textile industrialists" becoming supporters of Indian independence, see Beckert (2014, pp. 422–423).

weaving handicraft production inherited from previous periods. According to Morris (1983, p. 576), until "1896-7 to 1900-1, the average mill in India sold 80 per cent of the yarn it produced to handloom weavers at home and abroad". Farnie (2004, pp. 405–409) describes "three mill-building booms of 1872–1875, 1881–1884, and 1887–1893".

The growth of mechanized production in India was intense, and in 1909 there were 5,800,000 spindles (US Bureau of the Census, 1909, p. 24), the 6th position in a global ranking (see Table 3.3). This may be very important to understand India, still a colony but after 1891 the main importer of textile machinery from United Kingdom (Farnie, 1990, p. 152). This is important to investigate: strong forces driving the diffusion of cotton industry in India. Probably a combination between the strong historical roots of textile manufacturing in India, the formation of a nucleus of local entrepreneurs with skills to take advantage of opportunities available, and the interests of British machine-makers. This growth continued, and the textile industry became the most important in India by 1913 (Tomlinson, 2013, p. 93), with Indian mill production of textile surpassing British imports in 1918 (Farnie, 1990, p. 152) – "in 1938 mill production supplied almost two-thirds of the domestic market for cotton textiles" (Tomlison, 2013, p. 97).

3.5.2 China: Coastal Initial Nuclei of Capitalist Development

In China, it took more time for the first successful mechanized cotton production: in 1889 the Shanghai Cotton Cloth Mill was inaugurated (Yangzong, 1994, pp. 65–69). Its construction took eleven years, and its start up was not immediately after the beginning of the self-strengthening movement. According to Yangzong (1994, p. 64), "[i]mports of foreign cotton textiles to China helped the Chinese people realize the importance of developing their own cotton industry. A scholar, Feng Guifen, stipulated this in as early as 1861. Nevertheless, the government of the Qing Dynasty was concentrating on the development of the military industry, and thus, the civil industry was not put on the agenda until the 1870s". Feuerwerker (1980, p. 32) illustrates this change in the imperial agenda: "a number of official and semi-official mining, melting, and textile enterprises had been undertaken since 1872". Feuerwerker (1970, p. 346) mentions the involvement of Li Hung-chang in the first steps of the Shanghai Cotton Cloth Mill venture – and Li is an important actor in the self-strengthening movement, as Teng and Fairbank (1979, pp. 86–88) highlight. The coordination of the project involved A. W. Danforth, an engineer from the United States. The number of mechanized cotton firms in China grew, but not as fast as in India: in 1909 there were 800,000 spindles (US Bureau of the Census, 1909, p. 24) – see Table 3.3.

As discussed in Cerqueira and Albuquerque (2020, p. 1184), the initial industrialization in China may be understood as a process that involved unintentional and intentional changes. Intentional changes are related to the emergence of the self-strengthening process, a consequence of the limitations of the existing Chinese state – a declining imperial dynasty, unable to implement developmental measures (Feuerwerker, 1980, p. 59). Unintentional changes are consequence of how British commodities entered Chinese markets – the emergence of commercial intermediaries, the compradors that accumulated sufficient wealth to be later invested in manufacturing activities (Bastid-Bruguiere, 1980, p. 551).

In China, as in India, there is a combination between cotton mechanical production and handicraft weaving. As shown in Sect. 3.3.3, the initial impact of imported machine-made yarn was the strengthening of handicraft weaving. After the establishment of local production Feuerwerker (1970, p. 345) shows that "Kiangnan handicraft weavers in the early twentieth century became major purchasers of the output of the growing cotton mills of Shanghai".

These changes resulting from the first impact from the West established coastal nodes of capitalist initial developments (Cerqueira & Albuquerque, 2020, p. 1190). Although these nodes had limited effects, they started transformations that affected the handicraft industries with adaptations to new imports and new demands. This combination of nuclei of initial capital accumulation and the persistence of elements of customary, command and market economies of the early nineteenth century shaped a specific variety of peripheric capitalism.

3.5.3 Russia: Active Policies but Serfdom as a Limiting Factor

The "first mechanized spinning mill" was inaugurated in 1793 in Russia, according to Beckert (2014, p. 139).[18] The timing of this relatively early arrival – vis-à-vis the other regions in Table 3.2 – is a consequence of the active role of the Czarist state. This active role begins with Peter's "forced industrialization" in the early 1700s (Falkus, 1972, p. 22) – in the end of his reign there were 178 enterprises, "40 of them for armaments and iron metallurgy". Catherine II introduced another round of industrialization, leading to 2000 enterprises at the end of her reign (Ananich, 2006, p. 397). These initial efforts prepared the arrival of the first big bang, as Beckert highlights: "In Russia, the cotton manufacturing industry emerged from eighteenth-century linen and woolen manufacturing" (2014, p. 142).

These processes led to an initial industrialization that in 1804 had 2400 establishments – 199 in cotton textiles (Falkus, 1972, p. 33). According to Falkus (1972, p. 37), "[d]uring the 1830s cotton textiles overtook woolens as the major employer of industrial labor". These enterprises coexisted with serfdom until 1861 (see Table 3.1). The growth of industrial enterprises within this pre-capitalist landscape reached 5306 establishments in 1830, and 15,338 in 1860 (Falkus, 1972, p. 33).

---

[18] Thompstone (1984, pp. 44–45) mentions an establishment in 1793, "quickly going to decline" (2002, p. 3).

Zelnick (2006, p. 618) stresses that the growth of the textile sector in the 1830s had a new stimulus from "the decision of the British government to lift its ban on the export of cotton-spinning machinery in 1842".

Serfdom was an important factor blocking of, or at least restraining, the intensity of the industrialization process, as Gerschenkron puts forward: "The early development of the textile industry, even though large enough to enrich the owners concerned, was, prior to the abolition of serfdom, greatly handicapped by the competition of gentry factories and the cottage industry of the peasants. It could not give rise to a great spurt of Russian industrialization" (1970, p. 42).

A military event – the defeat in the Crimean War (1853–1856) – provoked internal debates and an era of reforms in the late 1850s and early 1860s: banking reform and emancipation of serfs were implemented and they "set a course for faster development of Russia industry" (Ananich, 2006, p. 405).

The role of machinery imports to Russia's textile industry is expressed an entrepreneur, Knoop, and his business with the British firm Platt Brothers (Thompstone, 1984). Gerschenkron describes Knoop's job: "[o]ver his lifetime he managed to establish in this fashion some 120-odd factories – surely one of the most remarkable examples of a massive borrowing of foreign technology (which, incidentally, for a year or two still proceeded in the face of the British prohibition against export of machinery)" (1970, p. 20). Thompstone (2004, p. 343) mentions 187 factories.

The textile industry in Russia attempted to produce machines, with limited success: Thompstone (2004, pp. 357–358) describes the domestic production of mechanical looms in 1881 by T. Morozov, a production that "increased when tariffs were raised against imports" (p. 357). However, Russian cotton manufacturers "preferred to buy West European equipment, even though it meant paying higher prices" (Thompstone, 2004, p. 358). In a general balance, "Russian continued to import the bulk of its textile machinery from abroad, despite the high tariffs it attracted" (p. 358).

In that "massive borrowing of foreign technology", one key factor was specialized personnel, given the tacit knowledge involved in the operation of textile machinery, resulted in the "dominance of English supervisory staff" (Thompstone, 2004, p. 360).

In 1913, although not an industrial country (Falkus, 1972, p. 11), textiles "employed 30 percent of the workforce" (Thompstone, 2004, p. 343). As one unintended and unforeseen consequence of this important role of textile industries in Russia, in February 1917 the unrest that led to the collapse of the Czarist regime had among them "women textile workers" (Zelnick, 2006, p. 635).

3.5.4 Sub-Saharan Africa: Very Late Arrival and the Survival of Artisanal Production

Colonial Sub-Saharan Africa did not produce an initial industrialization. Clarence-Smith (2014, p. 276) evaluates "modern colonial mills", identifying only in 1925 the first colonial initiative of textile production – Texaf -, an initiative of "two Belgian textile producers" (p. 276). As another example of superposition of different technological revolutions, in 1930 Texaf had a subsidiary to "generate its own hydroelectric power" (p. 276).

The colonial condition in Angola and Mozambique defined in the early 1930s a stimulus for the production of cotton and a formal prohibition of the "creation of textile mills" (p. 277). These colonial policies were reverted in the 1950s with Salazar stimulating metropolitan capitalists to build textile factories – a superposition of different technological revolutions, as the first "large textile factory" was located near "an abundant source of cheap hydroelectric power" (pp. 278–279).

Textiles did not have an important role in South African industrialization – a blanket factory in Cape Town was founded in 1891, and in 1933–1934 there were twelve textile establishments in South Africa. Clarence-Smith (2014, p. 280) mentions that only during the Second World War was there a growth in textile production in South Africa – European firms lacking electricity at home "relocated to South Africa" (p. 280).

"Independence from around 1960 was accompanied by policies of import substitution" (Clarence-Smith, 2014, p. 281), policies that were not well-succeeded (pp. 282–284) An important phenomenon in East Africa was the survival of "artisanal textiles in the era of Independence" (p. 284).

Kilby (1975) describes the introduction of cotton in Uganda and Kenya in the early twentieth century. Cotton became the leading crop in Uganda, and "the industrial processing associated with it – the mandatory ginning and the discretionary extraction of edible oil from the seed – early became the country's principal manufacturing activity". In 1962 the Nigeria Textile Mills opened and in 1965 Nigeria had 17 textile firms (p. 508).

The late and very limited diffusion of textile mechanization in Sub-Saharan Africa is shown in Mitchell (1998, p. 438): there are data only after 1950 – South Africa and Zaire with respectively 129,000 spindles and 49,000 spindles in that year -, with Ethiopia with initial data from 1958–35,000 spindles – and Nigeria from 1962–72,000 spindles.

Hopkins (p. 304) also presents evidence, for West Africa, on the survival of "traditional cloth industry" after the establishment of "modern textile factories". Hopkins lists areas where "traditional hand-weavers using hand-spun yarn" produced almost one third of the region's output: Nigeria, Mali, Upper Volta, Ghana, Ivory Coast and Senegal (p. 304). In another combination of different layers of technology, Hopkins indicates that "some crafts survived by employing new techniques" – sewing machines (p. 305).

3.5.5 Latin America: Initial Industrialization Induced by Exports

As discussed in Sect. 3.3, the arrival of cotton industrialization in Latin America was a process mediated through the specialization of the region in exports of primary products (Furtado, 1976, pp. 46–47). This export specialization led to an intra-regional differentiation as Furtado's typology suggests (1976, pp. 47–49).[19] This phase of the Latin American economies prepared the beginnings of industrialization: "industrialization induced by exports" (Furtado, 1976, p. 100).

However, for the very initial textile industrialization in Brazil – that defined its arrival date in 1834, in Table 3.2 – Suzigan (1986, p. 74) suggests another dynamic: cotton produced for export in the Northeast induced a diversification of activities in the nineteenth century, with mills for initial processing of cotton – ginning – and factories to produce textiles: the first three textile factories in Brazil were established in Bahia, respectively in 1834, 1835 and 1844 (Suzigan, 1986, p. 401). In the case of Brazil, there have been different rationales explaining different motivations for textile industrialization, and later the expansion of coffee production and exports stimulated both cotton textile industries and railways (Suzigan, 1986, p. 73) – an overlapping of the first two technological revolutions, as presented in the next chapter.

This Latin American phenomenon – industrialization induced by exports – is illustrated by the Brazilian case, as Suzigan (1986, p. 75) puts forward his research hypothesis: "industrial development in Brazil during the nineteenth century can be explained as an outcome of the growth of the industrial production induced by the expansion of the exporting sector".

This hypothesis involves a dynamic process that over time, as consequence of the growth of the industrial sector, the relationship between the primary products exporting sector and industrialization is mitigated, as the linkages generated by the "incipient domestic industrial sector" started to stimulate investments in other industrial sectors (Suzigan, 1986, p. 75). In the 1930s such link is broken and the process of import-substitution industrialization is started (p. 76).

Although an exporter of primary products, Mexico may have a peculiar trajectory in relation to textiles, defined by its political independence and by initial efforts towards industrialization, described by Beckert (2014, p. 159): "Mexico had a long-established and thriving nonmechanized textile industry" that was protected by tariffs in independent Mexico. This previous textile production might be related to the first "mechanized cotton mill", inaugurated in 1835, and Beckert (2014, p. 160) describes an early commitment to import substitution that led to the establishment of domestic cotton textile production large enough to in 1870 supply 60 percent of the local demand (p. 160).

[19] Furtado's typology of Latin American "economies exporting raw materials" is summarized in Chap. 4, Sect. 4.5.5, given their links to the railway building process in the region.

3.6 Conclusion: A Technological Revolution That Reshaped the International Division of Labor

The global impacts of the first technological revolution are associated with the emergence of modern industrial capitalism. Within this process there was the reconfiguration of the center-periphery divide (Furtado, 1987). The "astonishing reversal" identified by Darwin (2007, p. 196) is one big consequence of that reconfiguration.

Table 3.2 shows how a long-time lag between the first big bang (1771) and the arrival of cotton-textile mechanization at the periphery, confirming Beckert's puzzle (2014, p. 141). That list of arrival years in our five countries/regions shows how the time lag was big enough to reach India after the second big bang (in 1856) and China after the third (in 1889).

The analysis presented in this chapter explored the first big bang impacts on our five regions in this long time-interval organizing the discussions on the combined effects of expansionary and assimilatory forces. The outcome of this combined process is shown in Table 3.3.

Table 3.3 shows the arrival dates of cotton mechanization (dates presented in Table 3.2) and an indicator of the intensity of its diffusion – the number of spindles installed in 1909. A look at these data suggests that the earlier the arrival, the greater the diffusion – the case of Russia -, and the later the arrival, the smaller the diffusion – the case of China.

The long time-span of this spread is a consequence of one peculiarity of the propagation of this technological revolution: it involved two types of impacts. These two types of impacts are related to changes in the nature of expansionary forces – a transition from selling consumer goods to selling capital goods.

The first is the impact of cheap cotton textiles: the advanced condition of production in the United Kingdom supported successful exports to all regions, as this is the cornerstone of the "astonishing reversal" in global trade – the five countries/regions in Table 3.3 became importers of cotton textiles. These imports were a source of perturbations that affected the precapitalist economies in those five regions, starting a chain of events that led to their transition to different forms of peripheric capitalism during the nineteenth and early twentieth centuries. Initially, the expanding markets for cheap textiles led to an exponential growth of their production, which demanded more cotton (the core input), a demand that was matched by slave production in the Americas and slave trade from Africa – emerging modern industrial capitalism supported by slavery, with long-lasting consequences specially for Africa.

Related to this first type of impact, there is a route towards industrialization through intermediate steps. The first step is the new position of the United Kingdom in the international division of labor and an internal change derived from the industrial revolution. The second step is transformations in consumer behavior in the United Kingdom and in Western Europe, that led to growing demand for various agricultural products, a demand matched by countries at the periphery. This new role of some countries – Latin American countries are in this group -, in a third step, led to initial accumulation of some wealth that, among other consequences, financed imports of cotton textiles.

This first type of impact started almost immediately in the cases of India, Russia and Sub-Saharan Africa, less immediately in China and Latin America. But this type of impact – transformation of all regions in importers of British textiles – prepared the conditions for the second impact, that included elements of import-substitution industrialization.

The second type of impact – through imports of textile machinery – took more time to happen. It had as prerequisite an initial accumulation of wealth and knowledge to buy textile machinery from the United Kingdom. As discussed in Sect. 3.4.2, it took time for a specialized machine-making industry to develop in the United Kingdom, and that development contributed to a rearrangement in the international division of labor: the United Kingdom began to change its position from exporter of cotton textiles to exporters of textile machinery. This change is connected to a superposition between the first and the second big bangs, as the machines exported after the end of the export ban in the 1830s used steam-power.

The nature of the impact of this first big bang on the periphery is the redefinition of its role, after the reconfiguration of the global economy with this new international division of labor. This reconfiguration is at the core of Furtado's analysis (1987) – the center-periphery divide. Within the time span of its two types of impacts, the first big bang reconfigured the global economy twice: as the United Kingdom became an exporter of capital goods in the 1830s, it reorganized its role after the "astonishing reversal" of the early 1800s.

References

Alaev, L. (1982). South India. In T. Raychaudhuri & I. Habib (Eds.), *The Cambridge economic history of India. Volume 1 – c. 1200 – c. 1750* (pp. 315–324). Cambridge University Press.

Albuquerque, E. M. (2021). Revoluções tecnológicas e general purpose technologies: mudança técnica, dinâmica e transformações do capitalismo. In M. S. Rapini, J. Ruffoni, L. A. Silva, & E. M. Albuquerque (Org.), *Economia da ciência, tecnologia e inovação* (Fundamentos teóricos e a economia global, 2nd ed., Vol. 1, pp. 53–83). Cedeplar-UFMG.

Allen, R. C. (2017). Lessons from history for the future of work. *Nature, 550*, 321–324.

Ananich, B. (2006). The Russian economy and the banking system. In D. Lieven (Ed.), *The Cambridge history of Russia – Volume 2: Imperial Russia, 1689–1917* (pp. 394–427). Cambridge: Cambridge University Press.

Arrighi, G. (1994). *O longo século XX: dinheiro, poder e as origens do nosso tempo*. Contraponto/ Unesp (1996).

Bach, M. (2021). A win-win model of economic development: How Indian economics redefined universal development from and at the margins, 1870–1905. *Journal of the History of Economic Thought, 43*(4), 483–505.

Banaji, J. (2010). *Theory as history: Essays on modes of production and exploitation*. Brill.

Bastid-Bruguiere, M. (1980). Currents of social change. In J. Fairbank & K.-C. Liu (Eds.), *The Cambridge history of China. Volume 11: Late Ching, 1810–1911, part 2* (pp. 535–602). Cambridge University Press.

Beckert, S. (2014). *Empire of cotton: A global history*. New York: Vintage Books.
Boserup, E. (1981). *Population and technological change: A study of long term trends*. The University of Chicago Press.
Cerqueira, H. E. G., & Albuquerque, E. M. (2020). China and the first impact of the industrial revolution: Initial conditions and a falling behind trajectory until 1949. *Nova Economia, 30-* (Especial), 1169–1198.
Chaudhuri, K. N. (1983). Foreign trade and balance of payments. In D. Kumar (Ed.), *The Cambridge economic history of India, v. 2, c. 1757–2003* (pp. 804–877). Cambridge University Press.
Chaudhuri, K. N. (1990). *Asia before Europe: Economy and civilization of the Indian Ocean from the rise of Islam to 1750*. Cambridge University Press.
Chibber, V. (2003). *Locked in place: State-building and late industrialization in India*. Princeton University Press.
Clarence-Smith, W. G. (2014). The textile industry of Eastern Africa in the Longue Durée. In E. Akyeampong, R. H. Bates, N. Nunn, & J. A. Robinson (Eds.), *Africa's development in historical perspective* (pp. 264–294). Cambridge University Press.
Cookson, G. (2018). *The age of machinery: Engineering the industrial revolution, 1770–1850*. The Boydell Press.
Daniel, W. (1995). Entrepreneurship and the Russian textile industry: From Peter the Great to Catherine the Great. *The Russian Review, 54*(1), 1–25.
Darwin, J. (2007). *After Tamerlane: The rise and fall of Global Empires, 1400–2000*. Cambridge University Press.
Darwin, J. (2009). *The empire project: The rise and fall of the British world-system, 1830–1970*. Cambridge University Press.
Devine, W. D., Jr. (1983). From shafts to wires: Historical perspective on electrification. *The Journal of Economic History, 43*(2), 347–372.
Diamond, J. (2017). *Guns, germs and steel: The fates of human societies* (20th Anniversary ed.). W. W. Norton & Co.
Dutt, R. (1906). *The economic history of India in the Victorian age: From the accession of Queen Victoria to the commencement of the twentieth century* (2nd ed.). Kegan Paul, Trench, Trübner & Co. Ltd.
Escosura, L. P. (2006). The economic consequences of independence in Latin America. In V. Bulmer-Thomas, J. H. Coatsworth, & R. C. Conde (Eds.), *The Cambridge economic history of Latin America. Volume I: The colonial era and the short nineteenth century* (pp. 463–504). Cambridge University Press.
Fage, J. D. (2002). *A history of Africa* (4th ed.). Routledge.
Fairbank, J. (1978). The creation of the treaty system. In J. Fairbank (Ed.), *The Cambridge history of China* (Vol. 10, pp. 213–263). Cambridge University Press.
Falkus, M. E. (1972). *The industrialization of Russia*, 1700–1914. Macmillan. https://archive.org/details/industrialisatio0000falk/
Farnie, D. A. (1979). *The English cotton industry and the world market, 1815–1896*. Clarendon Press. https://archive.org/details/englishcottonind0000farn/
Farnie, D. A. (1990). The textile machine-making industry and the world market, 1870–1960. *Business History, 32*(4), 150–170.
Farnie, D. A. (2004). The role of cotton textiles in the economic development of India, 1600–1990. In D. A. Farnie & D. J. Jeremy (Eds.), *The fibre that changed the world: The cotton industry in international perspective, 1600–1990s* (Pasold studies in textile history, 13) (pp. 395–430). Oxford University Press.
Feuerwerker, A. (1970). Handicraft and manufactured cotton textiles in China, 1871–1910. *The Journal of Economic History, 30*(2), 338–378.
Feuerwerker, A. (1980). Economic trends in the late Ching Empire, 1870–1911. In J. Fairbank & K.-C. Liu (Eds.), *The Cambridge history of China. Volume 11: Late Ching, 1810–1911, part 2* (pp. 1–69). Cambridge University Press.

Freeman, C. (1987). *Technology policy and economic performance: Lessons from Japan*. Pinter Publishers.
Freeman, C., & Louçã, F. (2001). *As time goes by: From the industrial revolutions and to the information revolution*. Oxford University.
Fukazawa, H. (1982). Maharashtra and the Deccan. In T. Raychaudhuri & I. Habib (Eds.), *The Cambridge economic history of India. Volume 1 – c. 1200 – c. 1750* (pp. 308–314). Cambridge University Press.
Furtado, C. (1976). *Economic development of Latin America* (2nd ed.). Cambridge University Press.
Furtado, C. (1987). Underdevelopment: To conform or to reform. In G. Meier (Ed.), *Pioneers of development* (Second series) (pp. 203–227). Oxford University/World Bank.
Gerschenkron, A. (1970). *Europe in the Russian mirror: Four lectures in economic history*. Cambridge University Press.
Graham, L. R. (1993). *Science in Russia and the Soviet Union: A short history*. Cambridge University Press.
Grove, L. (2004). Rural manufacture in China's cotton industry, 1890–1990. In D. A. Farnie & D. J. Jeremy (Eds.), *The fibre that changed the world: The cotton industry in international perspective, 1600–1990s* (Pasold studies in textile history, 13) (pp. 431–460). Oxford University Press.
Hamilton, A. (1791). *Report on manufactures*. Senate (1913).
Headrick, D. R. (1988). *The tentacles of progress: Technological transfer in the age of imperialism, 1850–1940*. Oxford University Press.
Hopkins, A. G. (2020). *An economic history of West Africa* (2nd ed.). Routledge.
Inikori, J. E. (2002). *Africans and the industrial revolution in England: A study in international trade and economic development*. Cambridge University Press.
Jeremy, D. I. (1977). Damming the flood: British government efforts to check the outflow of technicians and machinery, 1780–1843. *The Business History Review, 51*(1), 1–34.
Jeremy, D. I. (2004). The international diffusion of cotton manufacturing technology, 1750–1990. In D. A. Farnie & D. J. Jeremy (Eds.), *The fibre that changed the world: The cotton industry in international perspective, 1600–1990s* (Pasold studies in textile history, 13) (pp. 85–127). Oxford University Press.
Kilby, P. (1975). Manufacturing in colonial Africa. In P. Duigan & L. H. Gann (Eds.), *Colonialism in Africa, 1870–1960 – Volume 4, The economics of colonialism* (pp. 470–522). Cambridge University Press.
Kondratiev, N. D. (1926). Long cycles of economic conjuncture. In N. Makasheva, W. J. Samuels, & V. Barnett (Eds.), *The works of Nikolai D. Kondratiev* (Vol. 1, pp. 25–60). Pickering and Chato (1998).
Krieger, C. L. (2009). 'Guinea cloth': Production and consumption of cotton textiles in West Africa before and during the Atlantic Slave Trade. In G. Riello & P. Parthasarathi (Eds.), *The spinning world: A global history of cotton textiles, 1200–1850* (pp. 105–126). Oxford University Press.
Kuo, T.-Y., & Liu, K.-C. (1978). Self-strengthening: The pursuit of Western technology. In D. Twitchett & J. Fairbank (Eds.), *The Cambridge history of China. Volume 10: Late Ching, 1810–1911, part 2* (pp. 491–542). Cambridge University Press.
Landes, D. (1969). *The unbound Prometheus: Technological change and industrial development in Western Europe from 1750 to the present*. Cambridge University Press.
Lemire, B. (2009). Revising the historical narrative: Indian, Europe and cotton trade, c.1300–1800. In G. Riello & P. Parthasarathi (Eds.), *The spinning world: A global history of global textiles, 1200–1850* (pp. 205–226). Oxford University Press.
Lovejoy, P. E. (2012). *Transformations in slavery: A history of slavery in Africa* (3rd ed.). Cambridge University Press.
Malm, A. (2016). *Fossil capital: The rise of steam power and the roots of global warming*. Verso.
Marks, S., & Gray, R. (1975). Southern Africa and Madagascar. In R. Gray (Ed.), *The Cambridge history of Africa – Volume 4: From c. 1600 to c. 1790* (pp. 384–468). Cambridge University Press.

Marx, K. (1867). *Capital* (Vol. I). Penguin Books (1976).

Metcalf, B. D., & Metcalf, T. R. (2002). *A concise history of India*. Cambridge University Press.

Michalopoulos, S., & Papaioannou, E. (2020). Historical legacies and African development. *Journal of Economic Literature, 58*(1), 53–128.

Mitchell, B. R. (1998). *International historical statistics – Africa, Asia & Oceania, 1750–1993* (3rd ed.). Macmillan Reference Ltd/Stockton Press.

Morris, M. D. (1983). The growth of large-scale industry to 1947. In Kumar (Ed.), *The Cambridge history of India, volume 2 – c. 1789-c. 1970* (pp. 553–676). Cambridge University Press.

Myers, R. H., & Wang, Y.-C. (2002). Economic developments, 1644–1800. In W. Peterson (Ed.), *The Cambridge history of China. Volume 9: Part one: The Ching Empire to 1800* (pp. 563–646). Cambridge University Press.

Nelson, R. R., & Winter, S. G. (1977). In search of useful theory of innovation. *Research Policy, 6*(1), 36–76.

Perez, C. (2010). Technological revolutions and techno-economic paradigms. *Cambridge Journal of Economics, 34*(1), 185–202.

Pomeranz, K. (2000). *The great divergence: China, Europe and the making of modern world*. Princeton University Press.

Raychaudhuri, T. (1982). Mughal India. In T. Raychaudhuri & I. Habib (Eds.), *The Cambridge economic history of India. Volume 1 – c. 1200 – c. 1750* (pp. 261–307). Cambridge University Press.

Raychaudhuri, T. (1983). The mid-eighteenth background. In D. Kumar (Ed.), *The Cambridge economic history of India. Volume 2 – c. 1757–2003* (pp. 3–35). Cambridge University Press.

Riello, G. (2013). *The fabric that made the world modern*. Cambridge University Press.

Rosenberg, N. (1972). *Technology and American economic growth*. M. E. Sharpe.

Rosenberg, N. (1996). Uncertainty and technical change. In R. Landau, T. Taylor, & G. Wright (Eds.), *The mosaic of economic growth* (pp. 334–353). Stanford University.

Rosenberg, N., & Trajtenberg, M. (2004). A general purpose technology at work: The Corliss steam engine in the late 19th century US. *Journal of Economic History, 64*(1), 61–99.

Saul, S. B. (1967). The market and the development of the mechanical engineering in Britain, 1860–1914. *The Economic History Review, 20*(1), 111–130.

Saxonhouse, G. R., & Wright, G. (2010). National leadership and competing technological paradigms: The globalization of cotton spinning, 1878–1933. *The Journal of Economic History, 70*(3), 535–566.

Suzigan, W. (1986). *Indústria brasileira: origem e desenvolvimento*. Editora Hucitec/Editora da Unicamp (2000).

Teng, S., & Fairbank, J. (1979). *China's response to the West – A documentary survey, 1839–1923, with a new preface*. Harvard University Press.

Thompstone, S. (1984). Ludwig Knoop, 'the Arkwright of Russia'. *Textile History, 15*(1), 45–73.

Thompstone, S. (2004). The Russian Technical Society and British textile machinery imports. In D. A. Farnie & D. J. Jeremy (Eds.), *The fibre that changed the world: The cotton industry in international perspective, 1600–1990s* (Pasold studies in textile history, 13) (pp. 337–364). Oxford University Press.

Thornton, J. (1992). Precolonial African industry and the Atlantic trade, 1500–1800. *African Economic History, 19*, 1–19.

Tomlinson, B. R. (2013). *The economy of modern India – From 1860 to the twentieth first century* (2nd ed.). Cambridge University Press.

Tripathi, A., & Tripathi, A. (2014). *Indian National Congress and the struggle for freedom: 1885–1947*. Oxford University Press.

Us Bureau of the Census. (1909). *Supply and distribution of cotton – For the year ending in 31 August 1909*. Government Printing Office/US Department of Commerce.

Wakeman, F. (1978). The Canton trade and the Opium war. In D. Twitchett & J. Fairbank (Eds.), *The Cambridge history of China. Volume 10: Late Ching, 1810–1911, part 2* (pp. 163–212). Cambridge University Press.

Wilson, J. (2016). *India conquered: Britain's Raj and the Chaos of Empire*. Simon and Schuster.

Wrigley, C. C. (1986). Aspects of economic history. In J. D. Fage & R. Oliver (Eds.), *The Cambridge history of Africa – Volume 7: From 1905 to 1940* (pp. 77–139). Cambridge University Press.

Yangzong, W. (1994). The establishment of the modern textile industry in the late nineteenth century China: A comparison with Japan. In *Transfer of science and technology between Asia and Europe – From Vasco da Gama to the present day* (Vol. 7, pp. 61–78). https://doi.org/10.15055/00003219

Zelnick, R. B. (2006). Russian workers and the revolution. In D. Lieven (Ed.), *The Cambridge history of Russia – Volume 2: Imperial Russia, 1689–1917* (pp. 617–636). Cambridge: Cambridge University Press.

Chapter 4
Railways and the Consolidation of an International Division of Labor: Hinterlands Join the Global Economy – 1829–1920

4.1 Introducion

The test of the Rocket steam locomotive in 1829 for the Liverpool-Manchester railway is, for Perez (2010, p. 190), the big bang of the second technological revolution.[1]

The invention of this second big bang had a long genealogy. As Wolmar (2010, p. 4) highlights, "[t]he railways were made possible by a series of technical innovations over the space of a couple of centuries involving the development of steam engines, locomotives and rails". The Rocket, a benchmark for steam locomotives, was produced by a firm – Robert Stephenson & Co – founded in 1824, "for the purpose of building locomotives" (Ross, 2006, p. 28).[2]

Freeman and Louçã (2001, p. 192) present a list of "major events of steam power", connecting James Watt's (1783, 1792) steam engines, Trevithick's locomotives (1804), Stephenson's locomotive (1829) and steamships (1838, 1839). The intertwinement between the first two technological revolutions is discussed by Freeman and Louçã (2001, p. 181): "the first two Kondratiev may be seen in Britain

---

[1]Kondratiev (1926, pp. 39–40), presenting the second long wave, associates it to a long list of inventions brought forward between 1824 and 1849. Among them, were the steam engine (1824)", "electromagnetic telegraphy (1832)", "Morse telegraphy (1837)", "the construction of the first wheeled steam-engine (1836)", "the cable system (1848)" (p. 39). Kondratiev identifies a lag before their use: "[a]fter a corresponding delay, many of these advances in technology and technical inventions found broad industrial use" (p. 39). The initial international spread of railways is noted: "in the United States, England and France from the 1830s to 1840s we see a rapid growth in railways and water transport" (p. 40). In this phase, Kondratiev identifies the "strengthening of the role of the United States in the world market" (p. 40). The articulation between different technologies is captured by Kondratiev, as his list includes the steam engine, its wheels and telegraphy.

[2]Wolmar (2010, p. 8) mentions Stephenson and "his company's locomotives".

E. da Motta e Albuquerque, *Technological Revolutions and the Periphery*, Contributions to Economics, https://doi.org/10.1007/978-3-031-43436-5_4

as two successive phases of the Industrial Revolution".[3] And in Europe, they note, "the catch up process combined features of the first and the second waves" (2001, p. 181).

This combination of different phases or technological revolutions seen in Europe is just an introduction to other forms of combination, overlapping and superposition that took place in the periphery. This second big bang occurred in the United Kingdom before the arrival of cotton textile mechanization in our peripheric regions, with the exception of Russia – see Table 3.2.

This chapter reviews the invention of railways and its initial expansion within the United Kingdom, presents the expansionary forces emanating from there, evaluates how railways were built in the United States – as an example of an almost full domestic exploitation of linkages for development, without dissipation effects -, presents the assimilatory forces and concludes analyzing the specificity of this technological revolution – the consolidation of an international division of labor.

4.2 Railways and Their Invention and Initial Expansion in the United Kingdom

The year of 1829 in the United Kingdom may be used as a starting point to review the connections between this second big bang and the mechanization of textile production.

The first connection has already been presented in the previous chapter: James Watt's invention and its use in the textile industry. In 1830 there was a turning point in the use of steam as motive power in textiles mills in England (Malm, 2016, p. 76). Improvements in the steam engine and experiments with it as a driving force of locomotives are described by Ross (2006). In 1804, Richard Trevithick developed the "primal railway engine" (Ross, 2006, p. 17). In this process an invention related to textiles and its later improvements led to an engine that began to be used in transports.

The second connection is the location of the first railway – the Liverpool-Manchester line: right within the region leading the first technological revolution. Wolmar (2010, p. 9) summarizes the roles of Liverpool and Manchester: Liverpool, a "booming port", "the main arrival port for raw cotton, which needed to be processed in Manchester's mills" (p. 9). Over time the volumes traded grew and the existing transport forms were becoming bottlenecks for the industry: the road between Liverpool and Manchester was "completely inadequate" and the "channel

[3] Marx (1867, pp. 505–506) begins his description of the industrial revolution with the cotton mill (p. 505) and concludes it with railways (p. 506). Marx's passage may be read as a dynamic model that combines perturbations that affect existing sectors, that also provoke the emergence of new sectors, and that completes the process with inter-temporal perturbations and effects. Intuitions on complex systems?

transport" was "expensive and slow" (p. 9). The opening of the Liverpool-Manchester railway, in 1823, was an attempt to solve that problem. This new railway provoked other events such as the creation of a firm to produce locomotives in 1824 – Robert Stephenson & Co, headed by the son of George Stephenson, an inventor who had in 1814 created his first steam locomotive – the Blücher. This firm, Robert Stephenson & Co, answered a call from the Liverpool-Manchester railway to join a competition – the Rainhill Trials, between 6 and 14 October 1829 – and they won with their locomotive, the Rocket. Thus, the "Liverpool-Manchester, the first railway to employ exclusively steam traction, was opened on 5 September 1830" (Wolmar, 2010, p. 44).

This railway, initially planned for freight transport, then opened up to passengers with great success – "the enormous demand for travel" was discovered (Wolmar, 2010, p. 9). Other new demands arose for the transportation of cattle and other products from farmers and fishermen (Wolmar, 2010, p. 10).

From the inauguration of this first commercial railway – the Liverpool-Manchester – the diffusion of railways was rapid and in 1855 there were 11,744 km of railways in the United Kingdom (Headrick, 1988, p. 55).

This proliferation of railways within the United Kingdom depended also upon developments of the credit system, given the capital intensity of railway investment – a public utility. The cyclical nature of railway expansion in the United Kingdom and the changes it brought to financial institutions is illustrated by a financial phenomenon: railway mania. Kindleberger and Aliber (2005) mention railway manias in the 1830s and in 1842 (pp. 44–45 and p. 238).[4]

This process within the United Kingdom led to the creation of a large railway network, a strong global advantage, based on the technology, the knowledge and the capital thus far accumulated. This advantage underlies what Wolmar (2010, pp. 45–64) defines as "the British influence". This process within the United Kingdom is an introduction for the investigation of the expansionary forces that shaped one component of the global spread of railways.

4.3 Expansionary Forces Emanating from the United Kingdom

In the United Kingdom there were early perceptions on how railways could become important global investments. Ross (2006, p. 57) identifies in the early 1830s this perception of "a growing international market for steam locomotives" (p. 57). Wolmar (2010, p. 45), discussing the British advantage until the 1870s, articulates

[4]Darwin (2009, p. 59) and Wolmar (2010, p. 45) also mention railway manias. Kindleberger and Aliber (2005, pp. 294–3003) present a "stylized outline of financial crises, 1618 to 1998" that shows how speculation with railways investments preceded crises in England in 1836, 1847 and 1857.

its domestic network with a "captive market in its expanding colonial empire, where it could export locomotives, rails and other railway supplies" (p. 57).

Between 1850 and 1914 Britain was at the height of its international power – it matters to be an Empire.[5] Darwin (2009, p. 114) describes the United Kingdom at the center of that Empire as an "octopus power" (chapter 2) and its development as a "commercial empire" (chapter 3). For Darwin (2009, p. 114), Britain was well positioned to take advantage of the tenfold increase in the world trade between 1850 and 1914 given its technology – specially steam power -, capital, institutions and personnel. British global investments in infrastructure gave railways a key role: "to open up the hinterland, without access to navigable water, dragging them from subsistence to commercial production" (p. 114). Under British leadership, the world's railway mileage grew from 66,000 in 1860 to 465,000 in 1910" (pp. 114–115).

The expansionary forces operating after the second big bang consolidated the international division of labor that emerged after the first big bang, expanding it through the capillarization of its networks within previously included regions.

The dominant form driving those expansionary forces was foreign capital investments.[6] Darwin connects the previous capital accumulation in Britain – outcome of the mechanization of textile production and its feedbacks – to the availability of incomes to be invested abroad (p. 116). Railways had an important role in those foreign investments, as "the major impetus came from the construction of railways overseas" (p. 116). The British leadership in railway technology, the previous development of financial instruments such as railway shares and the "role of British contractors overseas" (p. 116) supported those international capital flows.

Darwin provides a good picture of how British foreign capital investments were driving railway development abroad: "[a]s the international railway boom developed in the 1870s, a huge stream of British capital flowed abroad" (p. 116). A process that lasted until the First World War: "between 1870 and 1913, British investments in Indian, colonial and foreign companies rose fivefold to £ 1.5 billion – around 40 per cent of all British overseas investment" (p. 116).[7]

Another source, although with more intermediate steps in a causal chain, of railway expansion is a consequence of structural changes brought by the first big bang: the rise of a new European working class, that together with income-related changes in other sectors, transformed the nature of the demand at the center

[5]Darwin (2009, pp. 36–59) highlights the "domestic source of British expansion", a broad process within which the railway had an important role. It matters to be an Empire because United Kingdom could use its colonies as source for raw materials, as market for industrialized goods, and as nodes of its network of military and naval power.

[6]"A marked tendency to invest overseas was already visible before 1880" (Darwin, 2009, p. 116).

[7]There is a map (Darwin, 2009, p. 118) that shows the destinations of "British foreign investments to 1914". In that Map, India is the 5th destination of British investments, after the United States, Canada, Argentina and Australia. India was a more important destination than South Africa, Brazil, Russia, New Zealand, Mexico, Japan, China and Egypt. Note that all continents received British investments in that period – anatomy of an octopus power.

of global capitalism. These changes affected the demand for food and especially the "world wheat market" (Friedman, 2005, p. 234), built after "imports of cheap foods" (p. 234).

This new "food regime" was associated with changes in the international division of labor, with regions assuming new roles or struggling to preserve old roles in the global production of wheat: Nelson (2022) and Magnan (2016) describe those changes and the roles of Russia, the West of the United States, Canada, Australia, New Zealand, and Argentina. Friedman (2005, p. 235) links those changes to demographic movements and territorial expansion in new regions. New regions became producers of wheat for the United Kingdom imports because railways connected them to markets abroad. In a final step in this causal chain, Friedman (2005, p. 235) identifies territorial expansion "as a key driver of railway expansion" (p. 235).[8]

These expansionary forces emanating from the United Kingdom, with direct and indirect links strengthened British domestic industry because the building of railways increased the demand for its exports – from rails to locomotives. This process assumes different configurations in the five peripheric regions investigated in this book, with differences that now, in this second big bang, include transfer of technology from outside of the United Kingdom: the United States, since early 1840s, are already an alternative that Russia used (Westwood, 1964, p. 32). This is one reason why the next section focuses on the development of railways in the United States.

4.4 Railways in the United States

The United States as a source of technology transfer to Russia is an indication of a change in the dynamics of global capitalism, a step in the process of their transition to a new position replacing the British hegemony (Arrighi, 1994). In the next chapter the third big bang will be triggered in the United States, another evidence of technological basis for that hegemonic transition.

The building of the United States railway infrastructure is a key moment of their national market unification and formation, with broad macroeconomic and industrial consequences. Chandler (1977) presents a comprehensive analysis of that multifaceted process.

This section on the United States railways is a case study that provides a benchmark for the whole process of absorption of a new technology, a process that internalized almost all linkages – forward and backward – available from the

[8]Bruno C. Melo (2023) discusses those changes with a focus on their influence in the long-term behavior of wheat prices.

railway building. A railway building process with almost no dissipation effects – or with almost no leakages: a contrasting case is colonial India, which is an example of lack of backward linkages and strong dissipation effects (Hurd, 1983).

4.4.1 Technology Transfer and Sources of Learning

The transfer of railway technology, especially steam locomotive technology, is more difficult than that of cotton textiles –[9] the textile industry in the United States, as seen in Chap. 3, was created by one immigrant, Samuel Slater. For the absorption of railway technology other sources and other learning routes were necessary.

One learning route was to follow developments in the United Kingdom. Ross (2006, p. 34) reports imports of British locomotives already in 1829 – Horatio Allen, from the Delaware & Hudson Canal Company, ordered eight locomotives, one of them from Robert Stephenson. Allen and C. I. Miller, also from Allen's company, were present at the Rainhill Trails, in October 1829 (Wolmar, 2010, p. 2). In 1830, "the first US built engine" was produced at the West Point Foundries, with a design developed by C. I. Miller (Ross, 2006, p. 45). In 1831 W. Norris "set up a shop as a locomotive manufacturer in Philadelphia" (Ross, 2006, p. 58).

The second learning route is related to previous developments in textiles. In the 1830s, Lowell Machine Shop, a machinery-producing company like others that "emerged in the textile firms of New England", decided to produce locomotives. It was successful and in the 1840s concentrated on the production of steam locomotives (Rosenberg, 1972, p. 99). Baldwin Locomotive Works also had its origin related to textile (p. 99).[10]

The third learning route, described by Rosenberg (1972), came from the widespread use of steam-engines for navigation – in 1838 steamboats accounted for 60% of all power generated by steam in the United States (p. 69). For Rosenberg this is an early experiment with steam-engines as tractive power (p. 67).

All those sources of knowledge were supporting an early independence of the United States in the production of steam locomotives: in 1839 there were 450 locomotives there, but only 117 had been imported from the United Kingdom (Rosenberg, 1972, p. 73).

---

[9] In this comparison, the variable "ease of learning" (Cohen and Levinthal, 1989, p. 572) was greater in the case of textiles. Thus, on the one hand, more investments and more domestic knowledge are necessary for absorption of railway technology. On the other hand, the absorptive capacity in the United States had grown – more people and firms identifying the new technology and with resources to learn and adapt the new knowledge to specific United States conditions.

[10] According to Rosenberg (1972, p. 71, footnote 26), "[t]he Baldwin Locomotives Works in Philadelphia filled orders of large number of locomotives for Russian railways in the 1870s and 1890s".

4.4.2 *Chandler and the Revolution in Transport and Communication in Nineteenth Century*

Chandler's explanation of the rise of the modern multidivisional firm in the United States in the last decades of the nineteenth century attributes a central role to the railway infrastructure: this is the subject of *Visible Hand*'s Part II: "the revolution in transport and communication". This revolution is located between "the traditional processes of production and distribution" (Part I) and "the revolution in distribution and production" (Part III). Politically, Part I corresponds to the antebellum period and Part III to the post-Civil War period.[11] The Civil War in the United States (1861–1865) was an important political and institutional change, with implications for national and cross-country railway building. The stronger political capacity of the federal government enabled it to provide land concessions to railways that crossed different states.

For Chandler, "[m]odern mass production and mass distribution depend om the speed, volume, and regularity in the movements of goods and messages made possible by the coming of the railroad, telegraphy and steamship" (1977, p. 207). This is an excellent example of forward linkages provided by railway building.

The revolution in transport and communication is structured in four chapters by Chandler, covering its different phases: 1850s–1860s – the railroads: first modern business enterprise; 1870s–1880s – railroad cooperation and competition; 1880s–1890s: system building; and a final chapter on "completing the infrastructure" (Chandler, 1977).

The presence and strength of backward linkages is this process of building the railway network is shown in data presented in Chandler's Appendix A – "Industrial enterprises with assets of $ 20 million or more, 1917". In the "Group 37: transportation equipment" there are firms related to railways in the second, seventh and eighth positions; respectively Pulman Co., American Locomotives Works and Baldwin Locomotive Works (pp. 510–511). US Steel is the first in the "Group 33: Primary Metal Industries" (p. 508).[12]

The railway system built in the United States, especially after the Civil War, is a support of the process of national market formation – another forward linkage. This process is related to the geopolitical change that took place by 1875 when the United States GDP, according to Maddison data, overtook the United Kingdom GDP (Maddison, 2010). This process, beyond its backward linkages to the industrial sector, contributed to the development of the financial sector – there is a "Railroad Era" in the history of Wall Street (Geisst, 2004, chapter 2). The feedbacks between

---

[11] The antebellum size of railways influenced the outcome of the Civil War. According to McPherson (1988, p. 318), "[t]he Union had more than twice the density of railroads per square miles as the Confederacy".

[12] Freeman and Louçã (2001, p. 234) stress the importance of domestic production of steel rails after 1875. Rosenberg (1972, p. 73) explains that "America supplied most of her own rails by the late 1850s".

the railways and the emergence of the unified national market were sources of potential economies of scale and scope to be explored by Chandler's first-movers – leading firms that made investments in production, marketing and management and supported the United States technologic and economic leadership, basis of new steps towards the United States hegemony in the early twentieth century.

4.4.3 Emerging Global Leadership, Linkages and Lack of Dissipation Effects

This summary of the United States as a case study of railway development illustrates how railways can provide strong forward and backward linkages that generated positive feedbacks between that sector and other emerging industrial sectors. Those linkages blocked dissipation effects – that is when the case of the United States provides a benchmark to our investigation of the spread of railways across the periphery, in the five regions of this research.

4.5 View from the Periphery: Different Levels of Political Organization and Their Impact on Railway Building

Railways have peculiarities that affect their potential spread to peripheric regions: the amount and intensity of capital necessary for their building and the time required for each step in the networks' formation.[13] Another specificity is the knowledge needed to build and run a railway – from mechanics for its locomotives, metallurgy for its rails, civil engineering for its construction, and managerial skills to run and maintain a large and geographically dispersed firm. Those specificities increase the degree of needed absorptive capacity at the periphery. And the absorptive capacity depends on the level of political organization of backward regions.

The political organization of the five regions in 1850 is summarized in Table 3.1 (Chap. 3). Those different levels of political organization are determinants of different motivations for the initial spread of the railways. From colonial India and Africa to Czarist Russia, those different political organizations shaped different assimilatory forces. The combination of those different factors defined when and how railways were built in these five regions.

Those differences appear, again, in the different lags between this big bang (1829) and the first railway built in each of those five regions, as shown in Table 4.1.

[13] As an illustration, Hausman et al. (2008, p. 22) present a Figure that compares the capital/output ration between "steam railways" and "all manufacturing" for the United States in 1880: they were, respectively 16 and 0.5 (p. 22).

Table 4.1 Year of the first railway line opened in the Indian subcontinent, China, Russia, Sub-Saharan Africa and Latin America

Region	Year
India	1853
China	1876
Russia	1837
Africa	SA: 1860; NIG: 1886; MOZ: 1901
Latin America	MEX: 1850; ARG: 1857; BRA: 1854

Source: India: Ross (2006, p. 53); China: Ross (2006, p. 185); Russia: Westwood (1964, p. 24); Africa – South Africa, Nigeria and Mozambique: Nock (1978, p. 8); Latin America – Mexico: Nock (1978, p. 8), Argentina and Brazil: Ross (2006, p. 83)

The different motivations and the reasons of those different lags shown in Table 4.1 are the main topics of the subsections organized for those five regions.

4.5.1 *India: Railways as a Colonial Project*

The "astonishing reversal" that the initial impact imposed on the Indian subcontinent is behind the initial motives for railway building in India – the transport of cotton for export to the textile industry in Britain (Wolmar, 2010, p. 49). Wolmar (2010, p. 50) reports the pressure from cloth manufacturers in Manchester and Glasgow and "how the need for a stable cotton supply" was a "turning point" to build the first railway in India.

Not only this role related to cotton exports but also the timing of its construction are expressions of how that railway was related to a consolidation of India's new position in the international division of labor: Wolmar (2010, p. 49) identifies a failure in the US cotton crop in 1846 as the event that pushed the British textile manufacturers to search for stabler cotton suppliers.[14]

Hurd (1983, p. 738) evaluates that the motives for railway building in India were commercial but also political. MacPherson (1955) finds three different motivations, coming from the Indian government – the colonial power -, the investors, and promoters and business groups in the United Kingdom. In the first case, regarding the colonial Indian government, there were civilizatory and commercial reasons, including the desire to facilitate "the transport of primary commodities for both the internal and external market" (p. 178). There were also political and military aspects (p. 179): internal security and defense. MacPherson (1955, p. 179) highlights how the "Mutiny" (in 1857) provided a "greater stimulus to construction" (p. 179).[15] The British investors were motivated by the "5 per cent guarantee of interest offered by

[14]Headrick (1988, p. 60) also makes this causal connection.

[15]The 1857 "Mutiny" is dividing line in Indian colonial history: it is the end of the rule of the East Indian Company and the beginning of the administration directly by the British government. This institutional change had implications for the process of railway building.

the Indian government" (p. 180) – the "natives of India" paid "through their taxes the deficiency between the 5 per cent and the profits of the lines" (p. 186). Hurd (1983, pp. 738–739) explains this "system of subsidies known as 'the guarantee' (p. 738): "[a]ll of India's early railways, including the important lines leading inland from the port cities, were built in the context of the guarantee" (p. 739).

In sum, the policies of the United Kingdom related to railway building can be included within the broad topic that Tomlinson (2013, p. 125) calls "imperial commitment" – therefore the title of this subsection: railways as a colonial project.[16]

For Hurd (1983, p. 745) railways in India helped to tie India to the British economy. The railway network in India contributed to an "expansionism in the exports of products such as wheat, rice, jute, leather, oilseeds and cotton", and to an increase in the imports of cotton textiles, yarn and capital goods. Kerr (2007, pp. 114–115) associates railways with a trade surplus for Britain in its exchanges with India.

Before independence the building of railways is divided in different phases. For Headrick (1988), between 1853 and 1870 there was the building of trunk lines; between 1870 and 1879 an era of "state construction", between 1880 and 1914 a "new guaranteed period" – an expansion from 15,564 km in 1880 to 59,585 km in 1915 -,[17] and a final colonial period, the end in 1914 of the "golden age of Indian railways" (p. 78). Kerr (2007) suggests another periodization, with the final colonial period beginning in 1905 – "'nationalizing' the Indian railways" (p. 112), an indication of political changes in India exemplified by the foundation of the Indian National Congress in 1885 (Wilson, 2016, p. 332) and its increasing political influence.

The domestic economic impacts of this process of railway building are listed by Hurd (1983). Internal trade changed in at least four different ways. First, the new network changed the behavior of prices, evidence that "markets were not only widening, but were becoming national markets" (p. 746). Second, related to the increasing linking of Indian agriculture to the world market, a process of regional specialization took place (p. 747). Third, railways became the "largest single employer within the modern sector of the economy" (p. 748). Fourth, railways brought competition to local industries previously protected by the high costs of transport: the consequences of this impact on handloom industry are under debate – either it declined, given cheaper imported or domestically produced factory textiles, or it strengthened, given the availability of cheaper factory-made yarns that preserved the number of weavers (p. 748).

---

[16] Kerr (2007, p. 13) calls it "colonial railways", because between 1850 and 1947 there was a "development skewed to the political, administrative, military, and economic need of the Anglo-Indian connection. Headrick (1988, p. 53) stresses that among "colonial railway systems", "that of India is unique".

[17] In 1910 India was the fourth largest railway network, after the United States, Russia and Germany (Headrick, 1988, p. 55).

Hurd (1983, p. 749) points to the "absence of a basic structural change" in the Indian economy, a paradox for Headrick: although India in the end of the nineteenth century was one of the top railway countries, it was "the only one that failed to industrialize" (1988, p. 52). Hurd explains this paradox by "the way that railways were built and operated" (p. 749). Indian railways were the creation of British engineers (Headrick, 1988, p. 58) – the "1860s were boom years for British engineers and contractors" (p. 66). The first demands for technical education came from the Indian National Congress, only in 1887 (Headrick, 1988, p. 329).

In contrast with the case of the United States railways, the Indian case is an example of "the lack of linkages" (Hurd, 1983, p. 749): capital, management and skilled labor were British, "[r]ails, points, fishplates, machinery, locomotives, even sleepers, were almost all built outside India" (p. 749). Kerr (2007, p. 115) associates colonial power with the "retardation of 'backward linkages'".

The production of locomotives is investigated by Hurd (1983, p. 749), Headrock (1988, p. 81) and Kerr (2007, p. 27, p. 84). Headrick shows that in the nineteenth century countries that invested in railways also began manufacturing locomotives. Railway workshops were sites of technology transfer and India built its first locomotive in 1865 (Headrick, 1988, p. 82). However, until independence India produced only 700 locomotives, while importing 14,420 (p. 82), with the British exporting 12,000 (Hurd, p. 749). The potential but blocked linkages were also present in the production of rails, a dependence on British steel identified by the emerging Tata business group that since 1883 had tried to open a steel factory – but only launched Tata Steel in 1907 (Wilson, 2016, p. 385; Morris, 1983, p. 589).

The weight of imports of locomotives and rails illustrates the dimension of the dissipation effects by the colonial condition of India.

However, the formation of the railway network by the British colonial power had unintended political consequences: Indian railways were ground for the "building of the Indian state and economy" (Kerr, 2007, p. 109), on the one hand strengthening the colonial state, but on the other hand "facilitating the growth of the anticolonial nationalism" (p. 14).

4.5.2 *China: Very Late Beginning and a Post-1949 Priority*

The late beginning of railway development in China in 1876, even in comparison to Russia, India and Latin America (see Table 4.1) is an indication of peculiarities of this region. What happened to China's first railway illustrates those peculiarities: it was built with British capital but in 1877 it was dismantled by the Ching Dynasty (Wang et al., 2009, p. 768). This act of the Chinese empire is a consequence of doubts and fears raised by railway technology related to the fragile political situation in China after 1850.

Two military defeats in the Opium Wars, the loss of sovereignty in the Treaty Ports and the growing presence of Western powers initially, then Russia and Japan, establish a very peculiar geopolitical position for China. Although not a fully colonized country, China did not have complete control of its territory. Maps of China in late nineteenth century show various foreign-controlled cities and regions.[18] Furthermore, China's political leadership until 1911 – the Ching Dynasty – was a government "incapable of supplying positive assistance" to economic development (Feuerwerker, 1980, p. 59). These political conditions shaped the form and the speed of the spread of railways in China until 1949. It was only after the foundation of the People's Republic of China that railway building became a political objective (Wolmar, 2010, p. 315; Wang et al., 2009, p. 769).

During the late 1860s the self-strengthening movement (Kuo & Liu, 1978; Teng & Fairbank, 1979) was a response to the initial impact of Western powers and technology upon China. The need to learn Western technology and to use it began to be part of domestic debates in China. Probably those debates and the resulting emerging conscience of national backwardness stimulated the first governmental initiatives in railway building: in 1881 the 6 miles railway between Tangshan and Hsukochuang opened (Huenemann, 1984, Table 3, Appendix A). However, until 1885 China had only those 6 miles of railway.

Huenemann (1984) suggests a periodization of railway history in China divided into five phases: self-strengthening (1876–1894), "scramble for concessions" (1894–1900), "nationalist response" (1900–1911), "revolution and disintegration" (1911–1927) and "the Nanking decade" (1927–1937).

In Huenemann's first phase (1876–1894) only 410 km were built. Between 1895 and 1911, 87.3% of the railways were either "colonial concessions" or "financial concessions" (that involved foreign investments), evidence of the strength of foreign involvement in the Chinese railways, even during Huenemann's phase of "nationalist response". As Feuerwerker (1980, pp. 54–56) stresses, "China's pre-republican railways were financed mainly by foreign loans and constructed by foreign concessionaires". Huenemann reports that the railway boom between 1896 and 1914 "involved foreign middlemen ... and purchasing imported locomotives" (1984, p. 122). This form of building determined stronger dissipation effects and weaker linkages than the case of colonial India. The first Chinese-built locomotive was produced only in 1956.

Beyond this lack of backward linkages, the general impact of the relatively small railway network until 1911 was very limited. According to Feuerwerker (1980, p. 54), they "affected the economy and market system little, not only because their total mileage was, after all, extremely small, but also because the bulk of this track was opened only in the last few years of the dynasty".

Between the foundation of the republic in 1911 and the beginning of the war against Japan in 1937, another 12,417 km were built. Foreign financial concessions and railways with Japanese participation in Manchuria corresponded to 44.7% of the

[18] See, for instance, Spence (1990, p. 253) – a map that associates foreign zones of influence and railways in China (1880–1905).

network built.[19] However, this growth in the railway network during the republican period was not enough to improve transportation conditions. For Feuerwerker (1983, p. 91) "[p]oorly developed transport continued to be a major shortcoming of the Chinese economy in 1933". The contribution of railways and other modern forms of transport to the economy was three times less than the contribution of "old-fashioned forms of transport" (Feuerwerker, 1983, p. 93). Summarizing China's railway development until then, Huenemann evaluates that "China in 1937...had not solved the dilemma posed by railways" (1984, p. 97).[20]

After 1937, there was a war with Japan: "[a]ttacked by Japan in 1937, the Chinese economy disintegrated" (Harrison, 1998, p. 19). Between 1937 and 1945, according to Wang et al. (2009, p. 768), in Japan occupied Manchuria new lines were built "to exploit natural resources in the region".[21]

In 1949 there were 21,810 km of railway in China – almost the same length of colonial India in 1885 (Headrick, 1988, p. 55).

After 1949, an institutional change with the foundation of the People's Republic of China that made railways a priority, as a tool for national integration and a strategic part of Five-Year plans (Wang et al., 2009, p. 768). In 1974 China's railways network reached 45,093 km. Before the era of reforms, the condition of railways deserved a special attention from the central government that carried out a "[s]ystematic rehabilitation of key sectors such as railroads" (Naughton, 2007, p. 78).

In this process of railway building in the People's Republic of China, domestic production of steam locomotives was initiated. Based on the Russian LV class – a technology transferred by 1951 – the Datong Works built more than 4500 steam locomotives until late 1980s (Ross, 2006, p. 330). This very special case of technology transfer involved long lags – built in 1956, the first Chinese-made steam locomotive had a lag of more than 120 years vis-à-vis the British 1829 Rocket locomotive. In the United States, in 1956 the last steam locomotive was produced by Baldwin (Ross, 2006, p. 331). The source of the technology – the Soviet Union – in 1957 took the decision "to make a rapid transition to diesel and electric power, with steam to be phased out as early as possible" (Ross, 2006, p. 328). As Zhang et al.

---

[19]Naughton (2007, pp. 44–45) deals with the "beginnings of industrialization" in China (1912–1937), suggesting two patterns of industrialization: "Treaty Port industrialization" and "Manchurian industrialization". In Manchuria, "Japanese government sponsored industrialization", focusing on "heavy industries and railroads", the Japanese "developed a dense network of railroads and actively exploited the rich deposits of coal and iron ore in the region" (pp. 44–45).

[20]In their periodization, Wang et al. (2009, pp. 768–769) condensed the five phases from Huenemann in two: "preliminary construction" (before 1911) and "network skeleton" (1911–1949). After 1949 two other phases: "corridor building" (1949-early 1990s) and "deep intensification" (since mid-1990s).

[21]Naughton (2007, p. 47) mentions that in this period there was a "Japan-centered East Asian economic system", with Manchuria as one of the "raw-material and semiprocessed-goods suppliers" (p. 48).

(2006, p. 153) highlight, this is a case of transfer of "outdated" technology.[22] China was the last producer of steam locomotives globally (Ross, 2006, p. 330; Wolmar, 2010, p. 316).

Wang et al. (2009, p. 768) summarize the different strategies and decisions related to railways development after 1949, that combined expansion, access to new regions, and later initiatives for electrification and upgrades of old lines. Wolmar (2010, p. 329), in a chapter on "railway renaissance" – dealing with modern high-speed trains -, evaluates that China is "already the postwar star in railway development". Those data may identify China as one of the few exceptions that Headrick (p. 50) mentioned in his balance of 1914 global railway network.

4.5.3 *Russia: Railways and Spurts of Industrialization*

Railway development was a priority for Czarist economic policy (Westwood, 1994, p. 158). In the 1830s/1840s the Russian state had enough resources and political will to push industrialization measures. In the late 1890s railway construction was "central to the entire industrial economy" (Starns, 2012, p. 41).

In 1837 the first railway line was opened in Russia – a small, experimental 20 km railway. A second line was initiated in 1839 (Warsaw-Vienna) and a third in 1843 (Saint Petersburg-Moscow) (Westwood, 1964).

These initiatives show how closely Russia was following events in the United Kingdom and in the United States, and how its previous efforts in modernization and industrialization enabled the government to understand the importance of this new technology.[23]

---

[22] This case of transfer of outdated technology puts forward three questions. The first is the technological implications of China's reference for catch-up at that time: in the early 1950s the Soviet Union was its main source of new technology – but the Soviet Union was not able to go beyond a limited catch-up process. The second question looks for China's absorptive capacity in the early 1950s: there was no other choice, given the limited development in other sectors such as combustion engines and electricity, which made an impossibility to China to explore the "advantages of backwardness" at the time, skipping the steam age of locomotives and jumping to newer sources of traction. The third question is the implication for Chinese dependence on coal of the early 1950s choice to produce steam locomotives.

[23] Westwood (1964, p. 23) points to military motivations for those investments, as the "Tsar's attention had also been drawn by the British government's swift transfer by rail of troops from Manchester to Liverpool during an Irish emergency". Ames (1947) lists six motivations for railway building in Russia – one of them is the military motive. The other purposes are: stimulate export trade, connections with a single industrial complex, connections between existing industrial complexes, "opening up underdeveloped areas" and "development of regional lines along main transit routes" (p. 64). Starns (2012, p. 7) connects railway construction to Witte's industrialization policies, and Melnik (2020, p. 90) mentions List's influence on Witte.

The Russian government worried about the provision of locomotives and rolling stock since the construction of the Saint Petersburg-Moscow railway. According to Westwood (1964, p. 32), it was a Czar's wish to use material of Russian origin "as far as possible".

A previous industrial achievement – Aleksandrovsk, an iron foundry – in 1844 was reorganized to be transformed in a locomotive construction and repair center (Blackwell, 1968, p. 304). One firm from the United States – Hanson, Eastwick and Winas – was invited to present proposals and it won a contract to produce 165 locomotives in Russia.[24] The decision in favor of local production of locomotives instead of their import is a starting point of a learning process, that internalized parts of the backward linkages provided by railway building. Russian young engineers were recruited for railway construction (Westwood, 1964, p. 32), showing the importance of previous investments in engineering education (Balzer, 1996; Rieber, 1990).[25]

The subsequent process of railway building in Russia proceeded by cycles (Ames, 1947). There were three peaks, for Ames (1947, p. 59) in 1871, 1899 and in the First World War. Those cycles can be articulated with Gerschenkron's analysis of the 1890s as "the great upsurge of modern industrialization" (1960, p. 130).[26]

Over time, the domestic production of locomotive increased. Westwood (1964) presents data showing that between 1836 and 1865 two fifths of the demand for locomotives were satisfied by local production (p. 57), while in the 1890s only 806 locomotives out of 5196 used in Russian railways were imported (p. 93). Other backward linkages were at least partially internalized: between 1836 and 1865 one seventh of rails and one third of freight cars were domestically produced (p. 57). Capital and engineering skills were also Russian (p. 31).

[24]Why this invitation to a firm from the United States? For Rosenberg (1972, p. 75), such choice "may have reflected a shrewd awareness that Russia and America conditions closely resembled one another". Gerschenkron (1960, pp. 127–128) suggests that one advantage available for Russia in the nineteenth century was the opportunity to assimilate technology more advanced than the British, from Germany and from the United States – in the case of the United States, more capital-intensive options were available.

[25]There is a relationship between absorptive capacity in Czarist Russia and engineering education. For a discussion on "science in Russia in the nineteenth century", see Graham (1993, chapter 2). Rieber (1990, p. 563) mentions that "by the 1840s the general outlines of Russian engineering education were all established". Earlier, in 1830, "500 students were enrolled in a Mining Institute" (Rieber, 1990, p. 564). These steps in the engineering education explain why Russian engineers, although appreciating Western technology, they "opposed the idea of foreigners building Russian railroads" (p. 560).

[26]Falkus (1972, chapter 3) also identifies "the boom of the 1890s". Falkus claims that "[r]ailway construction dominated the industrial upsurge of the 1890s" (p. 65). Those cycles during the nineteenth century built the second largest railway network by 1905 (Headrick, 1988, p. 55). Gerschenkron (1960, p. 125) suggests a that railways might be a precondition for further industrialization in the Russian case, as "some railroad building had to antedate the period of rapid industrialization".

Institutional change brought forward by the fall of the Czarist empire in February 1917 and the beginning of the Bolshevik government in November 1917 – that opened a sequence of changes in economic systems between 1917 and 1991 – kept continuity in various dimensions. The size of the railway network built until 1915, the engineering skills accumulated and the domestic capacity in the production of railway equipment are strong roots for the post-1917 transport infrastructure. The production of steam locomotives was an element of continuity that survived until 1957 (Westwood, 1982, pp. 210–211; Ross, 2006, p. 328), crossing two world wars and different economic regimes – a variety of capitalism managed by Czarism, transition economy, "war communism", NEP, Stalinist model. This persistence – a lock-in with steam - delayed transitions to electric and diesel traction, related to the next two big bangs. Data from Westwood (1982, pp. 210–211) show that the first diesel locomotive was produced in 1931 and the first electric locomotive in 1932. This extended dominance of steam is documented in Westwood's chapter on "Steam's Indian summer, 1932–1952" (1982, pp. 125–198).[27] In this chapter the LV model in the 1950s is described (pp. 189–190) – the model that China used to produce its first locomotive (Ross, 2006, p. 330). In Russia this LV Model was produced until 1956 (Westwood, 1982, p. 190), the same year that China produced its first locomotive.

The lock-in of Soviet Union railway technology with steam until the middle 1950s is an indication of limitation within the Stalinist model to update technologies – one source of the limited catch up that the Soviet Union was able to perform. This might be connected with problems with planning decisions, that persisted supporting outdated technologies. Those decisions had impact on the rest of the economy, given the persistence of linkages that connected railways to coal and not to other emerging and new technologies – a negative contribution to a scenario preservation of technological relative backwardness identified in Russian economy during the 1960s and 1970s (Amman et al., 1977, p. 66).

4.5.4 Sub-Saharan Africa: Colonial Projects and Access to Natural Resources

In Sub-Saharan Africa there were two dynamics in railway building.

The first is located in Southern Africa, especially in contemporary South Africa – a late but active process of railway building connected to the exploration of natural resources discovered in the second half of the nineteenth century. Herranz-Loncán and Fourie (2018, pp. 75–76) identify a first period of intense railway building in the

[27] Westwood (1964, p. 275) reports that the "sixth five-year plan specified that in 1956–60 6000 steam, 2000 diesel and 2000 electric engines would be produced". This is another evidence on why the Soviet Union transferred outdated steam technology to China in the early 1950s: steam was still very important in Russia's railway planning establishment.

Cape Colony between 1875 and 1885, connecting the ports of the region to Kimberley – the diamond-producing area. Wolmar (2010, p. 173) associates a "railway boom in Southern Africa in the final fifteen years of the nineteenth century" with the "discovery of various minerals" – and a disease of cattle that led to a shortage of oxen. Railway building in South Africa can be related to a long process of formation of a "mineral-energy complex" (Fine and Rustomjee, 1996).

The second dynamic, in the rest of Sub-Saharan Africa,[28] is a more direct outcome – less mediated by initiatives from local populations – of colonial policies, that would culminate in the Berlin Conference (1885) and the partition of Africa. This political scenario in Africa is combined with the new international division of labor after the initial phase of the Industrial Revolution and, in the specific case of Africa, after the end of slave trade defined by the British Empire in 1807: European traders searched Africa for the natural goods available in its hinterland – railways would help to provide "direct access to the producing areas in the hinterland" (Fage, 2002, p. 329). The outcome of this specific dynamic is easily visualized in a Map of "colonial railways" prepared by Michalopoulos and Papaioannou (2020, p. 77): almost all lines connect one port with one area in the hinterland – the railways "did not connect the major African cities; rather railroads connected ports with the interior, as the Europeans strategy was to extract cash crops and minerals" (p. 76).

In their survey of historical legacies in Africa, Michalopoulos and Papaioannou (2020, p. 76) find that railways there were "largely nonexistent at the end of the nineteenth century", a condition that changed "partially" by "Europeans desire to exploit agricultural and mineral-rich areas and control the interior".[29] This desire led them to build railways and some roads (p. 76). However, at the end of the colonial era, "there were few railroads, as investments were limited" (p. 76). Data from Jedwab and Moradi (2016, p. A4) show a total of 57,872 km built before 1960 (including South Africa, that in 1912 had approximadly18,000 km).[30]

Michalopoulos and Papaioannou (2020, pp. 76–77) take a closer look to the geography of railways in colonial Mozambique, built between 1890 and 1960: there were 3 main and 2 subordinate rail lines connecting ports (like Lourenço Marques) and the interior (like Johannesburg), effectively splitting the colony into three zones – "[t]here was no effort to connect the Southern with Central and Northern provinces" (p. 77). This illustration shows that in the case of Mozambique, beyond the lack of domestic linkages, there were also very limited impacts on the process of formation of national integrated markets.

---

[28]The Sub-Saharan region outside South Africa is heterogeneous, given different long-term history, levels of political organization of native peoples, different contacts with different non-African nations. For example, Michalopoulos and Papaioannou (2020, pp. 59–60) mention a division of Sub-Saharan Africa in at least three regions: (i) Western Africa, (ii) Central Africa, and (iii) Eastern and Southern Africa.

[29]The relationship between railways and minerals had also an opposite causation: the dream of a Cape Town-Cairo line was a "project diverted by discoveries of minerals, which led to other railways being constructed" (Wolmar, 2010, p. 172).

[30]Jedwab and Moradi (2016, p. 282) divide railway building in colonial Africa in three periods: 1890–1918, 1919–1945, and 1945–1960.

Investigating what may have "stopped the technology adoption" of railways, Chaves et al. (2014) present three cases related to initiatives or reactions of African polities – "consolidated African states" (p. 349): the Assante Nation, Ethiopia and the Sultanate of Zanzibar. The Assante in 1892 signed an agreement with J. W. Herival "to finance and manage the construction of railroads" cooperating with their government (p. 349), but in 1895 the British government with a military intervention "blocked any chance of autonomous adoption of the railway" (p. 350). The case of Ethiopia is a long negotiation between the African state, Europeans powers and banks, starting in 1893 with the railway opened only in 1917. The case of the Sultanate of Zanzibar shows negotiations initiated in 1876 for a concession to the British to a railway there that later collapsed. Both the cases of Ethiopia and Zanzibar, according to Chaves et al. (2014, p. 351, p. 353) are examples of how fears of colonization and political risks contributed to limit the spread of railways.

After the Independence processes – after the 1960s – approximately additional 12,000 km of lines were built (Bullock, 2009, pp. 83–84). However, only 81% of these lines were being operated at the beginning of the twenty-first century (p. vi) – lines were "closed due to war, damage, natural disasters or general neglect and lack of funds" (p. vi). Xie and Wang (2021, p. 5) present data on "abandoned railways in African countries, during 1960–2010". They define this period as a second stage in the history of African railways that combines the slow construction of railways with the "desolation and abandonment of railways" (p. 5). After 1960 the availability of other transport options – the fourth big bang and its combustion engine – was also an important factor affecting the dynamic of railway construction. Jedwab and Moradi (2016, p. 283) comment how the road network increased after Independence.

The political fragmentation of Africa, a legacy of the colonial phase, has implications for the state of African railways, "that remain fragmented, with lines connecting cities within a single country or linking a port and its immediate regional hinterland" (Bullock, 2009, p. vii). There are few international networks.

The weakness of the impacts of railways in Sub-Saharan Africa – linkages and market formation – led to academic investigations of other long-term effects. Jedwab and Moradi (2016) evaluate the "permanent effects" finding how railway building had impact on "the spatial distribution and aggregate level of economic activity" and how "initial investments" induced "agricultural adaptation and trade integration" (p. 283).

4.5.5 Latin America: Railways, Exports and Beginnings of Industrialization

As in other regions, in Latin America the railways were related to the consolidation of their countries in the international division of labor. Between 1771 and 1850 the Latin American insertion in the global economy was based on the exports of raw materials. In a process that began in the 1840s, according to Furtado's analysis, these economies could be divided in three types: "economies exporting temperate agricultural commodities" – Argentina and Uruguay -; "economies exporting tropical agricultural products" – Brazil, Colombia, Ecuador, Central America and regions of Mexico and Venezuela -; and "economies exporting mineral products" – Mexico, Chile, Peru and Bolivia (Furtado, 1976, pp. 47–49).

In each of those economies the formation of a transport infrastructure, with a key role for railways, had an important contribution. In the case of temperate agricultural products, the availability of land and its extension, related to a vast area of agricultural producing areas, "necessitated the creation of a widespread transportation network". In the case of tropical products, there were old colonial products (sugar and tobacco) and new products (coffee and cocoa) involved in a "rapid expansion of world demand" (p. 48).[31] Old tropical products like sugar had a connection to railway that can be illustrated by the Cuban case – according to Summerhill (2006, p. 301), in this region "only Cuba executed its plans to build lines before the mid-century", and until 1870 it was the Latin American country with the largest railway network (p. 302). New products like coffee can be illustrated by the Brazilian case: on the one hand, Silva (1976, p. 56) considers that a coffee economy would not have been possible without railways, and on the other hand, according to Suzigan (2000, pp. 145–146), the resources from coffee were reinvested in railways shares and in cotton textiles factories. Furtado discusses the coffee-producing region of São Paulo, Brazil, as a case that "favored the creation of a modern infrastructure" (Furtado, 1976, pp. 48–49). Furthermore, for Furtado in those two types of economies the transport networks contributed to the formation of national markets.

This was not the case for the third type of economies: in mineral exporting regions where contribution was less significant, because the "infrastructure created to serve export mining industries was generally highly specialized" (p. 49).

Politically, Latin American countries in the 1850s were independent – see Table 3.2 – with some initiatives connected to their position in the international division of labor. The assimilatory forces from within this region combined with expansionary forces emanating from the center, with an important role for foreign investments, especially British investments. Darwin (2009) highlights how in the late nineteenth century there was an "economic connection between Britain and Latin America" (p. 135), with strong investments in the region, half of them in railways: "there were British-owned railways in every South American country, and in Mexico, Guatemala and Costa Rica" (pp. 136–137).

These dynamic forces for railway expansion in Latin America defined a late start (see Table 4.1: Mexico in 1850, Argentina in 1857 and Brazil in 1854) and a slow construction process – in 1870 Latin America as a whole had only half of the length

[31]The rapid expansion of demand for a tropical product like coffee illustrates diverse links and feedbacks that connect demand at the center, growth of export economies at the periphery, opportunities for railway building and beginnings of industrialization. Pendergrast (2004, p. 63) suggests a link between Industrial Revolution at the center and new tastes and demands from emerging working classes that led to demand for coffee. Brazil was a country that helped to create a market for coffee by producing enough cheap coffee to make it affordable to European and US working classes.

of the Indian railways. Only in 1900 did Latin America overtake India – 54,151 km and 40,396 km respectively (Summerhill, 2006, p. 302; Headrick, 1988, p. 55).

Evaluating the impacts of railway investments in the region, Summerhill (2006) highlights the greater importance, in Latin America, of "social savings" and "forward linkages" visa-vis "backward linkages" and "institutional externalities" (pp. 312–313).

Transportation costs reductions in the regions "widened the area of profitable cultivation, stimulating the rise of new agricultural enterprises, new settlements, new crops, and new investments in farming" (p. 312). Railways also "provided an impetus to new activities" (p. 312). Forward linkages were different across and within nations: in some, railways were a way to allow immigrants flow to the hinterland (Argentina, Southern Brazil), in other they "revitalized the mining industry" (Mexico). (p. 317). In common, railways "boosted export activities" (p. 318). This contribution to the growth of export activities impacted a specific Latin American dynamic of "industrial investment induced by the expansion of agro-exporting economies" (Suzigan, 2000, pp. 123–260).

Summerhill evaluates that "[r]ailways in Latin America did not have powerful domestic backward linkages" (p. 391), given the weight of "imported railway inputs" (p. 320). Those imported inputs explain the size of "leakages from the income stream" not internalized in Latin American economies. Later, before the 1930s, Summerhill estimates that domestic activities supplied part of the demand from railways: in Mexico, part of its rails, in Brazil, basic rolling stock (p. 319). In the Brazilian case, in 1909 there was a perception that the building of railways, among other factors, demanded high imports of iron and steel, a perception that led to pressure for their domestic production – an important determinant for the subsequent growth of the steel industry in Brazil (Suzigan, 2000, p. 275).[32]

4.6 The Second Big Bang and the Consolidation of the Previous International Division of Labor

The changes triggered by the second big bang and later spread of railways across the global periphery consolidated the international division of labor established by the mechanization of textile production in the United Kingdom.

This consolidation is articulated with improvements and expansion of the global economy. Railways at the periphery initially were built in previously already included regions, expanding from there. This expansion enabled new areas, in their hinterlands, to be accessed. This process of inclusion of hinterlands of Asia, Russia, Africa and Latin America has different impacts in different regions.

[32] Paula (2012, p. 212) also stresses that railways in early twentieth century induced an expansion of steel production and of the construction industry.

In the case of India, the impact of cheaper mechanical cotton textiles affected initially coastal regions, but with railways those impacts were extended to the hinterland – mediated by the expansion of cotton production for exports (Hurd, 1983, p. 745), by changes in handloom industry (Hurd, 1983, p. 748), or as reorganization of surviving weavers in "specialized urban centres" (Arnold, 2000, p. 96).

In the case of Latin America, railways were a source of inclusion of new regions in the hinterland of independent countries like Argentina and Brazil, with the occupation of new lands with crops of temperate and tropical agricultural products whose demand increased in the previous phase of industrialization at the center.

The case of South Africa is an example of an inclusion of a new region after the discovery of new mineral resources in the 1860s, a process that was combined with the expansion of railways.

One specificity of the spread of railways through the periphery is the differences in the sequencing of the first and second big bang. In the periphery, the order of the first mechanized cotton mill and the first railway to arrive in some regions was inverted. A comparison between Tables 3.2 and 4.1 shows that in India, in China and in the Sub-Saharan Africa the railways arrived first.

The differences in the arrival order of the two technologies may be a consequence of the different motivations in the leading force of spread of those technologies. In the case of India, as Darwin (2007, p. 269) puts forward, "[a]fter 1860 with the spread of railways, India developed much more rapidly as a source of raw materials and the greatest market for Britain's great export, cotton textiles".

This different sequencing between cotton textiles mechanization, industrialization in general, and railways may have other causal links beyond the consolidation of the international division of labor: there were backward linkages, that although limited and weak may have contributed for the beginning of new sectors, like iron and steel in India and Brazil. Indirectly, the expansion of old and new crops created new demands for textiles to pack those agricultural products and to cloth new workers.

The expansionary forces were led by British foreign investments – another peculiarity of the propagation of this second big bang. Given the capital intensity of railway investments – normally beyond the accumulated wealth and financial institutions of backward regions -, the initial spread played a large role for British foreign investments. Those foreign investments were enabled by previous accumulation of capital within the United Kingdom and by the need of outlets for its application – and the colonial power created guaranteed schemes to subsidize those flows to India.

The leading global role of British foreign investments is also explained by the focus of capital investments originated in the United States – it was the domestic expansion of their railways. The importance and extension of the United States domestic railways can be grasped by a comparison of their network and the world total of railways length: in 1900 the United States had more than half of the global

Table 4.2 Year of the first railway line opened and the size of the railway network in 1920 (Indian subcontinent, China, Russia, Sub-Saharan Africa and Latin America)

Region	Arrival year	Size in 1920 (in km)
India	1853	61,957
China	1876	11,283
Russia	1837	71,600
Sub-Saharan Africa		40,618
South Africa	1860	16,266
Nigeria	1886	1,812
Mozambique	1901	818
Latin America		101,463
Mexico	1850	20,800
Argentina	1857	33,884
Brazil	1854	28,535

Source: Year – India: Ross (2006, p. 53); China: Ross (2006, p. 185); Russia: Westwood (1964, p. 24); Africa – South Africa, Nigeria and Mozambique: Nock (1978, p. 8); Latin America – Mexico: Nock (1978, p. 8), Argentina and Brazil: Ross (2006, p. 83). SIZE – India: Headrick (1988, p. 55); China: Huenemann (1984, p. 78); Russia: Headrick (1988, p. 55); Africa and African countries: Mitchell (1998, pp.; 675–678); Latin America and Latin American countries: Summerhill (2006, p. 302); OBS: World railways in 1920: 1,033,136 km (Nock, 1978, p. 8); USA: 654,309 km; UK: 32,707 km (Headrick, 1988, p. 55).

railways – 416,461 km out of a world total of 790,551 km (Headrick, 1988, p. 55; Nock, 1978, p. 8).[33]

The assimilatory forces were very unequal among the five peripheric regions, given, in first place, the disparities in the political organization there, ranging from totally colonized regions – Sub-Saharan Africa, the Indian subcontinent – to Czarist Russia, with an active state with its policies and investments.

The combination of these expansionary forces (mainly British foreign investments) and those unequal assimilatory forces shaped the overall process of railway spread across the periphery – the initial dates of the first railways in each region, the size of the networks built, and each region's capacity to internalize linkages. Table 4.2 presents two of those sets of data: the year of the first railway and the size of the network in 1920.

The year of 1920 was chosen because Headrick argues that in 1914 the map of railway networks was basically the same as in the 1940s – a decade of huge institutional changes like the Independence of India, the foundation of the People's Republic of China and the conclusion of the hegemonic transition to the leadership of the United States after de Second World War.

[33] The limited geographical extension of the United Kingdom meant the very early the British investments would face a domestic limit, and that very early they should look for opportunities abroad. The Indian network overtook the size of the British network by 1890 (Headrick, 1988, p. 55).

In 1920 the world railway network had 1,033,136 km (Nock, 1978, p. 8), and the United States still had more than half of that total – 654,309 km – while the United Kingdom had 32,707 km (Headrick, 1988, p. 55).

Table 4.2 shows a simple relationship between the timing of the first railway and the size of the first railway and the size of the network in 1920. Focusing on big countries only, the earlier the railway, the larger the network: Russia, India, Brazil, China and Nigeria show this relationship. This might be an indication that the factors that retarded the opening of a railway also impacted the intensity of its spread and the strength of the building process.

A comparison between Table 4.2 (diffusion of railways) with Table 3.2 (diffusion of cotton textiles mechanization) also shows a relationship: the ranking of countries by the number of cotton spindles in 1909 is the same ranking by the size of railways built in 1920: Russia, India, China and Brazil.[34] This relationship might indicate some form of interaction between those two processes.

References

Ames, E. (1947). A century of Russian railroad construction: 1837–1936. *The American Slavic and Eastern European Review, 6*(3/4), 57–74.

Amman, R., Cooper, J. M., & Davies, R. W. (eds.) (1977). *The technological level of Soviet Industry*. https://archive.org/details/technologicallev0000unse

Arnold, D. (2000). *The new Cambridge history of India – Science, technology and medicine in colonial India*. Cambridge University Press.

Arrighi, G. (1994). *O longo século XX: dinheiro, poder e as origens do nosso tempo*. Contraponto/ Unesp. (1996).

Balzer, H. D. (1996). The engineering profession in Tsarist Russia. In H. D. Balzer (Ed.), *Russia's missing middle class: The professions in Russian history* (pp. 56–88). Armonk/London.

Blackwell, W. L. (1968). *The beginnings of Russian industrialization, 1800–1860*. Princeton University Press.

Bullock, R. (2009). *Off track: Sub-Saharan African railways*. Bird/World Bank.

Chandler, A., Jr. (1977). *The visible hand – The managerial revolution in America business*. The Belknap Press of Harvard University Press.

Chaves, I., Engerman, S. L., & Robinson, J. A. (2014). Reinventing the wheel: The economic benefits of wheeled transportation in early colonial British West Africa. In E. Akyeampong, R. H. Bates, N. Nunn, & J. A. Robinson (Eds.), *Africa's development in historical perspective* (pp. 321–365). Cambridge University Press.

Cohen, W., & Levinthal, D. (1989). Innovation and learning: The two faces of R&D. *The Economic Journal, 99*(397), 569–596.

Darwin, J. (2007). *After Tamerlane: The rise and fall of Global Empires, 1400–2000*. Cambridge University Press.

Darwin, J. (2009). *The empire project: The rise and fall of the British world-system, 1830–1970*. Cambridge University Press.

Fage, J. D. (2002). *A history of Africa* (4th ed.). Routledge.

Falkus, M. E. (1972). *The industrialization of Russia, 1700–1914*. Macmillan. https://archive.org/ details/industrialisatio0000falk/

[34] Using data for 1910 for railways, the ranking is the same.

Feuerwerker, A. (1980). Economic trends in the late Ching Empire, 1870–1911. In J. Fairbank & K.-C. Liu (Eds.), *The Cambridge history of China* (Volume 11: Late Ching, 1810–1911, Part 2) (pp. 1–69). Cambridge University Press.

Feuerwerker, A. (1983). Economic trends, 1912–1949. In J. Fairbank (Ed.), *The Cambridge history of China* (Volume 12: Republican China 1912—1949, Part I) (pp. 28–127). Cambridge University Press.

Fine, B., & Rustomjee, Z. (1996). *The political economy of South Africa: From minerals-energy complex to industrialisation*. Westview.

Freeman, C., & Louçã, F. (2001). *As time goes by: From the industrial revolutions and to the information revolution*. Oxford University.

Friedman, H. (2005). From colonialism to green capitalism: Social movements and the emergence of food regimes. In F. H. Buttel & P. McMichael (Eds.), *New directions in the sociology of global development* (Research in rural sociology and development) (Vol. 11, pp. 227–264). Elsevier.

Furtado, C. (1976). *Economic development of Latin America* (2nd ed.). Cambridge University Press.

Geisst, C. R. (2004). Wall Street: a history – from its beginnings to the fall of Enron. New York/ Oxford: Oxford University Press.

Gerschenkron, A. (1960). Russia: patterns and problems of economic development, 1861–1958. In A. Gerschenkron (Ed.), *Economic backwardness in historical perspective* (pp. 119–151). Harvard University.

Graham, L. R. (1993). *Science in Russia and the Soviet Union: A short history*. Cambridge University Press.

Harrison, M. (1998). The economics of world war Ii: An overview. In M. Harrison (Ed.), *The economics of world war II: Six great powers in international comparison* (pp. 1–42). Cambridge University Press.

Hausman, W. J., Herner, P., & Wilkins, M. (2008). *Global electrification: Multinational enterprise and international finance in the history of light and power, 1878–2007*. Cambridge University Press.

Headrick, D. R. (1988). *The tentacles of progress: Technological transfer in the age of imperialism, 1850–1940*. Oxford University Press.

Herranz-Loncán, A., & Fourie, J. (2018). "For the public benefit"? Railways in British Cape Colony. *European Review of Economic History, 22*(1), 73–100.

Huenemann, R. W. (1984). *The dragon and the iron horse: The economics of railroads in China, 1876–1937*. Harvard University Press.

Hurd, J. M. (1983). Railways. In D. Kumar (Ed.), *The Cambridge economic history of India* (volume 2, c. 1757–2003) (pp. 737–761). Cambridge University Press.

Jedwab, R., & Moradi, A. (2016). The permanent effect of transportation revolutions in poor countries: Evidence from Africa. *The Review of Economic and Statistics, 98*(2), 268–284.

Kerr, I. J. (2007). *Engines of change: The railroads that made India*. Praeger.

Kindleberger, C. P., & Aliber, R. (2005). *Manias, panics and crashes. A history of financial crises* (5th ed.). Wiley.

Kondratiev, N. D. (1926). Long cycles of economic conjuncture. In N. Makasheva, W. J. Samuels, & V. Barnett (Eds.), *The works of Nikolai D. Kondratiev* (Vol. 1, pp. 25–60). London, Pickering and Chato. (1998).

Kuo, T.-Y., & Liu, K.-C. (1978). Self-strengthening: The pursuit of Western technology. In D. Twitchett & J. Fairbank (Eds.), *The Cambridge history of China* (Volume 10: Late Ching, 1810–1911, part 2) (pp. 491–542). Cambridge University Press.

Macpherson, W. J. (1955). Investment in Indian railways, 1845–1875. *The Economic History Review, 8*(2), 177–186.

Maddison, A. (2010). Historical statistics of the World Economy – 1-2008 AD. Groningen Growth and Development Centre. http://www.ggdc.net/maddison/Historical_Statistics/horizontal-file_02-2010.xls

Malm, A. (2016) Fossil capital: the rise of steam power and the roots of global warming. London: Verso.
Magnan, A. (2016). *When wheat was king: The rise and fall of the Canada-UK wheat trade*. Ubc Press.
Marx, K. (1867). *Capital* (Vol. I). Penguin Books. (1976).
McPherson, J. M. (1988). *Battle cry of freedom. The Civil War era*. Ballantine Books.
Melnik, D. (2020). Soviet development model: A history of interpretations. In E. Trincado, A. Lazzarini, & D. Melnik (Eds.), *Ideas in the history of economic development: The case of peripheral countries* (pp. 75–93). Routledge.
Melo, B. C. (2023). *Estudo empírico de séries de preços com instrumental de sistemas complexos (Capítulo 3 da tese A economia como sistema complexo e o mercado como propriedade emergente: em busca de sinais de complexidade nos preços do trigo desde o séc. XIII)*. Cedeplar-UFMG.
Michalopoulos, S., & Papaioannou, E. (2020). Historical legacies and African development. *Journal of Economic Literature, 58*(1), 53–128.
Mitchell, B. R. (1998). *International historical statistics – Africa, Asia & Oceania, 1750–1993* (3rd ed.). Macmillan Reference Ltd/Stockton Press.
Morris, M. D. (1983). The growth of large-scale industry to 1947. In Kumar (Ed.), *The Cambridge history of India* (volume 2 – c. 1789–c. 1970) (pp. 553–676). Cambridge University Press.
Naughton, B. (2007). *The Chinese economy: Transitions and growth*. The MIT Press.
Nelson, S. R. (2022). *Oceans of grain: How American wheat remade the world*. Basic Books.
Nock, O. S. (1978). *World atlas of railways*. Mitchell Beazley Artists House. https://archive.org/details/worldatlasofrail0000nock_k9v9
Paula, J. A. (2012). O processo econômico. In J. M. Carvalho (Ed.), *A construção nacional, 1830–1889* (pp. 179–224). Madrid/Rio de Janeiro.
Pendergrast, M. (2004). *Uncommon grounds: The history of coffee and how it transformed the world* (Revised edition). Basic Books.
Perez, C. (2010). Technological revolutions and techno-economic paradigms. *Cambridge Journal of Economics, 34*(1), 185–202.
Rieber, A. J. (1990). The rise of engineers in Russia. *Cahiers du Monde russe e soviétique, 31*(4), 539–568.
Rosenberg, N. (1972). *Technology and American economic growth*. M. E. Sharpe.
Ross, D. (2006). *The steam locomotive: A history*. Tempus Publishing Limited. https://archive.org/details/steamlocomotiveh0000ross/
Silva, S. (1976). *Expansão cafeeira e origens da indústria no Brasil*. Editora Alfa Omega. (1981).
Spence, J. D. (1990). *Em busca da China moderna: quatro séculos de história*. Companhia das Letras. (1995).
Starns, K. E. M. (2012) *The Russian Railways and Imperial Intersections in the Russian Empire*. University of Washington (Thesis, Master of Arts in International Studies).
Summerhill, W. R. (2006). The development of infrastructure. In V. Bulmer-Thomas, J. H. Coatsworth, & R. C. Conde (Eds.), *The Cambridge economic history of Latin America, volume 2: The long twentieth century* (pp. 293–397). Cambridge University Press.
Suzigan, W. *(1986). Indústria brasileira: origem e desenvolvimento*. Editora Hucitec/Editora da Unicamp (2000).
Teng, S., & Fairbank, J. (1979). *China's response to the West – A documentary survey, 1839–1923, with a new preface*. Harvard University Press.
Tomlinson, B. R. (2013). *The economy of modern India – From 1860 to the twentieth first century* (2nd ed.). Cambridge University Press.
Wang, J., Jin, F., Mo, H., & Wang, F. (2009). Spatiotemporal evolution of China's railway network in the 20th century: An accessibility approach. *Transportation Research Part A, 43*, 765–778.
Westwood, J. N. (1964). *A history of Russian railways*. George Allen and Unwin Ltd.
Westwood, J. N. (1982). *Soviet locomotive technology during industrialization, 1928–1952*. The Macmillan Press Ltd.

Westwood, J. N. (1994). Transport. In R. W. Davies, M. Harrison, & S. G. Wheatcroft (Eds.), *The economic transformation of the Soviet Union* (pp. 1913–1945). Cambridge University Press.
Wilson, J. (2016). *India conquered: Britain's Raj and the Chaos of Empire*. Simon and Schuster.
Wolmar, C. (2010). *Blood, iron and gold: How the railways transformed the world*. PublicAffairs.
Xie, Y., & Wang, C. (2021). Evolution and construction differentiation pattern of African railway network. *Sustainability, 13*(13728), 1–13.
Zhang, B., Zhang, Z., & Yao, F. (2006). Technology transfer from the Soviet Union to People's Republic of China, 1949–1966. *Comparative Technology Transfer and Society, 4*(2), 105–171.

Chapter 5
Electrifying an Existing International Division of Labor: The Emergence of Multinational Firms in a Science-Based Technology – 1882–1937

5.1 Introducion

Thomas Edison's Pearl St. New York Electric Power Station, in the United States,[1] inaugurated in 4 September 1882 (Hughes, 1993, p. 42),[2] is the big bang of the third technological revolution (Freeman & Louçã, 2001, p. 141).[3] The fact that this big

[1]This starting point is different from Perez' scheme – her choice is the "The Carnegie Bessemer Steel Plant, in Pittsburg, United States" (2010, p. 190). However, a dialogue with Perez' elaboration is preserved, as she defines the "popular name for the period" as the "Age of Steel, Electricity and Heavy Engineering" – and in Freeman and Perez (1988, p. 51) this phase is the "Electrical and heavy engineering Kondratieff". Furthermore, for Freeman and Louçã (2001, p. 222) electricity is the "leading sector" of this third long wave – and they choose "Edison's Pearl St. New York Electric Power Station (1882)" as an example of highly visible, technical successful, and profitable innovation". The role of electricity in this third long cycle was highlighted by Kondratiev (1926, p. 40) and by Schumpeter (1939, p. 397) – For Schumpeter, "[i]n the same sense in which it is possible to associate the second Kondratieff with railroads, and with the same qualification, the third can be associated with electricity" (p. 397).

[2]For Schumpeter (1939, p. 395), 1882 is the reference year for the beginning of this long cycle, associating it with three Edison's stations: besides Pearl St. Power Station, there were also a hydroelectric station in Appleton and a thermoelectric in Chicago. Devine (1983, p. 354) also identifies 1882 as the year when electricity was "marketed as a commodity". Hughes (1993, p. 42) describes this inauguration on 4 September 1882.

[3]Kondratiev (1926, p. 40) introduces the third long cycle stressing its connection with scientific progress since the 1870s – "a period of significant inventions in engineering, and, in particular, in electrical engineering". Kondratiev lists inventions spanning from 1875 to 1898. Among them, there were "Gramme's DC dynamo (1875)", "the drilling machine (1875)", "the gas engine (1875)", "DC power transmission (1877)", "the electric telephone (1877)", "Thomas method for producing steel (1878)", "Westinghouse air brake (1879)", "Siemens electric locomotive (1878)", "the electric railway (1880)", "transformers (1882)", "petrol engines (1885)", "AC power transmission (1891)", "wireless telegraphy (1893)". This long list brings inventions related to previous technological revolution – Westinghouse air brake, electric locomotives, wireless telegraphy – and with the next technological revolution – petrol engines". In this phase Kondratiev highlight the inclusion of countries with a "young culture" such as Australia, Argentina, Chile, and Canada in the global economy (p. 41).

E. da Motta e Albuquerque, *Technological Revolutions and the Periphery*, Contributions to Economics, https://doi.org/10.1007/978-3-031-43436-5_5

bang occurred in the United States is an important indication of changes in the leadership of global capitalism, introducing further geopolitical changes related to a hegemonic transition concluded at the end of the Second World War (Arrighi, 1994).

Hausman et al. (2008, p. 11) describe the nature of Edison's invention: "the modern electric utility – that is, a system for production and delivery of electricity".[4] This big bang is a culmination of a long and cumulative series of findings and inventions, with a long scientific and technologic genealogy, summarized by Freeman and Louçã (2001, pp. 223–224) in their Table 8.1: the evolution of electric power begins in the early nineteenth century with Volta, Faraday and other scientists and their efforts to measure and analyze electricity, and their list ends with Thomson's discovery of the electron (1897) and Fleming's thermionic valve (1904) – connections with future electronics and computers.

As already mentioned, the location – or relocation – of the initial nucleus of this new technology is an expression of a new step in the long hegemonic transition from the United Kingdom to the United States – other signs in 1882 of that ongoing transition were their position as the world's highest GDP and their railway network as the world's largest. These achievements may have contributed both to the initial innovation and to their expansion through the United States economy. There are interactions between the previous phase and the emergence of electricity as a new technological paradigm – as Hausman et al. (2008, p. 63) put forward, "[t]he relationships between railroads and the spread of light and power companies were several": "experiences in international finance in railroad finance", construction companies in electrical utilities "had a background of experience in railroad endeavors", "train terminals were among the first places to be electrified", the "enclave form of electrification" depended on railroads, and experiences with regulation and government ownership (pp. 63–64). The telegraph is on the list of "science and technology in the evolution of electric power" (Freeman & Louçã, 2001, p. 223), an invention that had symbiosis with railways (Wolmar, 2010, pp. 81–82).[5]

Other relationships are shown by tracking the roots of two leading firms in the electric sector: General Electric and Westinghouse. The first had Thomas Edison among its founders, who worked with the development of telegraph systems for railways (Billington et al., 2006, p. 65), and as an inventor his first 100 patents were related to the application of telegraph technology. The Westinghouse company, on the other hand, was created as a firm to produce air brakes for trains (Billington et al., 2006, p. 83). The growth of railways and their linkages enabled subsequent advances

[4]Hughes (1993, p. 41) explains that "[t]he electrical network is, after all, the essence of the system. Edison's ultimate objective was to introduce the central-station supply".

[5]Garcke (1897, p. v) includes "telegraph" in a Table showing the "total registered nominal capital of the various classes of electrical companies registered in each year since 1856" in the United Kingdom – there are other five "electrical classes" listed there. The electrical class "manufacturing" only in 1871 has its first capital registered. "Electrical lighting" and "telephone" appear in 1878 and "traction" in 1885. Garcke's *Manual of Electric Undertakings* suggests that telegraph was an old sector in the new electricity industry.

for a more capital-intensive sector – electricity –, as they provided accumulation of resources, financial development, and a more connected world as a precondition for organizational innovation.

Two specificities of this new technology have implications for its global spread: the increase in the scientific dependence of electric products[6] and the growth in the intensity of capital required for the implementation of this modern electric utility. These specificities place a greater demand on the absorption capabilities of regions at the periphery.

The spread of the third big bang to the periphery begins in a global scenario where the uneven spread of the two earlier technological revolutions had increased the gap between the leading countries – United Kingdom and United States at this phase – and the regions at the periphery. The late and slow diffusion of the two earlier technological revolutions through the periphery (see Tables 3.2 and 4.2) now impact the speed, intensity and quality of the diffusion of electricity. The leading countries at the center have advantages at the start of a new technological revolution, among other things because there are relationships between the previous industrialization (cotton textiles in first place) and infrastructure building (railways mainly) and the birth and positive feedbacks with the emerging technology – first mover advantages. The regions at the periphery lack both the initial push and the early operation of positive feedbacks. Furthermore, the relative backwardness intensified by the late and slow diffusion of those two previous technological revolutions is now a new problem for the diffusion of the current big bang.

5.2 Electricity, Its Commercial Use and Peculiarities

The first modern electric utility, in September 1882, was developed by a new firm – Edison Illuminating Company of New York. This company created in 1880, is part of the Edison Electric Light Company, founded in 1878 to market Edison's invention of an electric lamp (Hughes, 1993, p. 39). The electric lamp was improved in his laboratory in Menlo Park, New Jersey (Billington et al., 2006, p. 65).[7] This com-

[6]This is an expression of changes related to an "increasingly scientific character of technology" (Freeman & Soete, 1997, p. 9). This change had two implications for assimilatory forces need to spread this technology to peripheric regions: first, a reduction in the "ease of learning", second, the need of more specialized education through Engineering Education – the first department to teach the new discipline of Electrical Engineering was created in 1882 in MIT, United States (Hughes, 1993, p. 145).

[7]Freeman and Soete (1997, p. 5, p. 10) locate in the 1870s and in the electrical (and chemical) sectors the creation of the institutional innovation represented by the modern Research and Development laboratory.

pany, in 1889, became Edison General Electric Company (Hughes, 1993, p. 41; Chandler, 1977, p. 427).[8]

Edison's patents, from the Menlo Park laboratory, shows the number of interrelated inventions necessary for the innovation of the first modern electric utility in 1882 – electric lamp,[9] improvements in a dynamo for electric generation,[10] a system for transmission of energy to lights,[11] and how to transform electricity in motive power.[12]

Those interrelated innovations at the origin of this new technological revolution are an expression of its peculiarity, a difference vis-à-vis previous big bangs and other contemporary emerging technologies – the leading firms in the new electric sector could not start selling their products and rapidly getting the cash flows as other industries did. In the electric sector, firms had "to fashion an integrated system of power-generating machinery, power stations, lamps, and power-using machines before they could begin to sell their products in volume" (Chandler, 1977, p. 426). This new industry dealt with technologies that were more complex, more costly and more time consuming compared to other sectors. Those specificities defined the relatively higher capital/output ratio vis-à-vis other industries in the United States, as presented by Hausman et al. (2008, p. 22): between late 1890s and late 1920s the "electric light and power" sector had the highest ratio, higher than "steam railways". This need for capital pressured the firms dealing with electricity in the United States to look for funds from capital markets – according to Chandler, the "first American industrialists not intimately connected with railroads" to do this.

The electric sector in the United States was led by first-mover firms, General Electric (created by the merger of Edison General Electric Company and Thomson-Houston Electric Company, in 1892) and Westinghouse (that diversifies to this sector in 1886).[13]

---

[8]Hughes (1993, p. 41) shows in a figure how The Edison Electric Light Company headed various different units: different The Edison Electric Illuminating Companies – for New York, Brooklyn, etc. –, The Edison Machine Works, The (Edison) Electric Tube Company, The Edison Lamp Works, The Thomas A. Edison Construction Department, and United Edison Manufacturing Company. All those firms were created between 1880 and 1889.

[9]Patent US 223,898.

[10]Patent US 222,881. David (1989) stresses the long development in dynamos technology necessary to reach an efficiency level high enough to become commercially feasible (p. 15) – the significant increase in that efficiency achieved by Edison's invention is graphically described in David's (1989) Figure 5 ("efficiency of electric generators"): from less than 50–90%.

[11]Patent US 248,422.

[12]Patent US 248,435.

[13]Chandler (1977, pp. 309–310) see those first-mover firms in electricity – Edison General Electric, Westinghouse and Thompson-Houston – as examples of companies that were in a business with fast technological development, that need integration between production and marketing, that had a salesforce with employees that knew "more about the technical nature of their equipment than did most of their customers" (p. 309) and they had to "finance new local central power stations in order to build the market for their machinery" (p. 310).

The subsequent process of diffusion of electricity within the United States is described by Paul David (1989, 1990). This process is an illustration of the powerful backward and forward linkages that reshaped the United States industry and economy after 1882 – Rosenberg (1998) is a discussion of those implications from the point of view of the elaboration of GPTs.

David documents the process of diffusion of "the new electric power technology", a "long-delayed and far from automatic business" (1990, p. 356). Three sets of data show this diffusion.

The first data set is related to "household electrification". In 1899, 8% of urban families and 3% of all families had home access to electricity, jumping to 47 and 35% respectively in 1919, and to 96 and 79% in 1939 (David, 1989, Table 3). The spread of household electrification is a precondition – an infrastructure necessity – for forward linkages to new products and industries that supplied homes with "electrical household appliances" (Gordon, 2016, p. 121).[14] David (1989, Table 3) presents data for two electric appliances: vacuum cleaners (9% of dwelling units in 1909 and 30% in 1929)[15] and mechanical refrigerators (0.5% in 1909 and 8% in 1929).[16] Gordon (2016, p. 115) presents data on the diffusion of the mechanic refrigerator and the washing machine[17]: both reached 40% by 1940.

The second data set is related to "factory electrification": according to Devine (1983, p. 353), in the year of 1883 "[e]lectricity was probably first used for driving machinery in manufacturing". Inventions during the 1880s and early 1890s allowed motors to become common in manufacturing, with an obvious connection with previous strengths in industrialization: "[m]echanical drive was first electrified in industries such as clothing and textile manufacturing and printing" (Devine, 1983, p. 355). In 1889, 3% of factories had electrified mechanical drive, in 1919, 53% and, in 1939, 86% (David, 1989, Table 3).

The third set of data is related to the form of electricity generation for factories – the diffusion of the use of electricity generated by electric public utilities – an important condition for the impact of this GPT on manufacturing through decentralization, cost reductions and flexibility (Rosenberg, 1998, p. 143). This transition also took time and depended on technical innovations in the sector of electric utilities. In the United States, according to Devine (1983, pp. 369–370), "[i]n 1909, 64 percent of the motor capacity in manufacturing establishments was powered by electricity generated on site; ten years later 57 percent of the capacity was driven by electricity purchased from electric utilities". The electrification of the United States made room for strong backward linkages, for new products that electrified existing commodities and other new products invented because there was electricity – both consumer and capital goods.

---

[14] Gordon (2016, pp. 115–122) discusses the impact of electricity in the US standard of living in a section intitled "the miracle of electrification: lighting and early appliances through 1940".

[15] The first patent of a vacuum cleaner was filed in 1907, by James M. Spangler, Ohio (US 889,828).

[16] The first patent of a mechanical refrigerator was filed in 1913, by Fred W. Wolf, from The Mechanical Refrigerator Company, Chicago (US 1,106,605).

[17] The first patent of a washing machine was filed in 1908, by Alva J. Fisher, from the Hurley Machine Company, Chicago (US 966,677).

David (1990, p. 359) evaluates the impacts of electrification on productivity growth in the United States economy, a careful evaluation that deals with "measurement bias" and other statistical problems to capture effects of factory electrification on production. The main point of David's paper is how the productivity growth generated by the diffusion of electricity took place: "factory electrification did not have an impact . . . . on productivity growth in manufacturing before the early 1920s" (p. 359).[18] The level of 50% of electrified industry was reached only then – this is an indication of how the dimension of the spread of electricity matters for productivity gains, an issue with important implications for the periphery.[19]

5.3 Expansionary Forces Emanating from The United States: Multinational Firms and Global Electrification

Hughes (1993, chapter 3) suggests that the International Electrical Exhibition in Paris, in 1881, was an important site for technology transfer of "Edison's incandescent-lamp system" (p. 51). There was also an International Congress for Electricians – mentioned by Hospitalier (1882, p. vii) –,[20] an event praised by one participant as the place where "electrical engineering was born" (Hughes, 1993, p. 50). The impact of those events in Paris on "motivated young engineers" and "stimulated investors" is highlighted by Hughes (1993, p. 51) as an example of informal technology transfer. After that, Edison's patents began to be negotiated in Europe.

Chandler (1992) shows a peculiarity of this technological revolution, the early international operation of those new firms: "[t]he newly formed enterprises that created and expanded these industries almost immediately began to compete in international markets" (p. 81). General Electric and Westinghouse Electric are among the "nation's first multinationals" (Chandler, 1977, p. 368).[21] Hausman

[18] Freeman and Louçã (2001, p. 261) mention a "post-1921 investment in electric power".

[19] One example of the impact of electricity on factory productivity is the assembly line, introduced by Ford in 1913 (Chandler, 1977, p. 280). Electricity was the driver of that process innovation, as the Highland Park factory, opened in 1910, had a power plant that "consisted of a three thousand-horsepower gas engine, which turned direct current generating equipment. Power was distributed through the factory by electric motors, which drove units of line shafting and belting" (Hounshell, 1984, pp. 228). This is an example of a phase in the process of lagged increase in productivity: new factories and new industrial plants designed to take a fuller advantage of electrification (David, 1989, p. 25; 1990, p. 358).

[20] Marx excerpted this book (Paula et al., 2020).

[21] Hausman et al. (2008, p. 77), reporting this very early international perspective, list between 1880 and 1883 a variety of "Edison Companies" organized "for business outside the United States": there were companies for Europe, Cuba and Porto Rico, Spain and Spanish Colonies, England, France, a company for the British Empire, Germany, Italy, Switzerland and Argentina. Garcke (1896) reports that in 1883 an Edison and Swan United Electric Company Limited was registered in the United Kingdom (p. 319) and a Manchester Edison-Swan Company Limited, registered in 1882, formed under an agreement with the Edison Electric Light Company Limited, "called Parent Company" (p. 333). Garcke (1897) informs that in 1889 was registered a Westinghouse Electric Company Limited (p. 431).

et al. (2008, p. 35) note that two phenomena took place "at identical time": "the beginnings of the diffusion of light and power facilities worldwide" and the emergence of the "modern multinational enterprise". Therefore, an important structural change in the actor of expansionary forces from the center: the multinational firm.[22] In the history of multinational companies, the electrical sector is one pioneer in this form of firms' organization.[23]

However, multinationals can assume different forms (Hausman et al., 2008, p. 36) and those different forms are important for the investigation of their global operation in the electric utilities sector. The "classic form" of a multinational firm – "that learned from its experience at home and developed international activities based on its accumulated knowledge" (p. 39) – is not enough to understand global electrification. Given the peculiarities of foreign direct investments in electric utilities, Hausman et al. (pp. 36–67) present a framework "for identifying and classifying the conduits for foreign investments into electric utilities and how these conduits altered over time" (p. 41).[24]

Hausman et al. (2008) present those various forms of "private-sector international capital" that were key for global electrification: "electrical manufacturing companies" and their satellites, and extended satellites (pp. 41–45),[25] "banks and other

[22] Multinationals acting in the electricity sector are "market-seekers" (Dunning & Lundan, 2008, pp. 69–71). But they were market-seekers in a very peculiar way, as at the center some subsidiaries were built, while at the periphery those more mediated forms took place: investments in electric utilities were important to push their exports to those countries. This mediated form may be the reason for American & Foreign Power – an international firm initially part of the global structure of General Electric (Hausman et al., 2008, p. 145) – becoming the "largest multinational enterprise in public utilities" by 1929 (Hausman et al., 2008, p. 185). Although the former was a spun-off company from General Electric after 1925, these two companies retained their "'network' relationship", a relationship strong enough to sell its equipment to utilities managed by the American & Foreign Power (p. 182).

[23] This precocity of multinational firms related to electricity could be indicated by the classic elaboration from Hymer (1970) that associates modern multinationals with "the new international economy created by the aeronautical and electronics revolution" (p. 443). This precocity is also in Freeman's (1987, p. 70) scheme, which identifies "multinational corporations" as typical "organization of firms" (his column 7) only in the fourth long wave – with an "upswing" in the 1930s.

[24] Mira Wilkins led the elaboration of this chapter of Hausman et al. (2008, p. 35). Wilkins is a scholar on multinational firms, thus her reflections on the specificities of multinational investments in this sector are well grounded.

[25] There is a dual relationship between the manufacturer and the electric supplier: on the one hand, the supplier acquired equipment from the manufacturers, on the other hand, the electric supplier provided to firms and homes access to energy necessary to use their electric goods (Hausman et al., 2008, p. 43). Manufacturer satellites are those firms involved, directly or indirectly in electric generation abroad (p. 44). Examples are firms like General Electric, Siemens, AEG, "stimulating the establishment of foreign public utilities" (p. 92).

financial intermediaries" (pp. 46–50),[26] "the enclave form" (pp. 50–51),[27] "large power consumers" (pp. 51–52),[28] "holding companies" (pp. 52–55),[29] "operating companies" – with their different forms (pp. 55–57),[30] "concessions and franchises" (pp. 57–59),[31] "clusters, networks, and business firms" – financial cluster, engineers and engineering firms, construction companies, accounting firms and trading companies (pp. 59–61). This variety of international capital forms was available to the global periphery, and changes in those forms rearranged their distribution between the center and the periphery. For example, over time the enclave form became present only in "the less-developed world" (Hausman et al., 2008, p. 66).

Hausman et al. (2008, pp. 30–33) present detailed information on "the extent of foreign ownership and control of electric utilities" – for 1913–1914 (the first period of their Table I.4) there are data for 74 countries (developed and underdeveloped), among them 46 had a foreign ownership and control of their electric utilities equal or greater than 20%. In India, Russia, South Africa, Mexico, Brazil and Argentina this participation was greater than 66%, in China less than 10% (pp. 30–33).

Over time, an institutional change took place (Hausman et al., 2008, chapter 6): at the second half of the twentieth century there was a global process of "domestication" of electric utilities ownership: in their Table I.4 (pp. 31–33), during the period 1970–1972, the foreign ownership and control of electric utilities was reduced to less than 35% in India, China, Russia, South Africa, Mexico, Argentina and Brazil. For Hausman et al. (2008, pp. 67–72) this is a consequence of another peculiarity of electric utilities: the importance of the political dimension.[32]

---

[26] Given how capital intensive this sector is, investments abroad always had banks involved (Hausman et al., 2008, p. 46).

[27] This "international structure", an association between multinational investments in "plantations, mining or oil drilling" and "some kind of power facilities", is a form that "introduced electrification in diverse areas around the globe, from Europe to Latin America, Africa, the Middle East, Asia and North America" (Hausman et al., 2008, pp. 50–51). In this form, electricity production follows the economic activity (p. 89).

[28] As new sectors emerged as more energy-intensive – aluminum production, pulp and paper – this form is different from the enclave form because its location is based on potential for cheap energy – the economic activity follows the location of electricity. After 1945, according to Hausman et al. (2008, p. 52), this is the case of foreign aluminum production in West Africa, a stimulant for the "development of power resources"

[29] Important form for initial spread of electrification around the globe (Hausman et al., 2008, p. 52). In Latin America, examples are firms that delivered electricity to Santiago and Buenos Aires (p. 99).

[30] Many firms in the enclave form or operating electric utilities began as free standing companies (Hausman et al., 2008, p. 56). In India, there were free standing companies in Bombay, Calcutta and Delhi (p. 123). Mexico is an example of relationships between different operating foreign-owned operating companies (p. 112).

[31] As before with gas and transport, concessions were operated by international firms.

[32] The process of "domestication" of electric utilities may be an indication of growing capabilities especially at the periphery, because it means that skills to run those companies were developed in those regions. And the management of those public utilities leads to further learning – a contribution to an increase in the general absorptive capabilities of countries and regions.

In 1914, according to Hausman et al. (2008, p. 123), "foreign investors had spread electrification on a vast, global but very unequal scale". The investigation of our five regions seeks to evaluate that uneven spread, looking for assimilatory forces in operation.

5.4 View from The Periphery: Slow and Uneven Increase in Assimilatory Forces

Until 1914 the expansionary forces from the center, in the form of different types of multinational firms, predominated in the electrification of the periphery – as well as in the world in general (Hausman et al., 2008, p. 124). The greater demand on capital and knowledge for the construction of electricity networks tested the limits of political formations existent at the periphery in the end of the nineteenth century. As in the previous big bang, the political organization in late 1890s ranged from colonial India and Africa and an active Russian national state – indication of uneven assimilatory forces in consequence of the stage of political formation at the periphery.

A summary of the changes in political organization in our five regions is presented in Table 5.1.

The importance of foreign control and ownership of electric utilities in our five regions was summarized by Hausman et al. (2008, pp. 30–33). Until 1914, the logic of electricity spread across the periphery through the expansionary forces emanating from the center, at least in part, followed a logic that had prevailed before: "[i]n Latin America, Oceania, Asia and Africa, often electrification was associated to mining or oil operations (and to a lesser extent agricultural ventures) – developed by companies from Britain, continental Europe, and the United States" (Hausman et al., 2008, p. 123).

Table 5.1 Political organization in the Indian subcontinent, China, Russia, Latin America and Sub-Saharan Africa (1890 and 1937)

Region	1890	1937
India	British colony. Post-1857 administration from British Monarchy. Foundation of the Indian National Congress (1885)	Strengthening of the Indian National Congress
China	Ching's imperial state in crisis. Self-strengthening movement	Treaty-port cities, areas under Japanese occupation. Republic after 1911
Russia	Abolition of serfdom in 1861 Czarist state	End of Czarism in 1917. A non-capitalist economy after 1918. Stalinist model after 1928
Africa	Post-Berlin Conference (1885) colonialism	Consolidated colonialism
Latin America	Independent and fragmented states. Slavery abolished in Cuba (1886) and Brazil (1888)	Independent and fragmented states

Source: Author's elaboration based on the literature reviewed in this chapter

There is another question related to these expansionary forces: how far was foreign ownership and control able to go in the electrification of the periphery? The main expansionary force from the center was in the form of multinational firms, of foreign direct investment, but this expansionary force had a limited capacity to spread electrification – Hausman et al. (2008, p. 122) suggest a relationship between the position of the country or region in the multinational firm – home or host country – and the level of electrification: “Latin America, Australia/New Zealand, Asia, and Africa had a far lower level of electrification; moreover, countries in these regions (Japan excepted) were hosts rather than homes to foreign investment (Hausman et al., 2008, p. 122).

There were areas, like “the rest of Asia”, where “FDIs were not very large, nor was electrification very extensive” (Hausman et al., 2008, p. 123). A preliminary indication of the limits of these expansionary forms to electrify the periphery is shown by statistics compiled by Hausman et al. (2008, p. 28): in 1933, while the United States had almost 70% of “population in areas supplied with electricity”, and other developed countries had higher percentages than the United States (for example: Switzerland, France, Germany), peripheral countries had 21% (as Mexico) or less (as China under 7%).

Hausman et al. (p. 25) present a Figure that may be an introduction to investigations of differences between the spread of electricity in the center and in the periphery: China reached a level of per capita output in electricity in 1950 that Italy had by the early 1900s and Japan by 1910.

These data suggest another causal connection between electrification and levels of development that is mediated through the level of urbanization: “urban areas became electrified before rural ones” (Hausman et al., 2008, p. 18). By 1914, “some electrification was present in every large city in the world”, although with different levels of access among them (pp. 123–124).

The arrival dates of electrification in our five regions are found in Table 5.2.

In all cases, the arrival expressed the predominance of the expansionary forces, with foreign investments taking the initiative – note that the lag in these arrival dates is shorter than the lags identified in the previous two big bangs (see Table 3.2, Chap. 3 and Table 4.3, Chap. 4).

Table 5.2 Year of the first electric utility opened in in the Indian subcontinent, China, Russia, Sub-Saharan Africa and Latin America

Region	Year
India	1899
China	1882
Russia	1883
Africa	SA: 1882; NIG: 1886
Latin America	MEX: 1883; BRA: 1883

Source: India: Madan et al. (2007, p. 155); China: Tan (2021, p. 7); Russia: Coopersmith (1990, p. 48); Africa – South Africa, Nigeria: Showers (2011, p. 196); Latin America – Mexico: Montaño (2021, p. 40); Brazil: Santos (2016, p. 561)

This section focuses on the specificities of those arrivals and how, over time, assimilatory forces developed and contributed to shape, to a certain and limited extent, the intensity of the spread of electrification in those regions until 1937.

5.4.1 *India: Late and Anemic Start, Increase of Local Initiatives*

The first electric utility in India arrived in 1899, when the Calcutta Electric Supply Corporation, British owned, opened its first line. Table 5.2 shows a shift related the Indian subcontinent: while the arrival of railways in India lagged only behind Russia, electricity only arrived there behind Russia, China, South Africa and Brazil. This difference in this relative timing may suggest differences in the logic of electricity diffusion vis-à-vis previous big bangs.

Kale (2014b) compares the involvement of British colonial power in railways, canals and electricity, pointing out that it was "more decisively involved in railroad and canal systems" (p. 455).

There might be technological reasons behind those differences. In first place, the colonial power – United Kingdom – was not the nation that triggered this new technology, and it had not completed its catch up in the end of the nineteenth century: "compared to Chicago and Berlin, London was a backward metropolis in the early twentieth century" (Hughes, 1993, p. 227).

Leading firms in electricity were from the United States (General Electric and Westinghouse) or from Germany (Siemens) – three firms whose British subsidiaries produced, by 1914, two-thirds of the United Kingdom output in this sector (Chandler, 1990, p. 276) – the "electrical-machinery industries" in Britain are cases of "entrepreneurial failure" (Chandler, 1990, pp. 274–286).

These differences reduce the colonial power motivation to push electrification, as differently from the railway building in the Indian subcontinent that led to British exports of locomotives and rails, the electrification would be translated in imports coming from the United States and Germany.[33]

Political changes within the Indian continent that contributed to initial development of assimilatory forces in India involve three different internal movements. The first would be the general repercussions of the creation and later strengthening of the Indian National Congress – in the long process that led to its Independence in 1947, the existence of a new force in the Indian politics affected all sectors, including the first initiatives in relation to education, universities and technology (Headrick, 1988,

[33]The strength of exports from the United States, Germany and Switzerland as suppliers to Indian public electric companies is shown by Speyer (1913, pp. 598–599). Evidence of how firms from the United States were aiming to markets in the British Empire is the creation, in England, already in 1882, of the Edison's Indian and Colonial Electric Company, Ltd. (Hausman et al., 2008, p. 77).

p. 329, p. 332).[34] Second, as unintended consequences of the impacts of the first and second big bangs, initial nuclei of capital accumulation in India were created – one example is the Tata Group, with capabilities to identify electricity as a new technology and to collect resources among Indians to fund the initiative related to a Hydropower Project (Speyer, 1913, p. 599; Headrick, 1988, p. 363).[35] Third, what Kale (2014b, p. 455) evaluates as "ambiguous freedoms of indirect rule" open room for regions in India governed with a logic different than that of colonial government – this led to a very heterogeneous process of electrification in India, with a "quasi-autonomous state" in Mysore implementing "India's first large-scale public electric development" (Kale, 2014b, p. 461).[36]

Those domestic initiatives are reflected in the data on foreign ownership and control in India reported by Hausman et al. (2008, p. 32): circa 80% for 1913–1914, falling to 31% for 1928–1939.

The lack of an aggressive policy of network building as had happened with railways led to a characterization of the first phase of electrification in India as an "anemic beginning" (Lanthier, 2016). His periodization of electrification in colonial India is divided in two phases. The first (1890–1918) is a phase of isolated installations: there were 121 firms, private and public, generating energy – 20 suppliers of electricity, 15 tramways and the rest dealing with electricity for the needs of textiles and mining (p. 571).[37] In this first phase, Lanthier mentions two larger projects: created in 1897, Calcutta Electric Supply Corporation (p. 579), and the Tata Hydroelectric Power & Supply, inaugurated in 1910.[38] The second (1919–1946) is a phase of "electrification by local initiative" (p. 580), with diversification of uses of electricity.[39] Local governments and states take more initiatives – with the heterogeneity described by Kale (2014b, p. 455).[40]

[34] Headrick (1988, p. 329) mentions how in 1887 the Indian National Congress assumed a demand for technical education in India. Headrick lists different initiatives in India for local education and research, as the foundation of the National Council of Education in 1905 and the inauguration of the Indian Institute of Technology in 1911 (p. 335).

[35] Speyer (1913, p. 599) lists this project in his Table 1, inaugurated in 1911, with prime-movers coming from Switzerland and the electric generating plant from Germany and United States.

[36] The Mysore Government initiative is reported by Speyer (1913, p. 599), a project inaugurated in 1900, with prime-movers coming from Switzerland and the electric generating plant from Germany and United States – Kale (2014b, p. 459) identifies General Electric as one supplier of this equipment.

[37] This "anemic beginning" of electricity in India coincides with the "new guaranteed period" for railway building (Headrick, 1988, p. 78). This coincidence might suggest that the British colonial power was focused in one technology (railways) and could not support electricity in the same way.

[38] Lanthier highlights that J. N. Tata was close to the Indian National Congress (p. 579).

[39] In this phase the Tata Group expands its involvement with hydroelectricity, creating a firm in 1929 with the participation of American & Foreign Power, that would survive until 1951 (Lanthier, 2016, p. 581).

[40] The colonial power contributed both for this heterogeneity and for the slow spread of electricity, as the case of a hydroelectric project in the Madras Presidency showed: the colonial Government of India did not sanction projects when initially proposed, thus it was implemented "only two decades after Mysore" (Kale, 2014b, p. 456).

Lanthier (2016) describes the growing awareness in India of the weaknesses and limitations in the electric system, a perception that influenced the preparation of industrial policies for Independent India. A case in point was the Bombay Plan, prepared with the participation of J. D. R. Tata, that included the production of electricity as a priority (p. 583).[41] And the Independence of India is a key institutional change in 1947, opening new two phases in Lanthier's periodization: between 1947–1990, "consolidation at the level of the states" (p. 583), and after 1991, "towards a national network" (p. 588).[42] After Independence there is a change in the participation of foreign ownership in electric utilities: for 1947–1950 its share is zero (Hausman et al., 2008, p. 32).

5.4.2 *China: Early Entry, Slow Diffusion with Interactions of Late Arrival of Machines and Railways*

In 1882 the first power station was built in Shanghai – Shanghai Electric Company (Tan, 2021, p. 21).[43] The influence of the political condition of China explains the location of this initial arrival: Shanghai was a Treaty Port. The expansion followed that political condition: after Shanghai, "British, American, French and Japanese capitalists invested in power stations in treaty ports all over China" (Tan, 2021, p. 7). This political condition also explains the presence of enclave-type foreign investments in China, as Hausman et al. (2008, p. 123) report: "In Chinese port cities, Belgium, French, German and Japanese companies provided some electrical power, especially for tramways".

[41] Kale (2014a, p. 26) mentions how "electrification became central to the project of infrastructural state building" – during the debates before Independence was suggested the idea of "electricity as new 'strategic railway'" (2014a, p. 32).

[42] Farnie (2004, p. 425) describes an interesting illustration of superposition of different technological eras, as "small-scale power-loom manufacturers" benefited from "large-scale electrification of the villages" during the second five-year plan. These manufacturers used "small scale electric motors to supply power to their looms" (p. 425). In 1997 there were 1.7 million power looms in India – three times the number of Liverpool power looms "at the height of its productive capacity in 1915" (p. 426).

[43] The history of this firm is a guide of political changes in China. It was founded with resources raised by Robert Little, a "former chairman of Shanghai Municipal Council" (Tan, 2021, p. 21) – a "British-controlled municipal council" (p. 23). Reincorporated in 1888, it was acquired by the Shanghai Municipal Council in 1893 (p. 22). In 1929 it was sold to American & Foreign Power – part of General Electric Corporation (Hausman et al., 2008, pp. 184–185) and renamed Shanghai Power Company (Tan, p. 32). After Pearl Harbor, December 1941, it was placed "under Japanese military administration" (Tan, 2021, p. 76; Hausman et al., 2008, p. 228). After 1945 its control returned to foreign ownership (Tan, 2021, p. 139, p. 144). During the Civil War there were disputes within it in 1948 (p. 148), and it was bombed by Nationalist forces on 6 February 1950 (Tan, 2021, p. 165). After the foundation of the People's Republic of China, it was nationalized on 18 December 1950 (Tan, 2021, p. 167).

That early arrival in 1882 was followed by a second investment in electricity in China only in 1888 – in one imperial palace in Beijing (Tan, 2021, p. 8). Outside Shanghai, Tan (2021) reports a power station being built in Canton in 1890, providing electric lighting, as in other cities. Tan (2021) suggests a dynamic of electrification in China that initially concentrated in electric lighting: in 1907, in Shanghai, 92% of electric power was used for lighting purposes (p. 21), and outside Shanghai the first power stations started "with electrical lighting as their core business" (p. 24).[44] Later, there was a transition to the increasing role of electric power for economic activities (p. 22) and promotion of electric motors (p. 24).

Here there is a specificity of the timing of arrival of electricity in China: in relation to cotton mechanization and to railways, their initial arrival is almost simultaneous: the first mechanized cotton mill was opened in 1889 – see Table 3.2, Chap. 3 – and in 1882 China had only 6 miles of railway network (Huenemann, 1984, p. 76).

In the case of urban cotton mills, electricity arrived earlier. The transition from mere providers of electric lighting to providers of electricity to industries puts forward a new phenomenon: "energy revolution in textiles" (Tan, 2021, pp. 24–29).

Initial nuclei of capital accumulation in China are present in the electric sector, contributing to the dynamic of industrial expansion. Feuerwerker (1980, p. 29) reports that in 1894 among a total of 84 foreign-owned industrial companies there were 4 in the sector "electric power and waterworks". For the period 1895–1913 there were 16 foreign and 3 Sino-foreign firms established in "electric power and waterworks" (p. 30). There were also 46 Chinese-owned firms establishes between 1895 and 1913 in this sector, "in the larger cities in all provinces", often in Treaty Ports (pp. 35–36).[45] These firms related to electric power and waterworks were part of a total of 685 new companies in industrial sectors established between 1895 and 1913 – discussed in Feuerwerker's section on "modern industry" –, of which 163 are related to textiles (cotton, silk, wool, hemp).

Focusing on Shanghai in this period between 1895 and 1914, according to Tan (2021, p. 25), "Chinese, British and Japanese businessmen established ten cotton-spinning mills" and those new firms demanded more power, beyond the capacity of existing power stations. This led to a heterogeneous framework, with cotton mills relying on their own generators, others purchasing electricity from power stations and other reluctant to abandon steam power (p. 27). Tan reports that after the inauguration of one new power station in Shanghai in 1912, "cotton mills became the largest consumer of electrical power" there (p. 24). But the transition to electric power purchased from electric utilities was uneven, a "source of contention between Chinese and foreign textile mills" (p. 25).

[44] Tan (2021) mentions "thirty-three power stations founded before 1911 solely on Chinese capital" (p. 24). Those initiatives with Chinese resources may explain the low share of foreign ownership in electric utilities shown by Hausman et al. (2008, p. 32): for 1913–1914, less than 10%.

[45] Lundquist (1918) presents an overall view of China before 1918: "not more than 90 to 95 cities and towns have electric service", with some cities with several plants (Beijing, Shanghai, Hankow and Tientsin) (p. 37). Among the installed electric stations, few "for power purposes, mainly by mining and manufacturing companies, as well as three street-railway systems" (p. 38).

Tan (2021, p. 24) highlights a causal connection running from electrification to industries, as the "diversification of electric companies catalyzed industrialization in places beyond Shanghai as well" (Tan, 2021, p. 24).[46]

The institutional change brought forward by the Republic in 1911 changed the importance of electricity in the country, as the leaders of the new regime, such as Sun Yat-sen, "called for the transformation of electricity into a public good by nationalizing or regulating the industry" (Tan, 2021, p. 42). Another important institutional building in 1918 is the establishment of electrical engineering as a department in Chinese university system (p. 43). At the same time, the interest of foreign investors expanded – Hausman et al. (2008, p. 32) shows an increase in foreign ownership in electric utilities to a share estimated between 51% and 65%.[47]

Those combined processes may have contributed to an expansion of electricity production in China between 1912 and 1936: data from Wright (1991, p. 362) show an increase from 65 to 3967 million kwh.[48] This increase occurred in a time that also witnessed the growth of cotton textile investments: between 1909 – as shown in Table 3.3, Chap. 3 – and 1937, the number of spindles grew from 800,000 to 5,071,000 (US Bureau of the Census, 1937, p. 44) – the largest absolute growth among our five regions.

In 1937 a new political scenario opened up in China – the Second Sino-Japanese War – or the beginning of the Second World War in the Pacific. The implications for the electricity production involved initially a capture by Japanese forces of 97% of China's capacity (Tan, 2021, p. 62).

During the Japanese occupation China had three different electric systems: North China Electrical Corporation, and Central China Waterworks and Electricity Co (both in Japanese-controlled regions) and Lakeside Electrical Works, in the Yunnan Province (controlled by the Nationalist Government). The war led to changes in the electricity sector, as it was "no longer concentrated in Shanghai, but extended outward to other regions of the nation" (Tan, 2021, p. 63).

During the Second World War, between 1937 and 1946 – data from Etemad and Luciani (1991, p. 118), the Chinese electricity production increased from 2422 million kwh to 3625 million kwh. This growth was regionally uneven: between 1937 and 1946, while in North China the electricity produced increased less than 2 times, in Sichuan its growth was 4.74 times, in Yunnan 5.18 times, and in Guizhou 11.16 times.

[46] Imports of electrical goods were the main source of technology transfer before the First World War. According to Lundquist (1918, p. 35), in 1914 the main suppliers of those goods were the British Empire (43.7%), Germany (23.4%), Japan (13.8%), United States (4.8%) and Belgium (3.7%).

[47] Feuerwerker (1983, p. 60) presents data on the participation of foreign ownership in electricity production: it was 77% in 1923 and 55% in 1936.

[48] According to Tan (2021, p. 89), before 1937 "almost all power generation and transmission equipment had to be imported – even basic components like wires". "On the eve of Japanese invasion", those imports were coming from Germany (34.08%), Japan (32.40%) and Britain (15.19%) (p. 90).

During the Second World War, as Tan (2021, p. 87) presents, there was a transformation of Chinese electrical equipment manufacturing: a state-run enterprise, Central Electric Manufacturing Works was a key actor. Two routes were pursued: technology transfer and "state-sponsored applied research" (p. 87). For technological transfer, the Lend-Lease Act provided the Nationalist Government with resources for "projects established through the technology transfer agreements" (p. 97). The Central Electric Manufacturing Works organized "in-house research" after 1942, being able to "replicate different types of electric motors, power generators, and transformers" (p. 101). Tan (2021, p. 109) evaluates that the wartime mobilization "broke down decades of foreign dependence" and that Central Electric Manufacturing Works was "a success story for state intervention". Another important initial learning process was related to dam construction: Tan (2021, chapter 5) describes efforts from 1944 to 1948 to develop a project in China inspired by the TVA (p. 123).

During the Civil War, electricity had a strategic value and the control over China's electrical industries "played a significant role in shaping the outcome of the Chinese Civil War" (Tan, 2021, p. 161). Data from Etemad and Luciani (1991, p. 118) show ups and downs in the period between 1946 to 1949: from 3625 million of kwh in 1946, it peaked in 1947–4671 million of kwh –, reaching 4308 million of kwh in 1949.

A new institutional change with the foundation of the People's Republic of China and electricity becomes an important topic of Five-Year Plans (Shabad, 1955) – in 1954 the production reached 10.9 million of kwh (p. 190), part of the "phenomenal growth of China's electric industry up until 1957" (Tan, 2021, p. 184).

This new economic system also meant a "domestication" of electric utilities in China: for the period 1947–1950 foreign ownership falls to zero (Hausman et al., 2008, p. 32).

5.4.3 *Russia: Electricity and Planning*

In 1886, the first commercial utility in Russia was inaugurated (Coopersmith, 1992, p. 42).[49] Siemens & Halske led this initiative[50] by building a thermal plant in Saint Petersburg – a "typical manufacturer's satellite" (Hausman et al., 2008, p. 116). Hausman et al. (2008) highlight that "Russian electrification came rapidly and soon was dominated by foreign direct investors" (p. 116) – in 1913–1914, foreign firms were controlling 90% of electric utilities in Russia (p. 32, p. 118).

---

[49] Coopersmith (1992, p. 48) mentions an initiative that in 1883 inaugurated the illumination of Saint Peterburg main boulevard with thirty-two lamps, but both he (p. 42) and Hausman et al. (2008, p. 116) consider 1886 as the year of the first "commercial utility".

[50] In a connection with railways building, Siemens & Halske "had entered Russia in 1853 to construct telegraph lines for the state" (Coopersmith, 1992, p. 48).

However, according to Coopersmith (1992), "[e]lectrification grew slowly in Russia, especially compared with the West. Over a decade passed between the first Russian commercial utility in 1886 and the first wave of utilities in the country" (p. 42). These two features set apart the electrification from the center of global capitalism: "[t]he later diffusion of utilities and their small size distinguished Russia from the West" (p. 45) – for Coopersmith, in the United States "electric stations spread like wildfire" and "tsarist Russia moved much more slowly" (p. 45).[51]

Absorptive capacity was being developed in Russia, that was following closely the development of electricity in Europe – Coopersmith describes earlier experiences with incandescent light (pp. 43–44). There was also the development of technical societies that contributed to Russia's capacity to identify new knowledge emerging abroad – in 1866 Russian engineers created the Imperial Russian Technical Society (IRTO) (p. 21), and in 1880 an electrotechnical section was founded (VI Section) (p. 22): events before the big bang of electricity triggered from the United States.[52]

Coopersmith organizes his analysis of electrification in Russia between 1886 and 1926 in different phases – 1886–1913: electrification[53]; 1914–1917: the rise of electrification[54]; 1917–1920: "hungry stomachs"[55]; 1920–1921: the creation of GOELRO; 1921–1926: NEP years.[56]

Initial electrification growth was uneven and with regional disparities: there were three tiers of electrification, related to the population of urban areas. The first tier involved Saint Petersburg, Moscow and Baku – the center of the oil industry (p. 47). In this first tier, the growth of factory demand was matched by its utilities, localized positive feedback between electrification and industrialization (p. 59). Given the lower urbanization rates of the second and third tiers, "electrification penetrated far less" (p. 60). Between 1905 and 1913 the growth in electricity production by utilities is related to a transition from lighting (41.66% in 1905 and 28.01% in 1913) as the

[51]Those two features – relatively late arrival of electricity and its slow spread – put forward by Coopersmith (1992, p. 45) are structural characteristics of diffusion of new technologies to the periphery. In the case of electricity, as a more complete picture of the periphery emerges, Russia is a region with smaller time lag and larger diffusion vis-à-vis other regions (see Table 5.3, discussed in the last section of this chapter).

[52]Electrical engineering in Russia before 1917 laid down roots that connect this technological revolution to the fifth – related to electronic computers. As Chap. 7 shows, Sergei Lebedev – the leader of the development of the first Russian electronic computer – entered in 1921 "the Electrical Engineering Department of the Moscow Higher Technical School" (Crowe & Goodman, 1994, p. 4).

[53]According to data available in Etemad and Luciani (1991, p. 164), a growth from 482 million kwh in 1905 to 1945 million kwh in 1913.

[54]Another growth phase, from 1945 million kwh in 1913 to 2575 million kwh in 1916 (Etemad et al., 1991, p. 164).

[55]The impact of Civil War is expressed in a fall of electricity consumption to 200 million kwh in 1920 (Etemad & Luciani, 1991, p. 164).

[56]Recovery years, starting from 520 million kwh in 1921; reaching 1146 million kwh in 1923 and the level of 1916 in 1925: 2925 million kwh; and later growing to 3507 million kwh in 1926; and 4205 million kwh in 1927 (Etemad & Luciani, 1991, p. 164).

most important service to industry (27.08% in 1905 to 38.58% in 1913) in the role of main consumer (Coopersmith, 1992, p. 68). There was also a movement from factories generating their own power to consuming it from utilities (p. 68) – this movement was uneven, as firms located in the first tier were significantly supplied by utilities (pp. 68–69).

During this initial period, some development of electric industries occurred as in the eve of the First World War, when "domestic firms manufactured half of Russia's electrotechnical needs", but not the most sophisticated material (p. 103).[57]

Coopersmith (1992, p. 99) points to the First World War as the "single most important factor in the transition from electrification in Russia to Russian electrification" – the war economy brought new tasks for engineers (p. 100), demand for domestic production of more sophisticated electric goods,[58] and nationalization of utilities in large cities – Petrograd, Moscow and Kiev (p. 104) –,[59] a process that moved Russian engineers up in the management tasks (p. 104). In this period there was a mobilization of the "electrical engineering leadership" towards assuming the idea of "widespread electrification", articulated with "state plans for economic and social transformation" (p. 114). During the war, the production of electricity grew (p. 110).

In 1917 other institutional changes – the end of Czarism (February) and the beginning of the Bolshevik government (October). Three consequences of those changes: the subsequent Civil War led to a fall in the electricity production, and its end led to a process of recovery to pre-war levels (see footnotes 141 and 142), the nationalization process initiated under Czarism proceeded (Coopersmith, 1992, p. 127; Hausman et al., 2008, p. 148), and electrification assumed a central role in the policies of the new regime (Coopersmith, 1992, p. 151; p. 188).[60]

The creation of GOELRO (State Commission for the Electrification of Russia) in 1920 is a benchmark. First, because it precedes other advances in planning that will be important in the economic system of the USSR – GOSPLAN was created 1 year later -[61]; and second because it is an expression of the importance of the relationship between the community of electrical engineers and planning (Coopersmith, 1992, p. 139).[62]

---

[57] For example, "large turbogenerators powering first-tier utilities" were foreign (Coopersmith, 1992, p. 103).

[58] Coopersmith (1992, p. 104) evaluates that domestic production "failed to meet demand".

[59] Hausman et al. (2008, p. 131) reports this "Russian shock": "when the war began, takeovers of enemy German properties in Russia occurred early, first undertaken by city councils, then by tsarist officials ".

[60] "In 1920, electrification replaced the railroad as the state technology" (Coopersmith, 1992, p. 16).

[61] "By 1921, the GOELRO plan had become the basis for the formation of the far better now State General Planning Commission (GOSPLAN) and a model of centralized state planning and development" (Cummins, 1988, p. 1).

[62] Tracking the trajectory of the first head of GOELRO – and later in GOSPLAN –, Krzhizhanovskii, he previously directed the 1886 Company (Coopersmith, 1992, pp. 26–27) – the firm that initiated electrification in Russia (Hausman et al., 2008, p. 116).

An important document of this phase and evidence of the strategic role of electrification is GOELRO's plan approved in December 1920 by the eighth Congress of Soviets (pp. 174–178, p. 185).[63]

The community of electrical engineers, according to Coopersmith (1992, pp. 185–186), understood the role of foreign technology for Russian electrification plans. This understanding, evaluates Coopersmith, expresses how the community of Russian electrical engineers "considered themselves part of the international electrotechnical community" (p. 185). The GOELRO Plan attributed a key role for Western technology (p. 185).

Sutton (1968, pp. 185–208) presents detailed information on technological transfer in the electric sector, a flow that began early and was intense: "[f]rom 1921 onward, the government invited a series of foreign experts and companies into the USSR to make recommendations for modernization" (p. 185). Sutton documents the involvement of leading multinationals in agreements with the Soviet government: General Electric, Siemens, AEG, RCA, Ericsson are examples of those foreign firms.[64] Sutton (1968, pp. 206–208) explains the processing of this transfer and learning, in the case of hydroelectric technology: first the import of turbines together with technical assistance, second some initial domestic production of that previous imported machinery, and a final stage when "only domestically produced equipment was used, with or without foreign assistance" (p. 207).

Sutton (1968, p. 338) presents an overall balance of the "direct and indirect impact of Western technology" (between 1917 and 1930), with a disaggregation by subsectors of the "electrical equipment industry": the "estimated direct impact" was "complete" in "high-tension equipment", "electrical motive equipment", "low-tension equipment", "accumulators", and "turbine and generators", while "heavy" in "hydroelectric technology".[65]

With other institutional changes within Russia, especially the beginning of the Stalinist model in 1928–1929 (Nove, 1992), indicate that the "tempo of electrification in the Soviet Union increased sharply after 1926" (Coopersmith, 1992, p. 258). Sutton (1971, p. 176) documents the role of foreign technology then: "the ten largest power stations built by 1933, in addition to numerous smaller stations, had Western equipment".

---

[63] As an element for understanding that lock-in with steam locomotives discussed in Chap. 4, railway electrification was part of GOELRO plans – Coopersmith (1992, p. 158) shows a "section on railroad electrification", led by Graftio, in its structure, but through his book he notes how that priority fizzled (p. 188, p. 200, p. 214).

[64] A good example of this precious documentation work organized by Sutton is his Table 11-1 (1968, p. 187), for 1922–1930, that lists agreements between "trusts formed from prerevolutionary plants" and "new Soviet undertakings" with "foreign companies": "Electroexploatsia" has an agreement with International General Electric.

[65] An illustration of this process is Electrosila (Sutton, 1968): a firm created in 1893 as Siemens-Schukert A-G (p. 191), transformed in Electrosila in 1922, a firm with cooperation with AEG, Metropolitan-Vickers and International General Electric (pp. 191–192), it received "groups of GE engineers" (p. 198), supplied equipment for at least three GOELRO projects (p. 204). Later, this firm supplied electric generators for the Aswan Hydroelectric, in Egypt (Power Technology, 2021).

For Coopersmith (1992) this "increased tempo" was part of the state's renewed industrialization drive and the five-years plans" – another institutional change that will be used in other regions of the globe. The Five-years plan is an institutional innovation developed in the USSR that expanded the idea of planning to the whole economy. The reality and problems of planning under Stalin and later is the USSR has been presented and discussed by authors such as Trotsky, Nove, Mandel, Kornai, among others.[66] But, this form of organization of a backward economy for development was later appropriated and used in different versions in countries like India, China, South Korea, Taiwan, and Turkey. Given the success in South Korea and Taiwan, and the ongoing development process in China, this planning tool may be an example of change at the periphery that starts a chain of events that in the end contributes to rearrangements in the global economy.

5.4.4 Sub-Saharan Africa: Colonial Electrification and Interaction with Mining

After the third big bang, colonialism in Africa was strong and consolidated during the 1885 Berlin Conference – Africa partition between European powers. Therefore, Showers (2011, p. 195) analyses the spread of this new technology in Africa as "colonial electrification" – with territorial control as the main interest (p. 196).

Showers (2011, p. 195) lists three main motives for colonial electrification: "amenity for non-African settlers", "source of power for mines and industry", or as "stimulus for industrial development". The limits of those motives are explained because "in most of colonial Africa, electricity was not seen as important for African or non-urban settlers" (p. 195).

The arrival of electricity in Africa – 1880s and 1890s – was the initiative of "colonial administrators and private entities" (Showers, 2011, p. 196).[67]

South Africa has a different dynamic, as discussed in the previous big bang – Kimberley, a mining center, was "the first African city with electric street lights in 1882" (p. 196). As Hausman et al. (2008, p. 89) comment about enclave type of foreign direct investment, mining activities in the end of the nineteenth century had new electric requirements, thus, among mining groups in South Africa "electrification came on the heels of the industrial activity". But the relationship between electricity and mining had broader implications: Fine and Rustomjee (1996, p. 8) stress the dependence of South Africa on electricity and its feature as an electricity-

[66] After the collapse of the USSR there are new investigations on archives that were opened and became available. Markevich (2005) and Gregory and Harrison (2005) are articles that show the real operation of planning. Gregory and Harrison (2005, p. 754) identify "resource allocation by intervention rather than by plan".

[67] Beltran et al. (2016) organize chapters that deal with processes in specific countries – see Kamdem (2016) for Cameroon, Loukou (2016) for Ivory Coast, Miescher (2016) for Ghana. Other reference is Ardurat (2002), for Senegal.

intensive country, explained by "its use in mining and mineral processing". Christie (1984) introduces another variable in this relationship, including the mechanization of mining activities in South Africa as an element in the demand for electricity (p. 22): mechanical devices for mineral exploitation were introduced before 1914 (p. 20). The interconnections between the mechanization of mining activities, electricity demands, and need for cheap energy led in South Africa to an early development of one of the "most sophisticated energy systems" created before the First World War (Christie, 1984, p. 6).[68] In 1922, Escom is founded (Christie, 1984, p. 77).

Showers (2011, p. 196) lists the timing of different arrivals of generators, street lines, or electric trams in different countries: 1894–1895 in Ethiopia, before 1900 in Tanzania, 1896 in Nigeria, 1906 in Zambia. Showers also presents initiatives more related to commercial interests: in Ghana, electricity supply began with generators operated by "industrial establishments", in the Gold Coast, in 1914, the first electric supply was at the railway headquarters (p. 196).

In a balance presented by Hausman et al.'s (2008, p. 123) on the electrification in Sub-Saharan Africa before 1914, South Africa is an exception. In their table on foreign ownership of electric utilities, for the period 1913–1914 Hausman et al. (p. 32) present seven Sub-Saharan countries, showing that "electrification was negligible" in Ethiopia, Mozambique, Sudan, and Uganda. There was some electrification "in coastal cities in the rest of Africa, where colonial administrators might have generators (isolated plants)" (p. 123), and in enclaves – "Belgian investors had barely started electrification in the Congo" (p. 123).

Between the 1920s and the 1940s, in areas near mineral operation small dams and hydroelectric plants were built (Showers, 2011, p. 198). Examples of those initiatives for Zambia, Nigeria, Kenya, and Ethiopia are presented by Showers (2011, pp. 200–201). These initiatives apparently follow the logic of "large power consumers" in the typology of foreign investments suggested by Hausman et al. (2008, pp. 51–52). Showers (2011, p. 199) mention a stimulus for "colonial hydroelectric generation" after the Second World War, following an increased demand for minerals: given that demand and potential power shortages in Europe, it made sense to locate overseas in Africa some processing of minerals like aluminum. In the case of Mozambique, a construction of a dam in the 1960s – Cabora Bassa, concluded in 1975 – was financed by "selling electricity to Apartheid South Africa" (p. 200) – earlier, in 1946, after new colonial policies including "development plans" leading to a hydroelectric plant in Chicamba Real that was related to some industrialization in the region (Hedges, 1999, p. 169).[69]

Political changes impacted the spread of electrification, as there was enthusiasm about hydroelectricity (Showers, 2011, p. 200) and hydroelectric dam construction – that "became a feature of most independent African countries" (p. 200). Examples of

---

[68] The formation of the Union of South Africa in 1910 as a British Dominion led to a government that had "electricity and railway expansion" as priorities (Showers, 2011, p. 206).

[69] Sopa and Fernandes (n.d.) suggest a relationship between this dam and a colonial project for a textile industry in the region – Sociedade Algodoeira de Fomento Colonial.

this new scenario are constructions implemented in Ghana (a project inherited from colonial times on the Volta River), Tanzania (within the framework of its Second Five-Year plan with electricity as priority), and Zaire. The relevance of the political change – Independence – for this process is shown by the fact that 75% of the 1281 dams surveyed by Showers (2011, pp. 201–202) were built after 1960.

After independence, in the 1960s, another important change was the beginning of "national electrification campaigns" – expansion of power networks towards grids to achieve broader access to electricity (p. 207), still an important challenge for development in Africa. Independent countries also began negotiations for "sub-regional power grids" (pp. 207–209) – an international trade.

Marwah (2014, p. 10) presents a balance of the post-independence scenario, evaluating that although post-independence governments have done more than colonial powers for electrify Africa, "progress remained slow" and the limited access of households remains.[70] For Marwah, the persistence of one colonial heritage – the priority to industrial consumers – explains that limited access.

5.4.5 Latin America: Electricity and Beginnings of Industrialization

In Mexico, in 1879, initial electrification was identified, as "cotton mills, and mining and refining activities acquired generators related to their activities" (Hausman et al., 2008, p. 122). Montaño (2021, p. 40) mentions a mines and refineries that introduced electricity "only one year after it was tested in the US mines", and Wionczek (1965, p. 527) highlights its early arrival, "in the wake of its emergence in the United States and Western Europe". Hausman et al. (2008, pp. 111–116), presenting "operating companies in Latin America", list foreign concerns that operated in Mexico from the early 1880s to 1914 – the first working electric system of street lamps was inaugurated in 1894 (Hausman et al., 2008, p. 112). Electricity was a priority for the Porfirio Diaz government, that granted concessions to Mexicans to develop power facilities, concessions that were sold to foreigners – Hausman et al. (2008, p. 116) explain this hand-over by the domestic lack of "know-how and ability" and capital.

In Brazil, Santos (2016, p. 561) identifies the first power station (thermal) in 1883, in Campos – near Rio de Janeiro – and the first hydroelectric in 1889, in Juiz de Fora, "to power a textile mill" (Santos, 2018, p. 53).[71] The spread of electrification is related to initial industrialization, associated with coffee production and railways – an important role for the state of São Paulo, where local entrepreneurs and investors "scattered through the state" took initiatives (Santos, 2016, p. 564). The first

[70] In 2019, the population with access to electricity was 85% in South Africa, 55.4% in Nigeria, and 29.6% in Mozambique (World Bank, 2023).

[71] A project prepared by the firm Max Nothman & Co and the equipment supplied by Westinghouse (Magalhães, 2000, p. 48).

hydroelectric in São Paulo was inaugurated in 1895 – Corumbataí (p. 561). Santos (2016, p. 561) mentions the Geographical and Geological Commission formed by the state of São Paulo in 1886, whose work compiled available hydraulic resources in the region – this may be an important knowledge asset for later dam construction. Those early hydroelectric projects underscore one feature of Brazilian electricity supply: a strong participation of hydroelectric generation.[72] As in the case of Mexico – and Latin America –, foreign capital was involved, with a Canadian firm – Light, since 1899, with investments and hydroelectric projects in the South-Eastern region – and American & Foreign Power – in 1927.

Mexico and Brazil are typical cases of the region, as the participation of foreign capital is very strong: among the 23 countries listed by Hausman et al. (2008, pp. 32–33), 15 had foreign control greater than 70%, 3 around 15% and only 5 without it.[73]

The interaction between the availability of electricity and industrialization is shown by Suzigan (1986), in his research on the beginnings of Brazilian industrialization, as he points to a transition to electricity in the first two decades of the twentieth century (p. 127). Suzigan (p. 155) stresses the availability of electric power from hydroelectric stations built by foreign capital, mainly in São Paulo and Rio de Janeiro to the industrial sector and how cotton textile factories in those states switched to electricity early (p. 156) – a process that may have contributed to the growing concentration of cotton textile industries in that region (p. 156).[74] Suzigan (1986, pp. 372–383) documents the beginning of imports of "electric motors" in 1913 (p. 379) – in 1939 their value was greater than "textile machines" (p. 382).

Latin America also witnessed a process of "domestication" of electric utilities: for the last period compiled by Hausman et al. (2008, pp. 31–33), 1970–1972, only five countries had foreign control greater than 50%. This important institutional change may have been the consequence of a growing perception of the importance of electricity for development and the limitations of existing institutional arrangements to provide the necessary power sources for new industries.

Tendler (1968), investigating the Brazilian case, identifies after 1946 chronic "shortages of power" as the existing electric systems "were never able to satisfy fully the demands made upon them" (p. 9). This reality led to initiatives such as the "1954 Joint Brazil-United States Economic Development Commission" (p. 14) that presented diagnostics and proposals to solve these shortages. Expansion plans led to increasing intervention of state agencies (p. 26).

---

[72] See Bulmer-Thomas (2003, p. 130), for data for 1910.

[73] While foreign ownership was very important in this first period of electrification in Latin America, some local initiative took place. Mexico, Argentina, and Brazil illustrate this, because in those countries foreign control was not 100% – at least 10% of local participation can be identified in the data from Hausman et al. (2008, pp. 32–33).

[74] In the Brazilian case, there might have been a process of electrification that initially followed existing industries – illustrated by the first hydroelectric plant in Juiz de Fora – but later the availability of electric power influenced the location of industrial activities.

Furtado (1976, p. 167) evaluates that this problem is a characteristic of Latin American economies in general, as "nearly all" had energy supply shortages after the Second World War. That "inadequate supply" had to be solved by new institutions, thus the need of resources coming from public funds and international financial institutions such as the World Bank. These new institutional arrangements led to an expansion of hydroelectric power between the mid-1950s and early 1970s.

Bulmer-Thomas (2003, p. 240) describes this growing involvement of the state in the electrical sector in the region, "to remove obstacles faced by the industrial sector". The state involvement with electricity later contributed to the profitability of domestic and foreign industrial firms, as illustrated by the Brazilian auto industry (p. 344). The growth of electric power under increasing state involvement in this sector is a structural element of the import substitution processes in the region during the 1960s and 1970s.

5.5 The Expansion Between 1882 and 1937

The spread of electrification throughout the periphery did not change the inherited international division of labor – electrification spread towards previously included regions, either lighting important cities or powering existing manufacturing and mining areas. Once initially installed, electrification of regions at the periphery impacted internal distribution of manufacturing activities, as availability of power resources attracted new industries.

The specificities of the spread of this third big bang, electricity, through our five regions are consequence of the peculiarities of the expansionary forces, of the weaknesses of the assimilatory forces and their combined operation.

The first peculiarity of the expansionary forces is their origin: they emanated from the United States that together with Germany replaced the United Kingdom as technological leaders. The second peculiarity is the institution that shaped those expansionary forces: the multinational firm, via foreign direct investments under different forms, free standing firms, holding companies, enclave investments etc.[75] The third is the nature of a technology whose products can only be sold if there is a supply of power for their use – thus the involvement of firms with investments in electric utilities across the globe. The fourth is the scientific content embedded in this new technology: electricity is a science-based technology, source of organizational innovation that is the research and development department, and a technology whose implementation depend on engineering skills. The fifth is the importance of politics, given the even greater capital-intensity – in comparison with railways – and its

[75] Multinational companies are learning machines, an indication of how the leading regions may assimilate information, knowledge, and technologies from the rest of the world, including the periphery, since then.

infrastructural nature – electricity has public goods features, with some forms of generation depending on public lands and public decisions, as illustrated by hydroelectric projects.

Although powerful, those expansionary forces did not have motives and/or resources to bring reasonable levels of electrification to the periphery.

The assimilatory forces, during the initial phase of propagation of electricity, needed major advances in absorptive capacities, given the intensity of knowledge and capital. The initially weak assimilatory forces may explain the relative strength of foreign control of electric utilities in our five regions, as described in Sect. 5.4.

The initial weaknesses of assimilatory forces are determined by the political configuration of late nineteenth century: colonial India and Africa, fragmented China, politically independent Latin America without business or governmental capabilities to direct this new technology. Although weak, assimilatory forces operated in those regions. They were based on two different sources.

The first source is the initial and limited accumulation of commercial wealth and capital, from small and localized nuclei of capitalist activities. In India it is illustrated by an economic group like Tata; in China by local mercantile sectors in Treaty Ports that siphoned commercial wealth into manufacturing activities; in Brazil by textile manufacturers that needed more reliable and cheap energy; and in South Africa by mining groups with increasing demands for energy.

The second source is maneuvering room for local political action, with initiatives taken by domestic actors. In Czarist Russia after decades of experiments with state intervention stimulating manufacturing that reached a new stage after the transition to a non-capitalist economy with a key role for planning. In the Indian sub-continent regionally dispersed as limits of the colonial power opened opportunities for action of Princely States and other local governments. In China as consequence of the self-strengthening movement. In South Africa after becoming a dominion in the British Empire, an apartheid regime with state action for electricity provision to the mining sector.

The interaction between those two sources of assimilatory forces over time, and after cumulative gains in both, strengthened them. Countries and regions with more nuclei of capital accumulation – and learning with those initial involvements with the new technology – and with more political autonomy have, on the one hand, a better perception of their relative backwardness, and, on the other hand, more resources to value the strategic significance of electricity. This is evident after the Independence processes and institutional changes in the 1940s, which always put electricity as priority in their policies and planning.

The combined operation of expansionary forces (Sect. 5.3) and assimilatory forces (Sect. 5.4) led to a stage of electrification of our five regions presented in Table 5.2. The two sets of data – arrival year and electricity consumption in 1937 – help the investigation of the speed and intensity of the initial spread of electricity throughout the periphery.

The timing of the arrival of electricity – the third technological revolution – shows the shortest lag vis-à-vis the two first big bangs. In two cases, China and Nigeria, the first big bang arrived after the third. The average lag between this big

Table 5.3 Year of the first electric commercial utility opened and total electricity consumption (million kilowatt-hours produced) in 1925 and in 1937 (Indian subcontinent, China, Russia, Sub-Saharan Africa and Latin America)

Region	Year	Million kwh (1925)	Million kwh (1937)
India	1899	470	1,200
China (*)	1882	1,950	3,930
Russia	1886	2,925	36,400
Sub-Saharan Africa (**)		1,888	5,962
South Africa	1882	1,761	5,336
Nigeria	1886	5 (1929)	14
Mozambique		5 (1929)	9
Latin America		4,504	10,135
Mexico	1883	1,220	2,480
Argentina		1,182	2,195
Brazil	1883	740 (1929)	2,030

Source: Year – See Table 5.2. Production – Darmstadter et al. (1971, pp. 652–691) – except Mozambique (Etemad & Luciani, 1991, p. 98) and Nigeria (Etemad & Luciani, 1991, p. 99)
(*) China – data from other sources: Wright (1991, p. 362) – 1925: 1075; 1936: 3967. Etemad and Luciani (1991, p. 118) – 1928: 890; 1937: 2422
(**) Calculated subtracting North Africa from Africa
OBS: United States in 1925: 81,142 million kwh; in 1937: 146,476 million kwh (Darmstadter et al., 1971, p. 653). World in 1925: 188,933 million kwh; in 1937: 436,246 million kwh (Darmstadter et al., 1971, p. 652)

bang's year and the year of its arrival in our five regions is 4.4 years (see Table 5.3), compared with 26.2 years for railways (see Table 4.2) and 87 years for cotton mechanization (see Table 3.3). Certainly, this shorter lag has roots in the emergence of the multinational firm as the main source of expansionary forces.

The order of the arrival in our five regions is different from the previous technological revolutions: China and South Africa became the first, and India became the last –[76] probably a consequence of British colonial priorities.

The intensity of the spread of electricity in 1937 (13.41%)[77] is similar to the spread of cotton mechanization in 1909 (12.48%), and lower than in railways in 1920 (27.69%).

As in other propagation processes, the imports of electricity-related goods, especially the equipment for electricity generation – now from multinational firms –, were the basic source. In the case of this technological revolution, given the knowledge requirements for absorption, the dissipation effects were very strong – very weak backward linkages: some production of electrical equipment was identified in Sect. 5.4 only in Russia, by the 1930s, and to a lesser extent, in China during

[76] Although in India the lag in electricity – 17 years – is shorter than in railways – 24 years.

[77] The intensity of the spread of a given technology here is calculated adding the total of its availability in our five regions (number of spindles, km of railways, or kwh of electricity consumption, according to Tables 3.3, 4.2 and 5.2) divided by the world total.

the war economy after 1937. As forward linkages, a phenomenon was the feedbacks with cotton textiles mechanization, identified in almost all regions.

At this stage, by 1937, after three technological revolutions with a late and limited propagation throughout their economies, there is a process of cumulative backwardness: the limited and incomplete diffusion of previous big bangs accumulates with the repetition of this problem with newer technologies.

Globally, those processes are expressed by the increase in the income gap of those regions vis-à-vis the leading country. Using available data compiled by Maddison (2010) and calculating the income gap with the leading country (the largest GDP per capita) in 1820 (United Kingdom) and in 1937 (United States) there was an increase in the income gap in the cases of India, China, Russia (former USSR in Maddison's data), and Brazil – the exceptions were South Africa (data for 1913 or 1950) and Mexico.[78] Therefore, the period involving those three big bangs – between 1771 and 1937 – may be described as a predominantly lagging behind phase.

At the periphery, these processes' superposition of limited and incomplete expansion of three technological revolutions had by 1937 established a growing heterogeneity both between and within those regions – a structural feature of peripheric forms of capitalism that had developed until then.

Politically and institutionally the superposition of backwardness and the lagging behind, apparently, had two implications. First, it is a real problem to face the next technological revolution, as the starting point is worsening each time, after each technological revolution. Second, as evidence of this superposition of backwardness is perceived by political actors of those regions, stimulus for development initiatives emerges: strengthening of pro-independence movements, the search of new policies to face that growing problem, and initiatives for formation of institutions of national systems of innovation.

References

Ardurat, C. (2002). L'électrification du Sénégal de la fin du XIXe siècle à la Seconde Guerre mondiale. *Outre-mers, 89*(334–335), 439–457. https://www.persee.fr/issue/outre_1631-0438_2002_num_89_334

Arrighi, G. (1994). *O longo século XX: dinheiro, poder e as origens do nosso tempo*. Contraponto/UNESP. (1996).

Beltran, A., Laborie, L., Lanthier, P., & Le Gallic, S. (2016). *Electric Worlds/Mondes électriques: Creations, circulations, tensions, transitions (19th–21st C.)*. https://www.jstor.org/stable/j.ctv9hj6hk

[78]The income gaps with the United Kingdom were in 1820 as follows: India 0.312; China 0.352; former USSR 0.403; South Africa 0.243; Mexico 0.234; Brazil 0.379. The income gaps with the United States in 1870 were: India 0.218; China 0.218; USSR 0.38; South Africa 0.351; Brazil 0.292; Mexico 0.276. The income gaps with the United States became in 1937 as follows: India 0.105; China 0.096; former USSR 0.335; South Africa 0.302 (in 1913) or 0.265 (in 1950); Mexico 0.279; Brazil 0.194.

Billington, D. P., Billington, J. R., & David, P. (2006). *Power, speed and form: Engineers and the making of the twentieth century*. Princeton University Press.
Bulmer-Thomas, V. (2003). *The economic history of Latin America since independence* (2nd ed.). Cambridge University Press.
Chandler, A., Jr. (1977). *The Visible Hand – The Managerial Revolution in America Business*. The Belknap Press of Harvard University Press.
Chandler, A., Jr. (1990). *Scale and scope: The dynamics of industrial capitalism*. The Belknap Press of Harvard University Press.
Chandler, A., Jr. (1992). Organizational capabilities and the economic history of the industrial enterprise. *Journal of Economic Perspectives, 6*(3), 79–100.
Christie, R. (1984). *Electricity, industry and class in South Africa*. Macmillan.
Coopersmith, J. (1992). *The electrification of Russia, 1880–1926*. Cornell University Press.
Crowe, G. D., & Goodman, S. E. (1994). S. A. Lebedev and the birth of Soviet computing. *IEEE Annals of the History of Computing, 16*(1), 4–24.
Cummins, Alex G. (1988) *The road to NEP, the State Commission for the Electrification of Russia (GOELRO): A study in technology, mobilization and economic planning*. PhD Dissertation, University of Maryland.
Darmstadter, J., Teitelbaum, P. D., & Polach, J. G. (1971). *Energy in the world economy; a statistical review of trends in output, trade, and consumption since 1925*. Johns Hopkins Press. https://archive.org/details/energyinworldeco0000darm/
David, P. (1989). *Computer and dynamo: The modern productivity paradox in a not-too-distant mirror* (Discussion Paper # 339). Stanford University.
David, P. (1990). The dynamo and the computer: An historical perspective on the modern productivity paradox. *American Economic Review, 80*(2), 355–336.
Devine, W. D., Jr. (1983). From shafts to wires: Historical perspective on electrification. *The Journal of Economic History, 43*(2), 347–372.
Dunning, J., & Lundan, S. (2008). *Multinational enterprises and the global economy* (2nd ed.). Edward Elgar.
Etemad, B., & Luciani, J. (1991). *World energy production 1800–1985*. Librairie Doz.
Farnie, D. A. (2004). The role of cotton textiles in the economic development of India, 1600–1990. In D. A. Farnie & D. J. Jeremy (Eds.), *The fibre that changed the world: The cotton industry in international perspective, 1600–1990s* (Pasold Studies in Textile History, 13) (pp. 395–430). Oxford University Press.
Feuerwerker, A. (1980). Economic trends in the late Ching Empire, 1870–1911. In J. Fairbank & K.-C. Liu (Eds.), *The Cambridge history of China. Volume 11: Late Ching, 1810–1911, Part 2* (pp. 1–69). Cambridge University Press.
Feuerwerker, A. (1983). Economic trends, 1912–1949. In J. Fairbank (Ed.), *The Cambridge history of China. Volume 12: Republican China 1912–1949, Part I* (pp. 28–127). Cambridge University Press.
Fine, B., & Rustomjee, Z. (1996). The political economy of South Africa: from minerals-energy complex to industrialisation. London: Westview.
Freeman, C. (1987). *Technology policy and economic performance: Lessons from Japan*. Pinter Publishers.
Freeman, C., & Louçã, F. (2001). *As time goes by: From the industrial revolutions and to the information revolution*. Oxford University.
Freeman, C., & Perez, C. (1988). Structural crisis of adjustment: Business cycles and investment behaviour. In G. Dosi, C. Freeman, R. Nelson, et al. (Eds.), *Technical change and economic theory* (pp. 38–66). Pinter.
Freeman, C., & Soete, L. (1997). The economics of industrial innovation. London: Pinter.
Furtado, C. (1976). *Economic development of Latin America* (2nd ed.). Cambridge University Press.
Garcke, E. (1896). *Manual of electric undertakings*. P. S. King & Son.
Garcke, E. (1897). *Manual of electric undertakings*. P. S. King & Son.

Gordon, R. J. (2016). *The rise and fall of American growth: The US standard of living since the Civil War*. Princeton University Press.

Gregory, P., & Harrison, M. (2005). Allocation under dictatorship: Research in Stalin's archives. *Journal of Economic Literature, XLIII*, 721–761.

Hausman, W. J., Herner, P., & Wilkins, M. (2008). *Global electrification: Multinational enterprise and international finance in the history of light and power, 1878–2007*. Cambridge University Press.

Headrick, D. R. (1988). *The tentacles of progress: Technological transfer in the age of imperialism, 1850–1940*. Oxford University Press.

Hedges, D. (Ed.). (1999). *História de Moçambique* (Vol. 2). Livraria Universitária.

Hospitalier, E. (1882). *La physique moderne: les principales applications de l'électricité*. G. Masson, Éditeur (Deuxième édition).

Hounshell, D. A. (1984). *From the American system to mass production, 1800–1932: The development of manufacturing technology in the United States*. The Johns Hopkins University Press. https://archive.org/details/fromamericansyst0000houn/

Huenemann, R. W. (1984). *The dragon and the Iron Horse: The economics of railroads in China, 1876–1937*. Harvard University Press.

Hughes, T. P. (1993). *Networks of power: Electrification in Western Society, 1880–1930*. The Johns Hopkins University Press.

Hymer, S. (1970). The efficiency (contradictions) of multinational corporations. *American Economic Review, 60*(2), 441–448.

Kale, S. S. (2014a). Structures of power: Electrification in Colonial India. *Comparative Studies of South Asia, Africa and the Middle East, 34*(3), 454–475.

Kale, S. S. (2014b). *Electrifying India: Regional political economies of development*. Stanford University Press.

Kamdem, M. W. P. (2016). Origine et perspectives de l'électrification rurale au Cameroun. In A. Beltran, L. Laborie, P. Lanthier, & S. Le Gallic (Eds.), *Electric Worlds/Mondes électriques: Creations, circulations, tensions, transitions (19th–21st C.)* (pp. 295–316). Peter Lang AG. https://www.jstor.org/stable/j.ctv9hj6hk.16

Kondratiev, N. D. (1926). Long cycles of economic conjuncture. In N. Makasheva, W. J. Samuels, & V. Barnett (Eds.), *The works of Nikolai D. Kondratiev* (Vol. 1, pp. 25–60). Pickering and Chato (1998).

Lanthier, P. (2016). Les quatre phases de l'histoire de l'électricité en Inde, de 1890 à nos jours. In A. Beltran, L. Laborie, P. Lanthier, & S. Le Gallic (Eds.), *Electric Worlds/Mondes électriques: Creations, circulations, tensions, transitions (19th–21st C.)*. Peter Lang AG. https://www.jstor.org/stable/j.ctv9hj6hk.29

Loukou, A. F. (2016). Le développement des technologies de l'information et de la communication en Côte d'Ivoire face aux contraintes d'énergie électrique. In A. Beltran, L. Laborie, P. Lanthier, & S. Le Gallic (Eds.), *Electric Worlds/Mondes électriques: Creations, circulations, tensions, transitions (19th–21st C.)* (pp. 343–363). https://www.jstor.org/stable/j.ctv9hj6hk

Lundquist, R. A. (1918). *Electrical goods in China, Japan and Vladivostok*. U. S. Department of Commerce.

Madan, S., Manimuthu, S., & Thiruvengadam, S. (2007). History of electric power in India (1890–1990). In *2007 IEEE conference on the history of electric power* (pp. 152–165). https://doi.org/10.1109/hep.2007.4510263

Maddison, A. (2010). *Historical statistics of the World Economy – 1-2008 AD*. Groningen Growth and Development Centre. http://www.ggdc.net/maddison/Historical_Statistics/horizontal-file_02-2010.xls

Magalhães, G. (2000). *Força e luz: eletricidade e modernização na República Velha*. Editora da Unesp.

Markevich, A. (2005). Soviet planning archives: The files that Bergson could not see. *Comparative Economic Studies, 47*, 364–386.

Marwah, H. (2014). Who's got the power? The electrification of Africa. In E. Frankema, E. Hillbom, U. Kufakurinani, M. Z. Selhausen, & Felix (Eds.), *The history of African*

development. An online textbook for a new generation of African students and teachers. African Economic History Network. https://www.aehnetwork.org/textbook/
Miescher, S. F. (2016). The Akosombo Dam and the quest for rural electrification in Ghana. In A. Beltran, L. Laborie, P. Lanthier, & S. Le Gallic (Eds.), *Electric Worlds/Mondes électriques: Creations, circulations, tensions, transitions (19th–21st C.)* (pp. 317–342). https://www.jstor.org/stable/j.ctv9hj6hk.17
Montaño, D. (2021). *Electrifying Mexico: Technology and transformation of a modern city*. University of Texas Press.
Nove, A. (1992) An economic history of the USSR – 1917-1991. London: Penguin, Third Edition.
Paula, J. A., Deus, L. G., Cerqueira, H. E. A. G., & Albuquerque, E. M. (2020). New starting point (s): Marx, technological revolutions and changes in the centre-periphery divide. *Brazilian Journal of Political Economy, 40*(1), 100–116.
Power Technology. (2021). *Aswan High Dam, Egypt*. https://www.power-technology.com/marketdata/aswan-high-dam-egypt/
Rosenberg, N. (1998). The role of electricity in industrial development. In N. Rosenberg (Ed.), *Studies on science and the innovation process: Selected works by Nathan Rosenberg*. World Scientific Publishing C. Pte. Ltd. (2010).
Santos, G. M. (2016). Is small really beautiful? Operating early Brazilian power plants. In A. Beltran, L. Laborie, P. Lanthier, & S. Le Gallic (Eds.), *Electric Worlds/Mondes électriques: Creations, circulations, tensions, transitions (19th–21st C.)* (pp. 559–573). Peter Lang AG. https://www.jstor.org/stable/j.ctv9hj6hk.28
Santos, G. M. (2018). Energy in Brazil: A historical overview. *Journal of Energy History/Revue d'Histoire de l'Énergie*. [Online], n°1, published 04 December 2018. http://energyhistory.eu/node/56
Schumpeter, J. A. (1939). *Business cycles: A theoretical, historical and statistical analysis of the capitalist process* (Vol. 1). McGraw-Hill Book Company, Inc.
Shabad, T. (1955). Communist China's five year plan. *Far Eastern Survey, 24*(12), 189–191.
Showers, K. B. (2011). Electrifying Africa: An environmental history with policy implications. *Geografiska Annaler: Series B, Human Geography, 93*(3), 193–221.
Sopa, A., & Fernandes, J. M. (n.d.). *Barragem da Chicamba Real*. https://hpip.org/pt/Heritage/Details/2124
Speyer, H. R. (1913). The development of electric power for industrial purposes in India. *Journal of the Institution of Electrical Engineers, 53*(246), 597–604.
Sutton, A. C. (1968). *Western technology and Soviet economic development – 1917 to 1930*. Hoover Institution Publication. https://archive.org/details/Sutton-Western-Technology-1917-1930
Sutton, A. C. (1971). *Western technology and Soviet economic development – 1930 to 1945*. Stanford: Hoover Institution Press/Stanford University. https://archive.org/details/Sutton-Western-Technology-1930-1945
Suzigan, W. (1986). *Indústria brasileira: origem e desenvolvimento*. Editora Hucitec/Editora da Unicamp (2000).
Tan, Y. J. (2021). *Recharging China in war and revolution, 1882–1955*. Cornell University Press.
Tendler, J. (1968). *Electric power in Brazil*. Harvard University Press. https://archive.org/details/electricpowerinb0000tend/
Us Bureau Of The Census. (1937). *Cotton production and distribution – season of 1936–37*. Government Printing Office/US Department of Commerce.
Wionczek, M. S. (1965). The state and electric-power industry in Mexico, 1895–1965. *The Business History Review, 39*(4), 527–566.
Wolmar, C. (2010). *Blood, iron and gold: How the railways transformed the world*. PublicAffairs.
World Bank. (2023). *World Bank indicators*. https://data.worldbank.org/indicator
Wright, T. (1991). Electric power production in pre-1937 China. *The China Quarterly, 126*, 356–363.

Chapter 6
Automobiles, Oil, Petrochemicals, and Roads – The Inclusion of New Regions After a New Core Input – 1908–1971

6.1 Introduction

Ford's T-Model, released in 1908, in Detroit, United States, is, in the view of Carlota Perez (2010, p. 190), the big bang of the fourth technological revolution.

This new big bang had its roots in the integration of existing products – the automobile, the combustion engine, and a by-product of refined oil, gasoline – brought by Ford's invention.

Although the maturing of this new\ phase was beyond Kondratiev's horizon, he lists inventions that prepared it in other long waves. Kondratiev includes "the construction of the first car (1831)" among the "series of technical inventions" of the second long wave (1926, p. 39). Field (1958b, pp. 414–437) presents a long list of "mechanical road-vehicles", divided between "electric road-carriages", "steam road-carriages",[1] and "petroleum motor-carriages". The first "petroleum motor-carriage" mentioned by Field (1958b, p. 426) is an invention from Siegfried Marcus (Austria, in 1864). Ford is at the end of Field's list for his 1896 invention – before him there were references to Benz, Peugeot, Austin, among others.

Those petroleum motor-carriages presuppose developments of internal combustion engines. Field (1958a, pp. 157–175) describes inventions from 1860 (gas-engine) to 1893–1901 (Benz's patent).[2] Kondratiev (1926, p. 40), in his observations related to the third long cycle, mentions "among the most important

[1] Probably this was the first car mentioned by Kondratiev.

[2] According to Billington and Billington Jr. (2006, pp. 194–195), Ford "was fascinated by engines at an early age, worked as a steam engine repairman in the 1890s and studied an Oto engine that came to the area".

E. da Motta e Albuquerque, *Technological Revolutions and the Periphery*, Contributions to Economics, https://doi.org/10.1007/978-3-031-43436-5_6

technological inventions" the "gas engine (1876)", "petrol engines (1886)", "the Diesel engine (1893)".[3]

In turn, all these inventions related to internal combustion engines depended on knowledge and availability of refined oil: Forbes (1958) summarizes a long history of "knowledge of mineral oil" that led to advances in technology to drill for oil, to refine oil, to transport oil.[4] In 1886 there was a patent on cracking (Forbes, 1958, p. 119), but "no demand for cracked petrol" (p. 121). There is even a debate on the invention of cracking technologies, with a possible first development in 1886 (Forbes, 1958, p. 120).

Ford's invention – Model-T – is a benchmark because it defines the "dominant design" in Klepper's (1997) automobile life cycle, an industry that started in 1895 (p. 154). Ford's T-Model triggered further changes, two of them highlighted by Freeman and Louçã (2001, p. 141): Ford's assembly line and Burton's cracking process, both in 1913. Larraz (2021, p. 133) explores those connections between innovations in transport and in the oil industry: Ford's innovation "drastically changed the oil industry" – among between the changes in the oil industry is the emergence of petrochemicals (Larraz, 2021, pp. 142–144; Rosenberg, 1998). Freeman and Louçã (2001, pp. 284–285) evaluate these interconnected changes, underlining the emergence of a new core input – oil.

Another impact of this fourth big bang is a demand for roads: these vehicles needed roads to circulate.[5] And roads added another product to the oil industry – asphalt (Larraz, 2021, p. 133).

This new core input – oil – became a new "strategic commodity" (Bromley, 1991, p. 46). As such, access to oil became a key factor for the inclusion of new regions in the global economy – see the Gulf region countries and the Middle East region – and a new reorganization of the international division of labor, with the emergence of oil-producing regions and conversion of countries into suppliers of oil.

The relationship between automobiles, oil and roads – a three-sided interaction – might be a peculiarity of this fourth big bang. Those relationships have multiple linkages and impacts that reconfigure, again, the global economy. Those three-sided simultaneous developments, at the center, impact the periphery in different ways, as one of those parts may be more important than others in different peripheric regions – some regions will be included in the global economy only as oil-producers, for example.

---

[3] All inventions mentioned by Kondratiev related to combustion engines are listed by Field (1958a), although sometimes with different dates. This inclusion of those inventions by Kondratiev in the same list of the long cycle of electricity – his third long cycle – may be an insight on how different inventions/innovations overlap in different moments, an important insight that may help the elaboration of our theoretical framework.

[4] Chandler Jr. (1977, pp. 254–255) comments how gasoline was part of the flow from a distillation process – his Figure 5 (p. 255) shows how gasoline represented 1.5 percent of the flow in one 1869 refinery: the Pratt Refinery. Larraz (2021, p. 133) stresses that "gasoline was a byproduct until the beginning of the 20th century". This status is derived from the fact that "in the first refineries, the most demanded products were kerosene and light distillates" (p. 133).

[5] Gordon (2016, pp. 157–159) discusses the "chicken and egg" relationship between automobiles and paved roads in the United States.

These relationships organize this chapter, which initially, in the second section, evaluates the nature of technologies in these three economic sectors. The third section presents how they shape the expansionary forces from the center – with an important role for multinational firms, now with two different motives for foreign investments. The fourth section summarizes how a new global political economy – especially after the Second World War – makes space room for different combinations of processes for technological absorption. The fifth section investigates how a new "core input" is related to inclusion of new regions in the world economy (and, among previous included regions, internal changes derived from discovery of oil reserves) -, with new included regions and countries forming new varieties of capitalism. It also evaluates how the spread of production of cars, oil extraction and refining, and roads occurred in our five regions.

6.2 The Fourth Big Bang and the Nature of Its Three Interrelated Technologies (and One Unfolding Field)

A peculiarity of this fourth big bang is the combined and interrelated development of other industries and sectors – this combination shows the strong and sophisticated linkages triggered by the automobile, representing an exercise of overlapping of technologies and positive feedbacks among them. Rosenberg (1998) has pioneered this line of investigation, suggesting how "the spectacular growth in the automobile industry" in the 1920s was an event that impacted the discipline of chemical engineering, whose history became "inseparable from the history of petroleum refining" (pp. 179–180).

There are feedbacks and also sequential development, as one sector grows and splits into new specialized sub-sectors that may become new sectors – as in the case of petrochemicals.

6.2.1 The Automobile

Billington and Billington Jr. (2006, chapter 5) describe Ford founding companies in 1899, 1901 and 1903 (pp. 195–198), and inventing the Model-T in 1908 – an invention that "depended on three core systems: electric ignition, chemical combustion of the fuel, mechanical transmission of power" (p. 201). The previous developments in different fields of engineering – electrical, mechanical and chemical engineering – were joined in one vehicle (p. 218).

In 1909, one year after the release of Ford's Model-T, there were 275 firms producing automobiles in the United States (Klepper, 1997, p. 154) – and a large amount of experimentation was taking place there. In Klepper's scheme, the emergence of a dominant design – Model-T in the case of automobiles – opens a new phase in the life cycle, with a shake-out that marks the beginning of increasing concentration in that industry: oligopoly-formation. This corresponds to Chandler's first-movers that explore economies of scale and scope, dominating industries (1992, pp. 82–83). Ford was one of those leading firms, with General Motors as an important rival (Klepper, 1997, p. 155). Ford was one of the first US multinational firms, according to a 1914 list compiled by Chandler Jr. (1977, p. 368).[6]

The consolidation of the automobile industry pushed the emergence of new firms and new specialized producers of components – one example is the automobile tires industry (Klepper and Simons, 1997, pp. 402–414). Over time, metamorphoses in the frontier of automobile firms reshaped the industry, with suppliers of different products assuming different roles in the sectoral division of labor.

6.2.2 The Automobile's Fuel: Gasoline and Oil Refining

The early history of Standard Oil illustrates the changes that the third and the fourth technological revolutions brought. An active and leading firm in oil refining to sell kerosene for lighting, Standard Oil, on the one hand, received the impact of the spread of electricity in the end of the nineteenth century, but, on the other hand, witnessed the new market for automobiles in the early twentieth century (Chandler Jr., 1977, p. 350): the rising demand for gasoline replaced the falling demand for kerosene.[7]

The demand for gasoline had two interconnected consequences.

First, it stimulated improvements in refining techniques, that led to the invention of the thermal cracking process in 1913 (Larraz, 2021, p. 134),[8] starting a long process of innovation in oil refining. Larraz (2021, p. 134) summarizes an "oil refining process timeline" with improvements in the cracking process such as the "catalytic cracking" in 1937, "fluid catalytic cracking" in 1942 (p. 134) – new techniques that pose challenges for their absorption at the periphery. Another important byproduct of oil refining improvements was the emergence of a new industrial sector: petrochemicals (Larraz, 2021, pp. 142–144). These developments

[6]According to Wilkins (1964, pp. 434–435), before 1914 Ford had branches in Canada, England, France and Argentina, with manufacturing operations in Canada and England, assembly operations in France. In Argentina its assembly operations began in 1916.

[7]A reference to this transition may be followed by the exports of petroleum refined products from the United States, comparing kerosene and gasoline: in 1913, 27,056 thousands of barrels of kerosene and 4629 thousands of barrels of kerosene; only in 1923 did gasoline overtake kerosene – 20,349 thousands of barrels of kerosene and 20,736 thousands of barrels of gasoline. If one compares kerosene to all other refined products, kerosene made up more than half of exports of all refined products in 1913, falling to less than a fifth in 1918 (American Petroleum Institute, 1930, pp. 22–23).

[8]Important developments of chemistry were necessary for this invention (Yergin, 1991, p. 111).

depended upon new knowledge and new technologies, and are connected with the rise of chemical engineering: Rosenberg (1998, p. 179) reports a "great expansion in the demand for chemical engineers" in the 1920s.

Second, it opened up exploration of new oil reserves globally, both within old oil-producing countries and regions (as the United States and Russia) and in new areas (as in the Middle East and Latin America) (Yergin, 1991). This search for new oil reserves did underly a new change in the international division of labor, with new regions now included in the global economy.

6.2.3 The Automobile's Way: Roads and Their Networks

Billington and Billington Jr. (2006, p. 218) comment how the automobile and its market expansion in the United States "stimulate the civil engineering of new roads and bridges".[9] Gordon (2016, p. 158) stresses that beyond the extension of paved roads – a construction process that involved support from federal and state resources -, between 1900 and 1930 there was an improvement in road building, including the "development of asphalt and concrete as durable road surfaces".

A document prepared by the US Department of Transportation (1976) shows the research necessary for road development – since 1916 (p. 208), and part of public support, as in the Federal Highway Acts of 1921 and 1956 (pp. 320–352) -, different forms of public support for highway building (pp. 80–89), including the awareness of their strategic role for defense (pp. 142–153). In 1925 the United States had 838,289 km of surfaced roads (US Bureau of the Census, 1960, p. 459) – for comparison, in 1925 there were 672,613 km of railways (Headrick, 1988, p. 55). This network of roads, that kept growing during the twentieth century, may be discussed following Chandler's (1977) elaboration on the impact of revolutions in transport and communication upon the economy and business – this huge and very tentacular network has impacts on market formation and new business opportunities, a type of indirect forward linkages triggered by this fourth big bang.

Montealegre (2019, pp. 90–107) in her work on "global history of the road" evaluates the role of the American model of road construction that spread world-wide, mentioning "mechanization of road construction" as an important topic. It is related to the emergence of an industry of earth-moving equipment – "[o]ver a dozen of earthmoving machine manufacturers were created in the US during the 1920s" (p. 92).

[9] And here one very specific feedback, pointed out by Billington and Billington Jr. (2006, p. 234): better roads made Model-T less attractive, making room for General Motor's growth with a more diverse set of cars.

6.2.4 The Combination Between Those Three Components

Automobiles, oil and roads are three processes interconnected by the very nature of this fourth big bang. This combination of different processes is an indication of the very broad effects and impacts of this big bang, with strong backward and forward linkages, and an example of overlapping of different technologies that is prerequisite for development in each one of them.

This combination in the leading country – the United States – meant powerful positive feedbacks that shaped what Freeman and Louçã (2001, p. 141) called the "motorization of transport, civil economy, and war".

New products for these sectors and new interactions between these developments opened up new business opportunities – and new challenges for technology absorption at the periphery.

6.3 Expansionary Forces: Multinational Firms in a Three-Pronged Process

Expansionary forces in this big bang are shaped by these three components discussed in Sect. 6.2. Different firms, with activities in different sectors, will assume different roles in this process. Multinational firms are the main institutional form of those expansionary forces. As in electricity, in this big bang early US multinationals were taking initial steps to produce or drill abroad. Chandler's (1977, p. 368) list – "American multinationals, 1914" – mentions three companies related to different activities in these sectors: Ford (producer of motor vehicles), Standard Oil (drilling and refining oil) and US Rubber (tires).[10]

These three multinationals illustrate the different but interrelated roles they assume, and also the different "motives for foreign production": automobile-producing multinationals are examples of market seekers, while oil companies are examples of resource seekers (Dunning & Lundan, 2008, pp. 67–71). Construction firms are mentioned by Dunning and Lundan (2008, p. 217) – in relation to highways, their example is a Chinese firm in Africa.[11]

During the initial phase of this big bang, the expansionary forces acted almost alone, imposing a new division of labor globally: especially in oil drilling and exploration, the multinational firms controlled this activity in all regions, and only very lately domestic forms of control emerged (Beyazay-Odemis, 2016) – a pattern similar to the late "domestication" of electricity provision (Hausman et al., 2008, chapter 6).

[10]Klepper and Simons (1997, pp. 403–404) report that in 1905 US Rubber acquired RGM Company, a firm with subsidiaries that produced tires.

[11]Chinese investment in infrastructure in Africa today may be an example of the role of foreign construction firms in extending road networks globally (The Economist, 2022).

6.3.1 The Search for Oil Reserves and Changes in the Production Chain

The search for oil reserves antedated the automobile industry, and it was truly global (Yergin, 1991). In the Dutch East Indies, in 1885, a first drill led to a firm launched in 1890 – Royal Dutch (Yergin, 1991, p. 73). By 1900 two foreign firms controlled over half of the "Russian and Far Eastern oil exports": Shell and Royal Dutch (p. 121). These two companies will merge in 1907, forming the Royal Dutch Shell (p. 126). In 1909 one sees the foundation of the Anglo Persian Oil Company (p. 148), in 1932 Royal Dutch Shell arrives in Venezuela, in 1938 SOCAL discovers oil in Saudi Arabia (p. 300) – an international presence that will be preserved until the 1950s, as the Gulf region was in the range of the "seven sisters' cartel" (Hanieh, 2011, p. 37).

This search is knowledge-intensive as it involves geological sciences and in the 1920s the "emerging science of geophysics" (Yergin, 1991, p. 218).[12]

Between the two world wars oil is consolidated as a "strategic commodity" (Bromley, 1991), connected to a geopolitical transition to the hegemony of the United States. Over time, oil production was organized globally, with metamorphoses in the frontiers of the multinational firms that increasingly orchestrated a "petroleum value chain" (Beyazay-Odemis, 2016, chapters 1 and 2). Changes in the localization of activities in this chain affect the division between the center and the periphery – before the late 1950s "the refining of crude oil took place in North America and Western Europe" (Hanieh, 2011, p. 37).

Changes in the petroleum value chain are followed by changes in leading firms' boundaries. Standard Oil is an example of a completely integrated international firm (Chandler Jr., 1977, p. 325, pp. 418–425; Beyazay-Odemis, 2016, p. 22), from oil extraction to selling gasoline to consumers. Over time, with the growing sophistication and specialization of upstream and downstream services, the "core firms" concentrated on coordination of the whole value chain.

Its upstream activities involve specialized services such as identification of targets (seismic research, from geologists and geophysicists), "drill exploration and appraisal wells", development of the field, extension of the field life, and field decommission (Beyazay-Odemis, 2016, p. 15). Downstream activities involve "services and equipment from the oil field to customer", including production in "onshore and offshore fields", transport to refineries, "refining", "transport from refineries to marketing and petrochemical plants", "marketing" (p. 17).

The reference to "petrochemical plants" is an example of a new sector originating from the petroleum industry. The innovations that led to this new sector took place, in the 1920s, within the Standard Oil of New Jersey and Union Carbide, "the first

[12]This line of scientific and technological development has a route that will lead in the 1950s, among other paths, to the emerging semiconductors' sector: Texas Instruments is a firm active in equipment for geophysical research, before diversifying towards electronics (Miller, 2022, p. 14).

companies to develop crackers for the production of ethylene and propylene" (Larraz, 2021, pp. 142–143).

Upstream and downstream services were provided by a growing set of specialized firms – "oil services companies" (OSCs) – divided in six segments: "seismic", "drilling", "well servicing", "engineering, procurement and services", "subsea", and "equipment producers and manufacturers" (Beyazay-Odemis, 2016, pp. 25–26).[13] There is a peculiar dynamic in the petroleum industry between them – the OSCs – and the "international oil companies" (IOCs), the core firms of the sector.[14]

The strategic role of these OSCs, given their knowledge and technology accumulation is shown by their localization following core firms.[15] As the international division of labor changes with the emergence and consolidation of big "national oil companies" (NOCs) in peripheric countries, OSCs are contracted directly by them (Beyazay-Odemis, 2016, p. 42).

6.3.2 Selling and Making Cars (and Trucks) Abroad

Ford Company establishes international operations since the very beginning (Wilkins, 1964). As a classical movement from selling cars abroad to assembling them and later manufacturing – the "internationalization process" explained by Dunning and Lundan (2008, pp. 206–231) -, Ford's foreign operations until the early 1960s did reach the six continents, which include large parts of our five regions – an indication of how expansionary forces driven by multinationals led to the arrival of automobile production in those regions.

Wilkins compiled data on the foreign operations of Ford showing how and when they were established in different regions: in India, assembly operations initiated in 1926; in China, marketing operations in 1928; in South Africa, assembly operations in 1926; in Latin America, assembly operations in Argentina (1916), Uruguay (1920), Chile (1924), Mexico (1925), and Brazil (1920), manufacturing operations in Argentina (1961), and in Brazil (1959).

[13]The leading OSCs are listed in Beyazay-Odemis (2016, p. 27). There are firms such as Schlumberger (founded in 1926), Halliburton (founded in 1919, as Howco) and Baker Hughes (Hughes Tool Co. founded in 1908).

[14]Listed in Beyazay-Odemis (2016, p. 20) – the leader in this list is ExxonMobil, that has its roots in Standard Oil.

[15]The influence of the core firm – "oil exploration companies" – on downstream investments is highlighted by Dunning and Lundan (2008, p. 226), as their presence "has frequently led to investment by foreign downstream specialists, such as petrochemicals or synthetic fibre companies".

6.3.3 Roads and Construction

The global diffusion of the advances of road construction in the United States to rest of the world is investigated by Montealegre (2019), focusing in some cases in the developing world. For this diffusion, institutions had an important role – as the International Road Federation (IRF), created "in 1948 by officials from firms such as Shell Union Oil of New Jersey and the Automobile Manufacturers' Association, among others", encouraged the "creation of national road associations abroad" (p. 100).

The objective of the IRF was to promote "road development worldwide" (p. 100), organizing transfer of knowledge and technology – including grants for foreign engineers to "take post-graduate courses in British and especially American universities" (p. 100). Montealegre (2019, p. 106) mentions an international network that circulated "engineering knowledge and experience".

For this process of mechanized road construction globally, the activities of earthmoving machine manufacturers were important, and the leadership of firms from the United States dominated that market globally (p. 95). This means that road construction until the 1960s was done using equipment produced by those leading firms – Caterpillar, for instance, is a reference since the 1920s (p. 92).

6.3.4 Motives and Impacts of Those Expansionary Forces

Although interrelated in the leading center – the United States -, at the periphery those technologies did not necessarily come together. On the contrary, initially those three technologies will be separated: some regions will become suppliers of oil, other will combine oil exploration with some processing, all regions will become populated by automobiles, trucks and tractors, that can be produced domestically or imported. The separation of these three components is a source of strong dissipation effects, as all linkages and all potential technological developments are not internalized at the periphery.

These multifaceted impacts, and the different possible arrangements that they may shape at the periphery are sources for more heterogeneous development.

In this fourth big bang, initially the multinationals operating in oil-related activities and in automobiles manufacturing combined resource and market-seeking motives. Resource-seeking motives were important to include new regions in the global economy – new oil-rich regions, like the Middle East –[16] and rearranged the international division of labor after this new strategic commodity came on board.

[16] As Hanieh (2011, p. 79) puts forward, "[t]he discovery and export of oil from the 1930s to 1950s shifted the way in which Gulf financial circuits were integrated into the global economy".

6.4 Political Changes: Decolonization and Domestic Policies

After the fourth big bang and after the two world wars, important political changes took place in our five regions, in line with a new world order of independent countries. The end of the British empire led to decolonization in the Indian subcontinent and Africa, the foundation of the People's Republic of China – China's reunification with national sovereignty under a modernization and Westernization project – reorganized East Asia, including a new dynamic within the context of the "cold war".

In oil-producing regions – new regions included in the global economy after the fourth big bang -, the formation of new nations, initially under colonial powers and later also part of the decolonization process, a very peculiar process took place. In the Arabian Peninsula, comments Bromley (1991, p. 108), states began to define borders "when the oil companies required to determine the extent of their concessions". During the 1950s and 1970s there was the formation of independent nations in the region.[17]

The implications of decolonization and independence movements, together with more assertive policies of some oil-producing Latin American countries (Mexico in the 1950s, Venezuela in the 1970s) led to a structural change. While the IOCs detained more than 85 percent of global reserves in the 1970s, nationalizations transformed the NOCs in controllers of, at least, 80 percent of the reserves and 73 percent of oil production (Beyazay-Odemis, 2016, pp. 18–19).

These political changes – the transition to a world order based on independent nations – impact absorption capacities specially because independent countries invest in universities and academic institutions in their initial actions. Independent countries may establish political goals and plan for active policies for insertion in the international division of labor. This new political scenario starts new dynamics, that may lead to structural changes such as the "domestication" of electric utilities created (see Chap. 5) and the emergence of national oil companies (NOCs). In sum, the political changes summarized in Table 6.1, led to a new dynamic in relation to assimilatory forces.

6.5 View from the Periphery: Different Arrivals, More Heterogeneity

One single innovation – Ford's Model-T – and various different lags: this is a specificity of this big bang for the periphery. Thus, a new question arises: how to deal with these three different technologies at the same time? Once more, without

[17] Under previous British colonial power, Oman became independent in 1951, Kuwait in 1961, and UAE formed in 1971 (Hanieh, 2011, p. 57).

Table 6.1 Political organization in the India, China, Russia, Latin America and Sub-Saharan Africa (1950 and 1971)

Region	1950	1971
India	Indian independence in 1947. First five-year plans (1951–1961). Import substitution industrialization	Third and fourth five-year plans
China	Foundation of the People's Republic of China (1949). First five-year plan in 1952. Catch-up project with USSR as a reference	Pendular policies related to the power of provinces in planning between 1952 and 1971. In 1971 the beginning of change in the catch-up project, now with the United States as reference
Russia	Stalinist model. Limited and incomplete catch up concluded	Consolidation of the bureaucracy. Beginning of the long stagnation. Attempts to localized reforms
Africa	Beginning of the end of the colonial period	Consolidation of the movement for independent African nations
Latin America	Independent and fragmented states. Beginning of import substitution industrialization	Independent and fragmented states. Import substitution industrialization

Source: author's elaboration based on the literature reviewed in this chapter

completing the absorption of the three first big bangs, our five regions must face a new technological revolution and its many dimensions. At the same time, investments in industrialization, railways and electricity were taking place after 1908 – our five regions were dealing with old and new gaps.

Another peculiarity of this big bang, given the three interrelated technologies (automobile, oil and roads) and new sector (petrochemicals), is the number of different arrivals of these technologies in the periphery: Table 6.2 shows four different initial years, with different lags and dynamics. Just to identify a reference date to organize the evaluation of each lag, the initial year of each technology in the United States are as follows: automobile – Ford Model-T – in 1908 (Perez, 2010, p. 190); oil drilling in 1859 (American Petroleum Institute, 1930, p. 10); oil refining in 1862 (atmospheric distillation) and in 1913 (thermal cracking) (Larraz, 2021, p. 134), petrochemicals in 1921 (ACS, 2021; Larraz, 2021, pp. 142–143).

There are many different arrivals.

In the case of motor vehicles, they were imported before local production – and their import triggers a specific dynamic that impacts the need for road construction and use of gasoline. In 1935, according to data from Mitchell (1993, 1998a, b) regarding "motor vehicles in use", they were 123,000 in India; 242,000 in South Africa; 96,000 in Mexico; 354,000 in Argentina; and 139,000 (in 1937) in Brazil. Wilkins (1974, pp. 416–417) describes how those car imports were related to imports of refined products and the operation of marketing organizations of multinationals during the 1920s in South America.

Table 6.2 Year of arrival of each of the three interrelated technologies and petrochemicals in India, China, Russia, Sub-Saharan Africa and Latin America

Region	Automobile production	Oil drilling	Oil refining	Petro-chemicals
India	1926 (a) 1954	1889	1901	1973
China	1955	1926	1958	1972
Russia	1901	1846/1863	1859	1959
Sub-Saharan Africa				
South Africa	1924 (a)		1954	
Nigeria	1961 (a)	1957	1965	
Mozambique				
Latin America				
Mexico	1925 (a) 1952	1901	1906	
Argentina	1916 (a) 1961	1907	1911	
Brazil	1920 (a) 1958	1942	1932	1957

Source: Automobile Production: India: Wilkins (1964, p. 435); Mitchell (1998a, p. 479); (The references from Mitchell (1993, 1998a, b) are based on the conjecture that his first data on "output motor vehicles" and on "crude oil production" correspond to the first year of that activity in that country. If other sources present earlier dates, one has the option to use them) China: Mitchell (1998a, p. 479); Russia: Sutton (1968, p. 243); Africa – South Africa: Wilkins (1964, p. 435); Nigeria: Mitchell (1998a, p. 478); Latin America – Mexico: Wilkins (1964, p. 435); Argentina: Wilkins (1964, p. 434); Brazil: Wilkins (1964, p. 435)
Oil Drilling: Mitchell (1993, 1998a, b), for Russia: Larraz (2021, p. 131); American Petroleum Institute (1930, p. 10); Argentina: American Petroleum Institute (1930, p. 10); Mexico: American Petroleum Institute (1930, p. 10)
Oil Refining: India: Tang (1994, p. 170); China: Kambara (1974, p. 701); Russia: Larraz (2021, p. 131); South Africa and Nigeria (Mbendi, 2018); Brazil: Morais (2013, p. 336); Mexico: Hydrocarbons (2023); Argentina: Wilkins (1974, p. 419)
Petro Chemicals: Russia (Sutton, 1973, pp. 146)
OBS: (a) Assembly only

Table 6.2 shows two arrivals dates for "automobile production" – the first defined only by expansionary forces from one multinational – Ford -, the second defined by policies established by each country, with or without participation of multinational firms.

In this section, before evaluating our five regions, the Saudi Arabia case is presented, as an opportunity to follow how one region, "a remote and inhospitable area surrounded by desert" (Hanieh, 2011, p. 57), had been included in the international division of labor after the oil discoveries. This inclusion started a process that led to exploration in the region, following a path that climbed some steps in the petroleum value chain, becoming a new variety of capitalism (Hanieh, 2011, pp. 103–148; Achcar, 2013, pp. 53–96). This case could be an opportunity to evaluate the potential of wealth creation and industrialization that an oil-based economy can achieve.

6.5.1 *Saudi Arabia as a Case Study: Desert, Oil Drilling, and Petrochemicals*

In 1908 in contemporary Iran the first oil well was drilled – a confirmation of the region's potential in that strategic input. The movements of countries and big companies in the region are described by Yergin (1991, chapter 15).

Saudi Arabia, relatively independent from Britain, that "inhospitable area" in 1932 assumed "its modern form" (Hanieh, 2011, p. 57). A Standard Oil controlled company – California-Arabian Standard Oil Company (CASOC)[18] was active in the region since 1933 (Yergin, 1991, p. 298), making an oil discovery in March 1938 (p. 300) that starts a new phase in the history of Saudi Arabia, transforming it in a leading oil producing region. In 1945 ARAMCO inaugurates the oldest oil refinery in the Persian Gulf – Ras Tanura (Yergin, p. 398).

The oil revenues will play a key role in the next decades – IOCs paid royalties and rents to rulers. Those revenues contributed towards the initial formation of a "domestic capitalist class", through their redirection "to leading merchant families and other elites" (Hanieh, 2011, p. 60) – the "migrant labor flows" were the other side of this process of class formation.

As countries became independent in the Middle East and in the Gulf region, the domestic control of their oil reserves increased, especially after the nationalizations "from the early 1970s onwards" (Hanieh, 2011, p. 66). In the case of Saudi Arabia, the government gradually increased its participation in the control of ARAMCO – 25 percent in 1973, 60 percent in 1974 (Sorkhabi, 2008), taking full control in 1980 (Hanieh, 2011, p. 69).

As a state-run company, renamed to Saudi-ARAMCO in 1988, a new variety of capitalism began to take shape, after the importance of "state contracts to capital accumulation". The Saudi state develops and becomes politically active – between 1970 and 1975 there was the first five-year economic development plan. The "redirection of state revenues accumulated" plays a strategic role, creating opportunities for other new industries. These opportunities "were either derivative to the oil sector or were initiated with state assistance from accrued oil revenues" (Hanieh, 2011, p. 69). Private sector developed initially in industries like construction, food, transport, simple manufacturing (pipes, wires), security services. Later, downstream industrialization was stimulated – in 1976 the Saudi Basic Industries Corporation (SABIC) was founded – a government decision to use their oil resources to "make chemicals, polymers, fertilizers" (p. 71).

Those movements of redirection of oil revenues organized an initial diversification of the Saudi Arabian economy from its initial position of an oil drilling country – the long-term consequences of these movements are summarized in their exports profile in 2020, which shows crude oil as 53.29 percent of the total exports,

[18] In 1944, CASOC, then owned also by Texaco, changed the name to Arabian-American Oil Company (ARAMCO) (Yergin, 1991, p. 398).

refined oil as 6.43 percent as and chemistry-related products as 19.92 percent (Atlas Complexity, 2023).[19]

6.5.2 *India: Entry Before Independence, Industrial Policies After*

During colonial India the three interrelated technologies arrive in the subcontinent: in 1889 the first oil drilling, in 1901 the inauguration of the first refinery (Tang, 1994, p. 190), in 1926 the assembly line of Ford (Wilkins, 1964, p. 435). These relatively early arrivals however did not initiate a strong diffusion process, even in terms of the periphery.

Independence in 1947 is a benchmark, a political change that made room for national development and industrial policies. A long political process, led by the Indian National Congress (founded in 1885), it had a long debate of development and industrial policies – in 1939 the INC created a National Planning Committee (Chibber, 2003, pp. 88–89) and there were in India nuclei of capitalist accumulation strong enough to organize proposals for economic planning after Independence, the Bombay Plan in 1944–1945 (Chibber, 2003, p. 94). The new Indian government prepared the First Five-Year Plan in 1950 (Metcalf & Metcalf, 2002, pp. 240–241).[20]

After Independence, in the 1950s, "India's modern refining industry started", with international companies building three refineries (Tang, 1994, p. 170). The first government company was built in 1962 – technology from Romania.- and there were more two companies built with assistance from the USSR. There were also two joint-ventures in the late 1960s – one with Philips, other with Amoco (p. 170). In the early 1970s the Indian government acquired "refineries owned by multinationals" (p. 170). Beyazay-Odemis (2016, p. 18) lists one Indian NOC – ONGC – among the "leading producers of oil and gas".

The production of automobiles arrived in India through a subsidiary of Ford, that implemented assembly operations since 1926 (Wilkins, 1964, p. 435), and General Motors in 1928 (Remesh, 2017, p. 105). In the 1940s, two Indian groups –

[19] A comparison with Venezuela, a country that has been drilling oil since 1915 and refining it since 1917, would show different strategies for use of oil revenues. Its exports of chemical-related products were 4 percent of the total in 1996 and 2.3 percent in 2014, while these participations in the case of Saudi Arabia were respectively 5.5 percent and 9.52 percent (and, as shown, 19.22 percent in 2020). It seems that Saudi Arabia implemented a set of policies more successful in industrialization and diversification than Venezuela. For the Venezuelan case and its oil economy, there are two Celso Furtado reports, prepared in 1957 and 1974, a diagnostic of a country with huge positive trade balance that could be used to industrialize and diversify the economy (Furtado, 2008).

[20] Muzaka (2018) identifies elements of continuity with the "institutional structures inherited from the colonial past" (p. 97). In terms of discontinuity, Muzaka stresses that the "independent Indian state" had as a "constitutive part" of its identity the "engineering and achieving economic development for the nation as a whole via planned *industrialization*" (her emphasis, p. 96).

Hindustan Motors and Premier Automobiles, in agreements through foreign firms – initiated production. In 1954, the Tata Group started trucks production with an agreement with Daimler Benz (Remesh, 2017, p. 105). During the 1950s, government policies stimulated the increase of domestic content (p. 106). Amsden (2001, p. 281) classifies industrial policies in India as "independent", one of the cases where "automobile assembly was a platform for national firm formation", that led to TELCO (the truck firm from the Tata Group) and Maruti Motors (p. 213).[21]

In 1969 the Indian Petrochemicals Corporation was created, starting production in 1973.

6.5.3 China: Changing the Source of Technological Transfer

Before the institutional change with the foundation of the People's Republic of China (PRC) in 1949, only oil extraction was initiated (see Table 6.2): 1926 is the first year reported by Mitchell (1998a, p. 361). However, Kambara (1974, p. 700) mentions that in 1907 there was the discovery of the Yenchang oil field – a very limited production. In 1939 the "largest oil field" before the PRC began production at Yuman (p. 700). The small-scale production before 1949 is explained by the lack of interest of international companies and "lack of knowledge of the petroleum geology" (Kambara, 1974, pp. 699–700).

After 1949, with planning and a national goal of development, the three technologies received a new priority, and the form of their absorption followed the main political changes of the period.

In oil exploration, the initial period – in the 1950s, since the First Five-Year Plan – is characterized by "technical assistance and material aid from the Soviet Union" (Kambara, 1974, p. 700): technological transfer from Russia, that may be characterized by an indirect transfer from the United States and other Western countries – see Sect. 6.5.4. Between 1952 and 1960 the production of crude oil increased from 436 to 5200 thousand of metric tons (Mitchell, 1998a, p. 362). During the 1960s, a second phase, when between 1958 and 1959 an attempt was made to use "pre-modern methods of oil production", "small scale, hand-made drilling equipment", a policy that was unsuccessful (Kambara, 1974, p. 702). Geological research led to oil discoveries in 1959, with an oil field in Taching opened in 1963 – a step toward self-sufficiency in oil production (p. 705). A third phase started in the early 1970s, with China focusing on the absorption of Western technology directly: Heymann Jr (1975, p. 32) documents purchases of plants related to "petroleum exploration and extraction plants" involving 40 contracts and US$ 127 million.

---

[21] The extension of the Indian road network in 1950–1951 was 157,000 km of surfaced roads and a total of 399,000 km. In 1970–1971 it grew to 398,000 km of surfaced roads and a total of 915,000 km (Government of India, 2019, p. 6).

Between 1970 and 1980 the crude oil production increased from 30,650 thousands of metric tons to 105,946 thousands of metric tons (Mitchell, 1998a, p. 362, p. 364).

Three oil refining periods can be demarcated. During the 1950s, a first period characterized by technology transfer from the Soviet Union: "both construction and operation of refineries was done by Russian technicians" (Kambara, 1974, p. 711). The first refinery was inaugurated in 1958 (p. 701). After 1960, a period that the Chinese had to maintain and expand the refineries by themselves (p. 711). In the early 1970s, a direct acquisition of plants from Western companies took place: Brown (1980, p. 162) lists contracts of acquisition of turn key plants between 1972 and 1978, mentioning 20 contracts in oil and gas.

The period after the Great Leap Forward and the subsequent crisis brought important changes related to this new phase with a focus on Western technologies (Lardy, 1987, p. 393), with Chen Yun engaged in a program to expand the production of fertilizers and petrochemicals. Heymann Jr (1975, p. 32) documents, between 1972 and 1975, 44 purchases of complete plants in "petrochemical and synthetic fibers" (totaling US$ 900 million) and 32 purchases of "chemical fertilizers plants" (totaling US$ 534 million). Brown (1980, p. 162) documents 4402 contracts of complete plants between 1972 and 1978, and 520 contracts related to fertilizers.

Li (2006, p. 33) reports a conversation between Mao and Stalin in January 1951, when Mao asks for help to "produce the Soviet version of Ford Model-T A3-51 automobile". This conversation illustrates how indirect technological transfer mediated by Russia took place in China also in the production of cars. In the First Five-Year Plan the production of motor vehicles was included, and in 1953 the First Automobile Works was founded.[22] The first motor vehicles are produced in 1955 (Mitchell, 1998a, p. 479). The Second Automobile Works was founded after the Cultural Revolution (Yi et al., 2017, p. 87).[23]

As in other sectors, the end of the Maoist system led to important changes in motor vehicles production: Yi et al. (2017, p. 87) divide the history of the automobile industry in China in two phases. First, "30 years under a planned economy", initially with technology coming mainly from the USSR. Second, "30 years of development under reform". Heymann Jr (1975, pp. 42–48) lists 32 "foreign industrial exhibitions in China, 1971-March 1975", and in at least 7, topics related to motor vehicles were presented to Chinese firms. Those foreign exhibitions may be intermediate steps for the second phase, when joint-ventures between Chinese firms and automobile multinational companies were established, beginning in 1984 (Yi et al., 2017, p. 88).

The late arrival of all three technologies in China is explained by the limitations of the pre-1949 political condition of China to focus on industrial policies, and the consequent limited absorptive capacities. The first Five-Year Plans designated those

---

[22] Amsden (2001, p. 213) mentions this company as a Chinese example of "automobile assembly" as "platform for national firm formation". Amsden (p. 281) classifies China between the "independents" – together with South Korea, Taiwan and India.

[23] The extension of Chinese road network in 1949 was 80,700 km, and 300 km of roads with "asphalt, oil or concrete". In 1970 it was 636,700 km – in 1975 roads with "asphalt, oil or concrete" were 92,000 km (Lyons, 1985, p. 306)

industries as important, and initial development took place – in a phase that the target of the catch up process, defined by geopolitical conditions, was the USSR. In the early 1970s another institutional reconfiguration took place, with a new focus of the Chinese catch up process: the United States and other developed nations – including Japan and emerging economies such as South Korea and Taiwan.

6.5.4 *Russia: Negotiated Technological Absorption from the West*

As discussed in the previous chapter, starting from 1917 Russia underwent important political changes: end of Czarism in 1917, the Bolshevik Revolution in October 1917, and then a sequence of economic regimes within a non-capitalist economy. In the three interrelated technologies those political changes had implications, because of the role of state-run enterprises and the emergence of five-year plans (Nove, 1992). Those state-run enterprises all had roots in initial developments during Czarism.

In oil extraction, for example, in 1898 Russia overtook the United States as the largest producer country (American Petroleum Institute, 1930, p. 8). Yergin (1991, p. 57) describes the early discoveries and oil exploration in Russia, going as far back as 1829 – Table 6.2 adopts the "date of first recorded production" listed by the American Petroleum Institute (1930, p. 10): 1863. The expansion of oil production with foreign companies and capital such as the Nobel Brothers Co. and Rothschild's investments – that articulated railways construction and connections of oil-producing regions to the world markets (p. 61). Those investments led to "the rise of Russian oil" (Yergin, 1991, pp. 58–61). Russia's leading position was reverted in 1902, by the expansion of oil drilling in the United States.

In oil refining, Larraz (2021, p. 131) documents a kerosene refinery built in Pirallahi Islands, Azerbaijan, in 1859. Yergin (1991, p. 59) mentions that in the early 1880s there were almost two hundred refineries in Baku, allowing the Russian kerosene to dominate the Russian market.

The oil extraction in Russia reached a peak in 1901 (85,168 thousands of barrels), a production only superseded in 1928 (87,800 thousands of barrels). The political situation of Civil War led to a fall to 25,430 thousands of barrels in 1920. The process of reconstruction of Russian oil drilling capacity is part of a broader politics of foreign concessions (Sutton, 1968, chapter 1). Massive transfers of Western technology took place in this process, illustrated by the concession to International Barnsdall in 1921 (p. 18). Various contracts were signed, involving Lucey Manufacturing Co (p. 21), Metropolitan-Vickens Ltd. (p. 21), Schlumberger (p. 31). The importance of this technological transfer to the modernization of Russian oil exploration can be measured by the introduction of rotary drilling by Azneft, in Baku, replacing traditional methods – while in 1913 there was no use of rotary drilling, in 1928 it was 81.3 percent of the oil drilling techniques adopted (Sutton, 1968, p. 24).

In the case of Russia, it is possible to document the introduction of cracking units in 1927 (Sutton, 1968, p. 36), after a policy decision: "in 1926 an extensive program of refining and cracking plant construction was begun to upgrade the products exported" (p. 36). In April 1927 construction started on a first refinery equipped with "latest United States technology" (p. 36). The construction of the "Batum refinery complex" was made by foreign companies: among others, Craig Co, Heckman, and Standard Oil Co. of New York. Inland refineries were constructed by Winkler-Koch, Borman, Pintsch (p. 39).

Automobiles were produced, according to Sutton (1968, p. 243) since 1901 by Russian firms (models Tansky – produced between 1901 and 1905 -, and Sevronski – between 1901 and 1905). Sutton also mentions the AMO Plant built during Czarism, that produced "few 1912-model Fiat" in 1929 (Sutton, 1971, p. 177). The first five-year plan included in its first version a production of "3,500 autos per year" (Sutton, 1968, p. 246). In this context there are negotiations with Ford that resulted in an agreement on 31 May 1929: purchase of automobiles and "technical assistance until 1938 in the construction of an automobile manufacturing plant at Nizhninovgorod", that was completed in 1933 (pp. 246–247).[24] Until 1930 other foreign firms had technical assistance contracts with Soviet automobile construction: A. J, Brandt Co., Brown Lipe Gear Ltd., Hercules Motor Co., Austin & Co, (p. 248).

The balance made by Sutton for this initial period – 1917–1930 (p. 336–339) – suggests that in all sectors related to combustion engines, the "direct impact of Western technology" had been "complete": in the "oil industry", divided into exploration, drilling and pumping technologies, oil-field electrification, pipeline and refinery construction, and market acquisition (p. 336); in "automobile construction" and in "truck construction" (p. 339).

For the period between 1930–1945, Sutton (1971, p. 180) organizes a table indicating the "Western origins of Soviet automobiles and trucks" – Ford Motor Co., Fiat spa, A. J. Brandt, Budd Co. are mentioned as sources of technology.

During the Second World War there was a huge transfer of technology under lend and lease agreements and other forms of military alliance (Sutton, 1973, pp. 3–14) – among them Hanson (2003, p. 30) highlights the reverse engineering of "trucks and Caterpillar tractors". During the mid-1960s there was an agreement with Fiat that led to the production of Lada – "a modified Fiat 124 model" (Traub-Mertz, 2017, p. 128).[25]

Regarding petrochemicals, this sector is an example of a "'belated' initiation of major new fields of technological development" (Hanson & Pavitt, 1987, p. 26). Sutton (1973, pp. 146–148) describes "Krushchev's Chemical Plan", that between 1959 and 1961 led to the purchase of "at least 50 complete chemical plants or equipment . . . from non-Soviet sources" (p. 146). Plants for petrochemical products such as polypropylene and ethylene were part of these purchases (p. 147, p. 149). In

[24] Wilkins (1964, pp. 217–225) describes this agreement and its implementation.

[25] The extension of the USSR road network in 1930 was 1,149,999 km (Montealegre, 2019, p. 235). In 1975 it was 1,421,600 km (Britannica, 1977, p. 676).

this general chemical lag, there was an important lag in the production of fertilizers (pp. 150–152).

The very detailed research prepared by Sutton (1968, 1971) is a source to track links between those three technologies of the fourth big bang and petrochemicals, as he documents contracts and agreements between the Soviet government and/or state-owned Soviet companies and multinationals from the United States and other Western countries. This transfer is important for our investigation of other peripheric regions, because the USSR, as seen in technologies from other big bangs, was an indirect provider of technologies originated elsewhere and that it could learn first and teach later – especially important for the first phase of the PRC's catch up process.

In the case of the USSR, there were multiple transfers of technology from Western sources, but once absorbed the new product or process did not have further (relevant) improvements. This is related to a more specific feature of the Soviet economy: the microeconomics of innovation under the Stalinist model – a command economy with bureaucratic planning, where innovation was basically the consequence of the construction of new plants (Hanson & Pavitt, 1987, pp. 9–12). Over time, this lack of continuity in the assimilated technology led to "obsolete competencies" diagnosticated by Pavitt (1997).

Oil had a role before and after the collapse of the USSR. Before, the falling prices of oil in the early 1980s at least contributed to the deterioration of an already problematic economy (Nove, 1992, p. 392) – a framework that shows the dependence of the Soviet economy on petroleum, an indication of the limited and incomplete catch up achieved during the 1950s and 1960s.[26]

After the collapse, with the shock therapy that organized the transition of a new variety of capitalism, there was the consolidation of Russia in the international division of labor as a source of oil – how Russia organized the oil production is a dividing line between two varieties of post-collapse capitalism: in the second form, after the rise of Putin in the late 1990s, oil production returns to state-owned companies (Albuquerque, 2018, pp. 222–227).

6.5.5 Sub-Saharan Africa: Late Emergence of Oil-Producing Countries

The extraction of crude oil in this region, although belated as shown in Table 6.2, reorganized the role of countries in the international division of labor – UNECA (2019, p. 168) divides Africa in five "economic groups", one of them is "oil exporters": a total of thirteen countries.[27] Among those thirteen countries, only

[26]Hanson (2003, pp. 121–122): "the core of the trade was an exchange of Soviet hydrocarbons, minerals, metals, furs, timbers and the like for Western farm produce and machinery".

[27]This group is defined as "countries whose oil exports are at least 20 percent higher than their oil imports" (UNECA, 2019, p. 168).

four extracted oil in 1965 (BP, 2022): Angola, Congo, Gabon, and Nigeria – a total of 312 thousand barrels daily (see Table 6.3).

The very late opening of oil exploration in Sub-Saharan Africa has roots in the lack of indications of oil production possibilities in the region: a document prepared by the American Petroleum Institute (1930, p. 6) discussed "production possibilities" in different regions, "production only on a small scale has been developed in Africa, and that chiefly in Egypt".

The demand for cars in the region was very limited in the 1930s, even compared to other regions: by 1935 the total number of "motor vehicles in use" Sub-Saharan Africa was 306,300 units (Mitchell, 1998a, pp. 746–747) – and in South Africa there were 242,000 units. The demand outside South Africa was small given the limited wealth accumulated in the previous decades. This limited demand weakens linkages that could stimulate import substitution process for cars and fuels, and weakens the pressure for road construction.

In South Africa, the wealth accumulated after the growth of the mineral-industry complex led to a multinational – Ford -, in 1924, to begin the assembly of automobiles there (Wilkins, 1964, p. 435). Later developments led to the construction of a refinery in 1954.

The construction of roads had similar motives as railways, as evaluated by Michalopoulos and Papaioannou (2020, p. 77): "colonial investments in roads were also limited", that is why in 1960 "at the end of colonization there were just a few paved and primary roads" (p. 77). The road network in Sub-Saharan Africa in 1970 was composed of 77,800 km of paved roads,[28] 142,000 km of improved roads and 899,000 km of "other" roads (Berg et al., 2016, p. 24). Independence is a benchmark for infrastructure development, in the Sub-Saharan case, although there was an important increase – for instance, paved roads increased from 77,800 km in 1970 to 185,000 km in 2005 –, it was a limited resource for development. Herbst (2014, pp. 162–164), working with data on road density (km of roads divided by the square km of land), evaluates that "during the independence period, overall road-building performance has been poor" (p. 164).

6.5.6 Latin America: New Resource for a Raw Materials Exporting Region

The rise of a new "core input" – oil – reconfigured the Latin American position in the international division of labor adding this natural resource in its exports. Celso Furtado (1976, pp. 51–54), analyzing the "new trends in the international economy" after the First World War highlighted that "the relative decline in natural fibres and the rise in petroleum are the main changes" (p. 52). In Furtado's typology, there is a change with the inclusion of Venezuela in the group of countries exporting mineral

[28] South Africa had 33,115 km of paved roads in 1970 (World Bank, 1994, p. 141).

Table 6.3 Year arrival of each of the three interrelated technologies, total production of motor vehicles, crude oil and refining capacity in 1965, in India, China, Russia, Sub-Saharan Africa and Latin America

Region	Automobile production (initial year)	Total (thousands) (*) (1965)	Crude oil production (initial year)	Total (thousand barrels daily) (1965)	Refining capacity (initial year)	Total (thousand barrels daily) (1965)
India	1926(a) 1954	72	1889	62	1901	231
China	1955	40	1926	227	1958	241
Russia	1901	814	1846/1863	4,857	1859	4,518
Sub-Saharan Africa		177 (a)		312		337
South Africa	1924(a)	173 (a)			1954	305
Nigeria	1961(a)	4 (a)	1957	274	1965	32
Mozambique						
Latin America		545		4,293		2,443
Mexico	1925(a) 1952	95	1901	362	1906	417
Argentina	1916(a) 1961	197	1908	273	1911	402
Brazil	1920(a) 1958	185	1942	93	1932	346

Source: Automobile Production: India: Mitchell (1998a, p. 479); China: Mitchell (1998a, p. 479); Russia: Mitchell (1998b, p. 551); Sub-Saharan Africa: Mitchell (1998a, p. 478); Latin America – Mitchell (1993, pp. 388–389)
(*) Total = passenger cars + commercial vehicles (Mitchell, 1993, 1998a, b)
Crude Oil Production – Data for 1965: BP (2022)
Refinery Capacity – Data for 1965: BP (2022)
OBS 1: Motor Vehicles in 1965 – United States: 11,058,000 units; World: 24,700.100 units. Crude oil in 1965 – United States: 7804 thousand barrels daily; World: 30,390 thousand barrels daily. Refining capacity in 1965 – United States: 10,390 thousand barrels daily; World: 34,785 thousand barrels daily
OBS 2: (a) Assembly only
OBS 3: Sources for the "initial years": see Table 6.2

products "in the 1930s as an exporter of petroleum" (p. 49).[29] Other countries, like Mexico, previously in that type of economy, during the first decade of the twentieth century – oil reserves were discovered in 1901 – included petroleum in its exports' portfolio (p. 50).

Earlier economic development – after the exports of agricultural products and mineral resources, that led to an initial industrialization and railway construction presented in Chaps. 3, 4 and 5 – generated income enough to create, through imports, a market for motor vehicles. That market was in the horizon of automobile multinationals that came to Latin America to sell, assemble, and manufacture motor vehicles.

In the case of Ford in Argentina, this succession took place in 1913, 1926 and 1961 (Wilkins, 1964, p. 434). In 1926 there were 273,000 passenger cars and 61,000 commercial vehicles in Argentina (Mitchell, 1993, p. 584). This market, on the one hand, created another market – for gasoline – and, on the other hand, started a process for domestic production of automobiles.[30]

Domestic markets for gasoline in Latin America, created initially by imports of cars, may explain why in some cases there were refineries before oil discoveries – like the first Brazilian refinery established in 1932, before the discovery of oil reserves in 1942.

The manufacturing of motor vehicles in Latin America contrasted with the cases of India, China, and Soviet Russia: Mexico, Argentina and Brazil are examples of "integrationists" in Amsden's evaluation (2001, p. 281). In Latin America, the institutional change represented by states with active policies of import substituting industrialization, led in the case of automobile industry to a strong participation of multinational companies in this sector. But industrial policies had requirements that induced automobile producers to buy components from domestic suppliers – an indirect stimulus for development of local firms (Amsden, 2001, p. 153). These policies in the end were able to lead some countries – Mexico and Brazil are examples of this – to an "advanced phase of underdevelopment", because they internalized part of the capital goods sector (Furtado, 1986, pp. 144–146).

An overall impact of motor vehicles in Latin America is suggested by the concluding section of Summerhill (2006) – "the rise of the motor road and the eclipse of railway" (pp. 324–326). Motor roads "complemented and substituted railway services" (p. 324–325), as they are "highly flexible" (p. 324) and have the "advantage of point-to-point delivery". Road construction in Latin America, as

[29] Venezuela began the production of crude oil in 1915, the refining in 1917, reaching in 1965 a production of 3503 thousand barrels daily of crude oil and 1102 thousand barrels daily of refined oil (BP, 2022). Furtado (2008) discusses the potential – not realized – of the use of oil export resources to industrialize the Venezuelan economy.

[30] This process in relation to motor vehicles is one illustration of a much more general trend uncovered by Furtado (1976, p. 176) as one feature of the import-substituting industrialization: "demand proceeds industrialization, which means that the demand schedule is defined before industrialization gains momentum".

illustrated by the Brazilian case, involved state-run programs that made room for local development of construction firms and learning in the field of civil engineering.[31]

6.6 The Spread of Three Interrelated Technologies and Their Uneven Impact

The impact of this fourth big bang has two peculiarities. First, it involved three interrelated technologies that shaped a three-pronged expansion process, and opened the possibility of a three-pronged assimilation process. Second, a reconfiguration of the international division of labor, with new regions in the global economy after the emergence of a new core input – oil-rich countries, included at different speeds and under different conditions.

The expansionary forces in this technological revolution were led by multinational firms, selling cars, searching and exploring for oil and eventually refining it at the periphery. This process demanded a new infrastructure, involving roads and services distributed across countries.

The assimilatory forces at the periphery faced now a larger portfolio of available technologies, with a broader set of technologies derived from the three earlier big bangs and from their transformation after the impact of the succeeding technological revolutions upon them. This broader portfolio poses new challenges, as there is the need to choose a reasonable combination of technologies that are able to be assimilated by the existing innovation system of each country/region.

This fourth big bang, as the third, was triggered in the United States, a country that completed its transition to hegemony. There is a new geopolitical scenario, after the end of the British empire and, after the Second World War, within the context of the "Cold War" (Kaldor, 1990).

In this phase institutional changes created new conditions for the strengthening of assimilatory forces: the beginning of Five-Year plans organizing the economy of USSR, India's independence in 1947, the foundation of the PRC, the beginning of the decolonization of Africa and the Middle East, and the Latin American countries with import-substituting industrialization. These changes will be related to important

[31]This process (rise of roads, eclipse of railways) lasted longer in Latin America than some other countries and regions. According to data compiled by the World Bank (1994, pp. 140–142), in 1960 the "railroad tracks" were larger than "paved roads" in Argentina (respectively 43,905 km and 22,712 km) and in Brazil (respectively 38,287 km and 12,703 km) but not in Mexico (23,369 km of railroad tracks and 25,667 km of paved roads). Brazilian paved roads overtook railroad tracks in 1970 (respectively 50,568 km and 31,847 km) and Argentinean roads overtook railroad tracks in 1980 (respectively 52,194 km and 34,077 km). For the United States and for India, already in 1960, roads were longer than railways: the data for the United States in 1960 were 2,202,101 km of paved roads and 350,116 km of railroad tracks; and in India 254,446 km of paved roads and 56,962 km of railroad tracks.

steps in the formation of national systems of innovation at the periphery, in special with the formation of national firms, national universities and research institutions that will be part of absorptive capacities in development.

These new institutional conditions face greater challenges, as there is a combination of previous relative backwardness – the assimilation of the three first technological revolutions were, at least, very incomplete – with new backwardness created by this fourth big bang. Assimilation of technologies of previous big bangs coexisted with initial efforts to absorb this last technological revolution.

At the center, especially in the United States, there is a dynamic that integrates the three technologies through various positive feedbacks, various mutual reinforcing mechanisms. These interrelated dynamics include even the appearance of a new industry as almost a by-product of oil refining: petrochemicals.

At the periphery, on the contrary, these three interrelated technologies may operate isolated. One illustration is the possibility of countries that only produce crude oil. This means a specific form of dissipation of potential linkages. Here, the political outcome of independence processes may contribute to this lack of positive feedbacks: regional fragmentation leads to economic structures that have oil resources in a small country disconnected from larger countries with potential demand for oil-processing industries. This fragmentation is the situation of Latin American and African regions.

This possibility of isolated development of these three interrelated technologies in their spread through the periphery increases its heterogeneity: there are now oil-producing and oil-exporting countries as a new category of countries. These oil-producing countries face different paths to use their accumulation of resources derived from oil exports: paths that may either allow the country to go up in the technological ladder – moving to refining and even petrochemicals -, or trap the economy in their crude oil operations.

The heterogeneity at the periphery increased also by the economic systems that were developing at that stage: in 1965 there were multinational firms drilling and refining oil, and producing motor vehicles at the periphery, but also domestic firms – private or state-run firms – in those three activities. These diverse firms are part of a more diversified periphery, now with two forms of non-capitalist economies – command economies under a reformed Stalinist model in USSR and a pendular Maoist model in China –, and different varieties of peripheric capitalism – defined by the diversification of each economy and by the role of private, domestic or foreign, and state-owned companies in their economies. These different economic forms led to different absorptive capacities: different learning paths, different forms of technological transfer, and different forms of continuity in the innovation – or improvement – processes after the initial learning and introduction of each new technology. In turn, these different absorptive capacities led to different insertions in the global economy – with variated ability to search for active insertion and changing the international division of labor.

Table 6.3 shows the outcome of the arrival and initial spread of those three interrelated technologies in our five regions.

The intensity of the spread of these three technologies is not homogeneous. In 1965, the five regions had 33.4 percent of global crude oil production, 22.3 percent of global refining capacity and 3.4 percent of global motor vehicle production. This ranking of spread intensity follows a logic related to resource availability and technological sophistication (and ease of learning): the greater participation of these five regions in crude oil production is defined by the presence of two known oil-rich regions (Russia and Latin America) and the presence of multinational companies in those regions – in Russia before 1917.[32] Refining was also done by multinationals initially. Motor vehicles production in 1965 was implemented by that variety of forms – multinationals in Latin America and Africa, private domestic firms in India, state-run firms in USSR and China.

Over time, during the period covered by Table 6.3, changes in the division of labor among firms occurred. An illustration is the process, analyzed by Beyazay-Odemis (2016, pp. 42–99), between existing oil producing firms – IOCs – and emerging specialized OSCs – providers of services and equipment for drilling and refining processes, downstream and upstream activities. As the knowledge and technology became more specialized, the role of those OSCs increased, with an interplay with metamorphoses in the frontiers of IOCs. After the nationalization of oil reserves and oil drilling activities, new NOCs had different interactions with established firms, depending on the knowledge held by these new national firms. NOCs with a greater number of strong technological skills interacted directly with OSCs, while NOCs with less accumulation of knowledge needed to interact with IOCs (Beyazay-Odemis, 2016, p. 42). Similar transformations within the international division of labor may take place for refining and motor vehicles production: what is initially produced by multinationals becomes produced by national firms, but these domestic firms will buy machines and services from specialized firms located at the center – a process that has in common a preservation of the more sophisticated technological parts of the process at the center.

Comparing with previous big bangs, this fourth had, on the one hand, the technology with the larger spread – crude oil production –, and, on the other hand, the technology with the smaller spread – motor vehicles production.

References

Achcar, G. (2013). *The people want: A radical exploration of the Arab uprising*. Saqi Books.

ACS (2021) Birth of the petrochemical industry. https://www.acs.org/education/whatischemistry/landmarks/petrochemical-industry-birthplace.html

[32]However, there were changes in the leading position of crude oil production. From 1857 to 1897, the United States were the leading country, between 1898 and 1901, Russia overtook the United States, that reassumed the leading position in 1902 (American Petroleum Institute, 1930, p. 8).

Albuquerque, E. M. (2018). Natureza da transição e tipo de capitalismo: notas sobre o fim da economia de comando na URSS e a emergência de um capitalismo dirigido pelo estado. *História Econômica & História de Empresas, 21*, 203–232.
American Petroleum Institute. (1930). *Petroleum facts and figures*. American Petroleum Institute. https://archive.org/details/petroleumfactsfi0000unse/
Amsden, A. (2001). *The rise of "the rest": Challenges to the West from late-industrializing economies*. Oxford University.
Atlas of Economic Complexity. (2023). https://atlas.cid.harvard.edu/
Berg, C., Blankespoor, B., & Selod, H. (2016). *Roads and rural development in Sub-Saharan Africa* (Policy research working paper 7729). World Bank.
Beyazay-Odemis, B. (2016). *The nature of the firm in the oil industry: International oil companies in global business*. Routledge.
Billington, D. P., & Billington, D. P., Jr. (2006). *Power, speed and form: Engineers and the making of the twentieth century*. Princeton University Press.
BP. (2022). *Statistical review of world energy, the excel data (1965–2021)*. https://www.bp.com/content/dam/bp/business-sites/en/global/corporate/xlsx/energy-economics/statistical-review/bp-stats-review-2022-consolidated-dataset-panel-format.xlsx
Britannica. (1977). *Britannica book of the year – 1977*. Encyclopaedia Britannica. https://archive.org/details/britannicabooko00ency/
Bromley, S. (1991). *American hegemony and world oil*. The Pennsylvania State University Press. https://archive.org/details/isbn_9780271007465
Brown, S. R. (1980). China's program of technology acquisition. In R. Baum (Ed.), *China's four modernizations: The new technological revolution* (pp. 153–173). Routledge.
Chandler, A., Jr. (1977). *The visible hand – The managerial revolution in America business*. The Belknap Press of Harvard University Press.
Chibber, V. (2003). *Locked in place: State-building and late industrialization in India*. Princeton University Press.
Dunning, J., & Lundan, S. (2008). *Multinational enterprises and the global economy* (2nd ed.). Edward Elgar.
Field, D. C. (1958a). Internal combustion engines. In C. Singer, E. J. Holmyard, A. R. Hall, & T. I. Williams (Eds.), *A history of technology, volume V – The late nineteenth century, c. 1850 to c. 1900* (pp. 157–175). Oxford University Press.
Field, D. C. (1958b). Mechanical road-vehicles. In C. Singer, E. J. Holmyard, A. R. Hall, & T. I. Williams (Eds.), *A history of technology, volume V – The late nineteenth century, c. 1850 to c. 1900* (pp. 414–437). Oxford University Press.
Forbes, R. J. (1958). Petroleum. In C. Singer, E. J. Holmyard, A. R. Hall, & T. I. Williams (Eds.), *A history of technology, volume V – The late nineteenth century, c. 1850 to c. 1900* (pp. 102–123). Oxford University Press.
Freeman, C., & Louçã, F. (2001). *As time goes by: From the industrial revolutions and to the information revolution*. Oxford University.
Furtado, C. (1976). *Economic development of Latin America* (2nd ed.). Cambridge University Press.
Furtado, C. (1986). *Teoria e política do desenvolvimento econômico*. Nova Cultural (2ª edição).
Furtado, C. (2008). *Ensaios sobre a Venezuela: subdesenvolvimento com abundância de divisas*. Contraponto/Centro Internacional Celso Furtado.
Gordon, R. J. (2016). *The rise and fall of American growth: The US standard of living since the Civil War*. Princeton University Press.
Government of India. (2019). *Basic road statistics of India – 2016–2017*. Government of India/Ministry of Road Transport & Highways. https://morth.nic.in/sites/default/files/Basic%20_Road_Statics_of_India.pdf
Hanieh, A. (2011). *Capitalism and class in Gulf states*. Palgrave Macmillan.
Hanson, P. (2003). *The rise and fall of the Soviet economy*. Routledge.

Hanson, P., & Pavitt, K. (1987). *The comparative economics of research, development and innovation in East and West: A survey*. Harwood Academic Publishers.
Hausman, W. J., Herner, P., & Wilkins, M. (2008). *Global electrification: Multinational enterprise and international finance in the history of light and power, 1878–2007*. Cambridge University Press.
Headrick, D. R. (1988). *The tentacles of progress: Technological transfer in the age of imperialism, 1850–1940*. Oxford University Press.
Herbst, J. (2014). *States and power in Africa: Comparative lessons in authority and control* (New ed.). Princeton University Press.
Heymann, H., Jr. (1975). *China's approach to technology acquisition: Part III: Summary observations*. Rand.
Kaldor, M. (1990). *The imaginary war: Understanding the East-West conflict*. Basil Blackwell.
Kambara, T. (1974). The petroleum industry in China. *The China Quarterly, 60*, 699–719.
Klepper, S. (1997). Industry life cycles. *Industrial and Corporate Change, 6*(1), 145–202.
Klepper, S., & Simons, K. L. (1997). Technological extinctions of industrial firms: An inquiry into their nature and causes. *Industrial and Corporate Change, 6*(2), 379–460.
Kondratiev, N. D. (1926). Long cycles of economic conjuncture. In N. Makasheva, W. J. Samuels, & V. Barnett (Eds.), *The works of Nikolai D. Kondratiev* (Vol. Volume 1, pp. 25–60). Pickering and Chato (1998).
Lardy, N. R. (1987). The Chinese economy under stress, 1958–1965. In D. Twitchett & J. K. Fairbank (Eds.), *The Cambridge history of China. Volume 14: The People's republic, part 1: The emergence of revolutionary China 1949–1965* (pp. 360–397). Cambridge University Press.
Larraz, R. (2021). A brief history of oil refining. *Substantia An International Journal of the History of Chemistry, 5*(2), 129–152. https://doi.org/10.36253/Substantia-1191
Li, H.-Y. (2006). *Mao and the economic stalinization of China, 1948–1953*. Rowman & Littlefiled Publishers, Inc.
Lyons, T. P. (1985). Transportation in Chinese development, 1952–1982. *The Journal of Developing Areas, 19*(3), 305–328.
Mbendi. (2018). *Africa: Oil and gas – Oil refining – Overview*. https://mbendi.co.za/indy/oilg/ogrf/af/p0005.htm
Metcalf, B. D., & Metcalf, T. R. (2002). *A concise history of India*. Cambridge University Press.
Michalopoulos, S. & Papaioannou, E. (2020) Historical legacies and African development. *Journal of Economic Literature, 58*(1), 53–128.
Miller, C. (2022). *Chip war: The fight for world's most critical technology*. Scribner.
Mitchell, B. R. (1993). *International historical statistics – The Americas, 1750–1988* (2nd ed.). Stockton Press.
Mitchell, B. R. (1998a). *International historical statistics – Africa, Asia & Oceania, 1750–1993* (3rd ed.). Macmillan Reference Ltd/Stockton Press.
Mitchell, B. R. (1998b). *International historical statistics – Europe, 1750–1993* (3rd ed.). Macmillan Reference Ltd/Groves' Dictionaries, Inc.
Montealegre, A. A. (2019). *A global history of the road: Road construction and maintenance and use in Colombia, Argentina, French West Africa and the Algerian Sahara, 1930–1970*. Thesis for Doctor of Philosophy, King's College, London.
Morais, J. M. (2013). *Petrobrás em águas profundas*. IPEA.
Muzaka, V. (2018). *Food, health and the knowledge economy: The state and intellectual property rights in India and Brazil*. Palgrave Macmillan.
Nove, A. (1992). *An economic history of the USSR – 1917–1991* (3rd ed.). Penguin.
Pavitt, K. (1997). Transforming centrally planned systems of science and technology: The problem of obsolete competencies. In D. A. Dyer (Ed.), *The technology of transition: Science and technology policies for transition countries* (pp. 43–60). Central European University Press.
Perez, C. (2010). Technological revolutions and techno-economic paradigms. *Cambridge Journal of Economics, 34*(1), 185–202.

Remesh, B. P. (2017). An "automotive revolution" in neoliberal India: Evolution, industrial structure, trends and prospects. In R. Traub-Mertz (Ed.), *The automotive sector in emerging economies: Industrial policies, market dynamics and trade unions. Trends & perspectives in Brazil, China, India, Mexico and Russia* (pp. 105–126). Friedrich Ebert Stiftung.

Rosenberg, N. (1998). Chemical engineering as a general purpose technology. In E. Helpman (Ed.), *General purpose technologies and economic growth* (pp. 167–192). The MIT Press.

Sorkhabi, R. (2008). The emergence of Arabian oil industry. *Geoexpro, 5*(6) https://geoexpro.com/the-emergence-of-the-arabian-oil-industry/

Summerhill, W. R. (2006) The development of infrastructure. In: Bulmer-thomas, V.; Coatsworth, J. H.; Conde, R. C. (eds) The Cambridge Economic History of Latin America, v. 2: The long twentieth century. Cambridge: Cambridge University Press, pp. 293–397.

Sutton, A. C. (1968). *Western technology and Soviet economic development – 1917 to 1930.* Hoover Institution Publication. https://archive.org/details/Sutton%2D%2DWestern-Technology-1917-1930

Sutton, A. C. (1971). *Western technology and Soviet economic development –1930 to 1945.* Hoover Institution Press/Stanford University. https://archive.org/details/Sutton%2D%2DWestern-Technology-1930-1945

Sutton, A. C. (1973). *Western technology and Soviet economic development –1945 to 1960.* Hoover Institution Press/Stanford University. https://archive.org/details/Sutton%2D%2DWestern-Technology-1945-1965

Tang, F. C. (1994). Analyzing the oil refining industry in developing countries: A comparative study of China and India. *The Journal of Energy and Development, 19*(2), 159–178.

The Economist. (2022, February 19). *How Chinese firms have dominated African infrastructure.* https://www.economist.com/middle-east-and-africa/how-chinese-firms-have-dominated-african-infrastructure/21807721

Traub-Mertz, R. (2017). Automotive industry in Russia: Between growth and decline. In R. Traub-Mertz (Ed.), *The automotive sector in emerging economies: Industrial policies, market dynamics and trade unions. Trends & perspectives in Brazil, China, India, Mexico and Russia* (pp. 127–147). Friedrich Ebert Stiftung.

UNECA. (2019). *Economic report Africa 2019.* UNECA.

US Bureau of the Census. (1960). *Historical statistics of the United States, colonial times to 1957 – Chapter Q: Transportation* (pp. 423–470). Government Printing Office/US Department of Commerce. https://www2.census.gov/library/publications/1960/compendia/hist_stats_colonial-1957/hist_stats_colonial-1957-chQ.pdf

US Department of Transportation. Federal Highway Administration. (1976). *America's highway: A history of the federal-aid program.* Federal Highway Administration.

Wilkins, M. (1964). *American business abroad: Ford on six continents.* Wayne State University Press. https://archive.org/details/americanbusiness0000wilk

Wilkins, M. (1974). *The maturing of multinational enterprise: American business abroad from 1914 to 1970.* Harvard University Press.

World Bank. (1994). *Infrastructure for development: World development report 1994.* World Bank.

Yergin, D. (1991). *The prize: The epic quest for oil, money and power.* Simon & Schuster.

Yi, C., Ying, H., & Xueling, G. (2017). Development and structure of the automobile industry in China. In R. Traub-Mertz (Ed.), *The automotive sector in emerging economies: Industrial policies, market dynamics and trade unions. Trends & perspectives in Brazil, China, India, Mexico and Russia* (pp. 86–104). Friedrich Ebert Stiftung.

Chapter 7
The Microprocessor and the World Wide Web – Two Technological Revolutions and a Second Reversal? – 1971, 1991

7.1 Introducion

For Carlota Perez (2010, p. 190) the invention of the microprocessor in 1971 by Intel,[1] in the United States, is the big bang of the fifth technological revolution. This invention triggered a subsequent stream of innovation that led to another technological revolution – the sixth, with the invention of the world wide web (www) in 1991, at the CERN, Switzerland, Europe (ACM, 2016).[2]

This chapter evaluates those two successive big bangs in an integrated way, as this intertemporal sequence is related to interactions and ramifications that are peculiarities of these technological revolutions: there are innovations in four different technologies that have positive feedbacks and virtuous cycles among them – in the case of the leading country for those developments: the United States. As Sect. 7.2 summarizes, based on available literature, these four technologies are in the following sectors: components/semiconductors (Intel's 1971 microprocessor is here), computers, software, and networks (Berners-Lee's 1991 www is here).

This summary, focusing on these four technological paths, is an introduction to an investigation of their diffusion across the periphery, because in the interplay between expansionary and assimilatory forces, the number of options available to countries becomes larger over time. These different technologies evolve, become more specialized, and reorganize the international division of labor as different locational logics are defined and redefined.

[1] USPTO 3,821,715, filed in 01/22/1973.

[2] The invention of the www as the sixth big bang is suggested, tentatively, in Albuquerque (2019). Evidence of this invention as a starting point for a new phase of capitalism may be inferred by important publications that use different expressions to name something new that could be taking place in global capitalism: "platform capitalism" (Srnicek, 2017), "digital economy" (UNCTAD, 2019), "data economy" (World Bank, 2021).

E. da Motta e Albuquerque, *Technological Revolutions and the Periphery*, Contributions to Economics, https://doi.org/10.1007/978-3-031-43436-5_7

This dynamic, for the first time, faced by a set of independent countries that may build domestic policies for development – a new geopolitical context, consolidated after the end of the Second World War and the creation of the United Nations (see Table 7.2).

This new geopolitical scenario – the hegemony of the United States – passed through different phases after 1945, demonstrating the strong flexibility that the new hegemonic country had to have to reshape and rearrange the world order under different realities: Cold War – and its different phases –, end of the USSR, emergence of China (Panitch & Gindin, 2012). For this strong flexibility, technological leadership is an important factor.

In this new scenario, the five regions/countries investigated here had, in 1971, some form of industrial policy or development policy. In 1971, as the conclusion of Chap. 6 has shown, all regions faced a superposition of backwardnesses – no previous technological revolution had spread very broadly there, with a combination between the renewal of technological gaps and different – and heterogeneous – industrial and technological structures. These different industrial and technological structures – beginnings of innovation systems at the periphery – were also uneven within each country, leading to a phenomenon that is related to underdevelopment: the polarity of modernization and marginalization" (Furtado, 1987, p. 223). This uneven internal structure, related to what Furtado (1986, pp. 144–146) mentions as "advanced phase of underdevelopment",[3] enabled peripheric countries to follow and to attempt to internalize the production of new technologies and industries related to these four technologies. The sequence of innovations within these four technologies puts forward new questions for the formulation and implementation of industrial policies: is it possible to absorb all technologies together? Is there an order in this absorption process? Can these technologies be disaggregated, and a country should focus on only one of them?

This chapter is organized to follow these major changes that led, as the last section shows, to an even more heterogeneous periphery, with nuclei of capitalist accumulations stronger, and a new geopolitical framework that may suggest a new reversal. This new reversal involves the rise of East Asian economies and China. In the case of China, the formation of a national system of innovation – underpinning its growing absorption capabilities acquired by learning with development experiences of other countries (Lee, 2022; Prates, 2022) – has allowed it to internalize almost all technologies generated at the center since 1771. This process of Chinese growth led, in 2013, its GDP (measured in PPP constant 2011 international $) to overtake that of the United States (World Bank, 2023).[4] A new reversal, because according to Maddison data, between 1870 and 1890 the United States GDP

[3]In Portuguese: "fase superior do subdesenvolvimento" (Furtado, 1986, p. 145).

[4]In 2013 China's GDP (PPP in constant 2011 international $) was 16.22 trillion and the United States' 16.13 trillion (World Bank, 2023)

overtook the Chinese (Maddison, 2010).[5] In current dollars China is still behind the United States, but the Chinese growth has probably changed the geopolitical scene: Miller's book on "the most critical technology" – semiconductors – begins his conclusion with a long discussion on "China's challenge" (2022, pp. 243–291).

7.2 Before the Microprocessor and After the WWW

This section summarizes the interactions between four interrelated technologies that shape the computer industry. Based on a broad available literature, this summary is presented in Table 7.1. There are different feedbacks between those dimensions, all four taking place in the United States – a reference to backward and forward linkages, within one economy: a phenomenon that is very difficult to be repeated elsewhere, as size matters. Size in terms of market demand but also in terms of available capabilities – scientific, technological, and industrial. These capabilities, in special the scientific capabilities, are important for this new technological revolution given its increasing scientific dependence.

A country with a national innovation system has strong learning capabilities (see Appendix 1, chapter 1, topic A.2). This feature is well illustrated by an analysis of international knowledge flows before the invention of the transistor in the Bell Labs – two patents (US 2,524,035 and US 2,569,347) registered that invention. The three inventors in these patents (Bardeen, Brattain and Shockley) received the Nobel Prize in 1956 "for their researches on semiconductors and their discovery of the transistor effect" (Nobel Prize, 2023). Alferov (2000, p. 414) indicates B. Davydov as an author of "the first diffusion theory of the p-n heterojunction rectification, which became the base for W. Shockley's p-n junction theory". One of B. Davydov's papers is cited by Bardeen (1947, p. 718), that by its turn is cited by Shockley (1950, p. 34). A. I. Offe is also cited by them, an indication of the awareness in the Bell Labs of the research done at the Russian institute.[6] In his Nobel Lecture Bardeen (1956, p. 319) again cites Davydov, and Bardeen's Lecture is cited by Shockley (1956, p. 345, p. 350).[7]

These international knowledge flows traced by citations of scientific papers show how the research done at the Bell Labs assimilated knowledge produced in the USSR during the invention process of the transistor. This is an illustration of assimilation before the big bang, showing that there is an interplay between assimilation by the

[5]In 1870, China's GDP was 189,740 million (1990 International Geary-Khamis) dollars, and the United States' GDP was 98,374 million dollars, while in 1890 China's GDP was 205,379 million dollars and the United States' GDP was 214,174 million dollars (Maddison, 2010).

[6]Graham (1993, pp. 209–210) presents the Soviet works on semiconductors and solid-state physics during the 1930s and 1940s. The Institute created by A. F. Ioffe is highlighted by Graham (p. 209).

[7]Another form of tracking this international knowledge flow, is through the patent US 2,524,035 that cites Joffe (1945) that cites B. Davydov (Joffe, 1945, p. 224).

Table 7.1 Timeline of innovations related to components, computers, software and networks in the leading countries (United States and Europe) (1904–2013)

Year	Components/semiconductors	Computers	Software	Network	Other
1904	Thermionic valve				
1946		ENIAC (17,468 valves)	1945–1964: "Stored programs"		
1947	Transistor (AT&T)				
1952	Beginning of semiconductor industry				
1953		IBM 701 (valves)			
1954					Pocket radio transistors
1957					Fairchild founded
1958	Integrated circuit – IC – (Fairchild and TI)	IBM 7090 (>50,000 transistors)			
1959		PDP-1 (minicomputer)			
1964		IBM 360 (ICs) Univac, Burroughs, RCA: ICs in minicomputers	1965–1978: "Software vendors"		
1968					Intel founded
1969				ARPANET	
1970					
1971	Microprocessor (Intel)				Pocket calculator
1975		Microcomputer			
1977		Beginning of microcomputer industry	1978–1994: "Package software"		
1982		IBM PC			ASML founded
1983	Motorola 68,000–68,000 transistors	Apple Lisa – Two million users			
1985				NSFNET	
1990	Motorola 68,030–273,00 transistors	Next comp – 53 million users			
1991				WWW	
1992					Intel: $200 million EUV
1996			1994 – ???: "Networking"		ASML invests in EUV
2010	ASML – First EUV lithography machine				

Source: Author's elaboration, based on Freeman and Louçã (2001), Miller (2022), and Reid (2001) for components/semiconductors; Campbell (1976), Malerba and Orsenigo (1996), and Chandler (2005) for computers; Mowery (1999) for software; Greenstein (2015) for networks; Miller (2022) for other.

center of knowledge available in the whole world before the unleashing of the expansionary forces of a new technological revolution – the fifth big bang in this case, as shown in Table 7.1.

This international flow for the invention of the transistor is just an example of one peculiarity of the processes summarized in Table 7.1: the high level of internationalization in key events described there. Three comments may illustrate other features of this level of internationalization.

First, the invention of the microprocessor, in 1971, as described by Reid (2001, p. 174): "[t]he story of the microprocessor begins in Tokyo". In 1969, a Japanese manufacturer of calculating machines, Busicon, presented to Intel a demand for "the design and production of twelve interlinked chips for the new line of machines" (p. 174). The outcome of this demand in 1971 was a "general-purpose CPU-on-a-chip" (p. 176). Why did the demand come from Japan? Chandler (2005, chapter 3) describes the rise of Japan in consumer electronics, an industrial achievement related to the consolidation of its national system of innovation (Freeman, 1987). A process that would be emulated in East Asia, initially by South Korea and Taiwan, and later by China.

Second, the invention of the www, in 1991, took place at an international research center, the CERN, in Switzerland. It is an invention that is international by definition: a network that crosses national boundaries and triggers a global dynamic to occupy economically a new global – and digital – sphere, the www.

Third, in an industry populated by multinational firms (IBM, Intel, Apple, Microsoft etc.) there is the development of a specialized sector producing machines for chipmaking. Among those machine-producing firms, there is a Dutch-headquartered multinational firm – ASML (The Economist, 2020; Clark, 2022; CNBC, 2022) – that in 2010 shipped its first EUV lithography machine (ASML, 2023) – a technological development in chipmaking. This development led to new models of EUV machines that are composed of 457,329 parts (Miller, 2022, p. 322) and produced by a network of 4700 suppliers from different countries (ASML, 2022). This level of international sourcing is a necessary technological step to produce chips for a steady growing demand which intensified in this post-www phase.

All these developments are interconnected and Table 7.1 should be read as a guide for these multidimensional interactions.

The invention of the microprocessor in 1971 (Table 7.1 column of semiconductors) took place within an industry whose beginnings can be traced back to 1952 (Chandler, 2005, p. 123). The microprocessor was a precondition for a change in computers and the emergence of the microcomputer in 1975 (Table 7.1 column of computers), thus bringing in a new era – the era of PCs (Chandler, 2005, p. 134). This lag – 4 years – between the invention of semiconductors and their application in computers was the shortest, compared to the first transistorized computer – 11 years – and the first computer using integrated circuits – 6 years.

The development of PCs led to an explosion of computer users – in 1983, two million Apple Lisa PCs, equipped with a 68,000 transistors chip, and, in 1990, 53 million of Next Comp PCs, equipped with a 273,000 transistors chip. This quantitative growth opened new opportunities and drove the need for networking, already in development after the ARPANET in 1969 and the NSFNET in 1985, setting the stage for the invention of the www in 1991 – the first website, a number that grew to 255 million in 2010.

This new digital and global sphere – the www – will be occupied by a set of new firms, exploring a new strategic commodity – the search. After the invention of a browser in 1992 – by Mosaic – there is a path that led to a new algorithm – Google, invented in 1998.[8] This new algorithm triggers a new chain of events that reinforces the growth of the www, leading to new sources of value production through data production, extraction, generation, and processing. This new dynamic in a new sphere demands a huge data infrastructure both for data development – data centers, populated by computers and servers – and for users' access – computers, laptops, cell phones, smart phones –, all chip-based commodities: in 2021, 1.15 trillion semiconductors were sold globally (Semiconductor Industry Association, 2022).

Table 7.1 is an attempt to show how those developments are interconnected and how those interconnections are part of a dynamic formed around semiconductors. One example of those interconnections not presented in Table 7.1 is a movement from firms created in the www – as Google, for example – that recently established divisions to produce chips, a necessary development given the very specific demands for semiconductors able to support their artificial intelligence investments (CNBC, 2021). Other post-www firms are doing the same – Amazon, for instance, bought a chipmaker firm, Annapurna Labs, in 2015 (The Information, 2021).

Table 7.1 could also be read as a guide for the genealogy of these processes. The Intel microprocessor invented in 1971 was a device to integrate twelve different integrated circuits – the integrated circuit is a 1958 invention by two firms, TI and Fairchild, to answer to a big problem – "tyranny of numbers" (Reid, 2001, p. 61),[9] as the number of connections between transistors had limits – and computers needed more and more transistors. Transistors, by their turn, invented in 1947,[10] overcame limits of vacuum tubes (Kilby, 2000, pp. 475–476) – that is why Table 7.1 begins in 1904, with the invention of the vacuum tube – thermionic valve, by J. A. Fleming in the United Kingdom, an invention related to the third big bang.[11] The vacuum tube was improved during the twentieth century and was the component of the first computer – ENIAC, invented in 1946 –,[12] and equipped the IBM 701 in 1953.

As is well known, the evolution of integrated circuits from 1958 onwards had a logic – Moore's Law – that reduced costs and improved the quality of the chips – more transistors in less space – that had impacts on firms and countries trying to enter

[8] USPTO 6,285,999, filed in 01/09/1998.

[9] USPTO 2,981,877, filed in 07/30/1959; USPTO 3,138,743, filed in 02/06/1959.

[10] USPTO 2,524,035, filed in 06/17/1948, and USPTO 2,569,347, filed in 06/26/1948.

[11] GB patent 24,850, filed in 11/16/1904.

[12] USPTO 3,120,606, filed in 06/26/1947.

in this industry. On the one hand, this process means ongoing improvement, changes that demand more sophisticated machines to print those smaller circuits on smaller chips. On the other hand, this increasing sophistication of the manufacturing process extended the production chain, adding more and more stages to it. These two processes had different impacts for entry: the constant improvement creates more difficulties for entry, and tougher conditions for surviving in this industry. The extension of the manufacturing chain opened the possibility of slicing it up and distributing its different stages among different countries – opportunities for backward countries to join less sophisticated stages of this chain.

Those processes mapped in Table 7.1 led to the supply of cheap and powerful semiconductors that impacted all existing industries – as electricity had done before: new machines using semiconductor devices transformed all industries, from textile machines, transport vehicles, electricity grids – new challenges and opportunities for the periphery. This is another example of how the last big bang impacts all previous technologies.

7.3 Expansionary Forces in Four Interrelated Technologies

The fifth big bang took place in a global scenario that had the multinational firm as a key organizational form (Hymer, 1970; Freeman, 1987, p. 70). In the early 1960s, IBM had an international position and a global dominance without precedence: "less than a decade after the creation of the first electronic computer, IBM had approximately 80 percent of U.S. and global markets" (Chandler, 2005, p. 81). IBM was an international firm before its entry in the emerging electronic computer industry: in 1940 IBM had subsidiaries in 17 countries (Machado, 2017, p. 25). After its entry in the computer industry, IBM's global presence grew, reaching 34 countries in 1970, the year before the invention of the microprocessor (Machado, 2017, p. 25). In many countries the arrival of the first IBM computer is an important event in their history of electronic computing: examples are Mexico (Nava et al., 2015, p. 13), Argentina (Carnota, 2015, p. 40) and India (Sharma, 2015, pp. 55–57).

The four different technologies summarized in Table 7.1 had different expansionary forces – inter-sectoral differences and intertemporal differences, which include intertemporal differences within the same technology.

In semiconductors, for instance, Fairchild was the first firm to offshore production, in 1963 (Miller, 2022, p. 54) – TI, Motorola and others followed. As the sector grew and the manufacturing processes became more complex – the level of miniaturization and the progress following Moore's Law intensified, subsectors were created – memory chips, logic chips – and a new specialized machine-making sector developed. This more diversified and segmented sector made room for other forms of international distribution of labor within new global value chains, that could be split in different stages of the chip production process through different countries.[13] Over time, this fragmentation led to the rise of fabless firms, with newer possibilities of international distribution of chip production – a foundry/fabless model (Miller, 2022, pp. 209–214). The sophistication of this process involves increasingly complex chipmaking-machines: an internationally orchestrated process coordinated by multinational firms such as ASML, a Dutch firm (Chuma, 2006; Miller, 2022, pp. 186–189).

The logic of expansion in computers changed as the phase of mainframes was followed by the phase of PCs.

In software, changes in semiconductors and computers, especially after the rise of PCs and the concomitant new era of package software (see Table 7.1), made room for a new distribution of international labor in this regard, both within multinationals and under their coordination.

The emergence of the www brought new changes: the www affected the boundaries of multinational corporations – affecting both their internal division of innovative labor (Cantwell, 2009), and their capacity to orchestrate global chains and contract suppliers abroad (UNCTAD, 2011, 2013). New firms populating that digital continent became international instantly, given the global reach of www. The growth of leading firms of this new digital continent led to strong global market concentration. According to a survey of *The Economist* (2018, p. 11), the global market share of sectors of a post-www economy conquered by leading firms were: 91% for Google in search, 37% for Amazon in online retail, 66% for Facebook in social media, and 45% for Apple in "smartphone web traffic".

All these changes combined presented new challenges and new possibilities for development in a global scale, specially to countries and regions at the periphery. These changes affected the nature of the expansionary forces during those two big bangs – with new capacities to expand and to integrate different countries with very specific roles in a changing international division of labor.

7.4 A Note on Institutional Changes: A Qualitative Change in Absorptive Capacities at the Periphery

The fifth big bang, in 1971, is the first technological revolution to be witnessed by independent countries at the periphery, and in the case of our regions, by an independent India, by a reunified China – without colonial presence in its territory –, and by a largely independent Africa (see Table 6.1). Independent countries are important for stronger absorptive capacities, given the ability to at least formulate developmental policies and to take initial steps for the formation of national systems

[13] See Accretech (2023) for a graphic display of the chip manufacturing process divided into its different stages: device design, mask manufacturing, wafer manufacturing, front-end, wafer test, and back-end.

of innovation. Independence is a step necessary to changes discussed in Chaps. 5 and 6 – such as the "domestication" of electric utilities after the Second World War and the nationalization of oil companies in the 1960s and 1970s. Further, those processes of attaining local control of those companies involve an increase in the technological skills.

Independent India and the PRC created in the early 1950s important institutions of their innovation systems: research institutes like the Indian Institute of Technology and the Chinese Academy of Sciences. In Africa, it is not uncommon to find an association between independence movements and the creation of national universities.

Institutional change in the United States and in East Asia has important implications for the two technological revolutions investigated in this chapter, as they shape key events presented in Table 7.1, as evaluated in the next section.

In the United States, the Second World War and the post-war phase introduced a structural change in their innovation system, the rise of military involvement in science and technology, a characteristic that may be quantified by the defense-related investments in basic research (Mowery & Rosenberg, 1993). This institutional change has direct influence on the emergence of the technologies described in Table 7.1. The ENIAC was "built by the US Army at the University of Pennsylvania" (Miller, 2022, p. 7); the initial demand for transistors, integrated circuits, and microprocessors was basically for defense purposes (Miller, 2022, pp. 74–75), the revitalization of US semiconductor industry included the Department of Defense among its institutional leaders (Miller, 2022, p. 99–100), Arpanet is a project initiated by DARPA (Greenstein, 2015, p. 24), IBM is a firm with strong involvement in defense contracts (Pugh, 1995, chapter 15; Miller, 2022, p. 99) and even a computer language such as COBOL had the Department of Defense involved (Pugh, 1995, pp. 196–197).

In the case of East Asia, the catch-up process of Japan during the 1950s and 1960s (Freeman, 1987; Odagiri & Goto, 1993), and the lessons that it taught to South Korea (Amsden, 1989) and Taiwan (Wade, 1990) reshaped the region – new lessons for China (Weber, 2021, p. 237) and a new geography of semiconductor industry (Kimura, 1997, Mathews & Cho, 2000). The strength of Japan in consumer electronics in the late 1960s (Chandler, 2005, chapter 3) contributes to the initial movements of the fifth big bang – a demand from a Japanese electronic calculator manufacturer (Busicon) to Intel in 1969 led to the invention of the microprocessor (Reid, 2001, pp. 174–176).

Table 7.2 summarizes the main changes in our five regions, in 1991 and 2011. The collapse of the Soviet Union in 1991 is a major institutional change, shaping a new geopolitical scenario (Buzan, 2004) and a new phase in the United States hegemony (Panitch & Gindin, 2012). Two new varieties of capitalism are consolidated in 2011, both as consequences of different transitions from non-capitalist economies – and these forms of transition have implications on absorptive capacities, shaping them. The consolidation of China as the second largest economy is a tectonic change that opens another new phase in the geopolitical scenario. A new variety of capitalism is consolidated in India (Drèze & Sen, 2002, 2013). In Latin America there is the end of import-substituting industrialization (CGEE, 2013).

Table 7.2 Political organization in the India, China, Russia, Latin America and Sub-Saharan Africa (1991 and 2011)

Region	1991	2011
India	Reforms. End of political hegemony of the INC	A new variety of peripheric capitalism
China	End of Maoist model by late 1970s – Dual-track gradual reforms leading to a new variety of capitalism. Catch-up project with the United States as reference	State-led variety of capitalism
Russia	Crisis of the Stalinist model. Gorbachev. End of the USSR. Transition through shock therapy leading to a new variety of capitalism	Post-shock therapy variety of capitalism. Crisis. State-led variety of capitalism
Africa	Consolidation of independent African nations. Final crisis of apartheid in South Africa	Post-apartheid South Africa.
Latin America	Independent and fragmented states. End of import substitution industrialization	Independent and fragmented states

Source: Author's elaboration based on the literature reviewed in this chapter

These changes, especially the collapse of the Soviet Union and the rise of China may be directly related to the fifth and sixth technological revolutions: during Gorbachev's reforms, the "computer test case" faced by Russia (Mandel, 1989, pp. 10–11) may have been one of the factors behind the final crisis of the Stalinist model, and the entry of China in all those four technologies listed in Table 7.1 might be related to its persistent economic growth after the early 1970s (Naughton, 2007).

7.5 Assimilatory Forces: More Resources to Cope with Even Bigger Challenges

The institutional changes summarized in Tables 6.1 and 7.2 created a new framework for assimilatory forces: all countries and regions investigated in this book could now as independent countries design and implement policies for industrial and economic development. And they did: both Independent India and the PRC had their first Five-Year plans in early 1950s, the USSR after the Second World War prepared its fourth Five-Year plan, newly independent African countries had development plans and Latin America entered a new phase following import-substituting industrialization.

In the early 1950s, all those policies and plans had to deal with a backlog of technologies not completely incorporated – see concluding sections of Chaps. 3, 4, 5 and 6 (Tables 3.3, 4.2, 5.3 and 6.3) – and with those new emerging technologies – transistors and computers.

Again, these five regions face this combination between old backwardness and new gaps after new big bangs. Once more, this new big bang does not appear as a single and isolated technology, but as a set of interrelated technologies, as described in Table 7.1. It took some time for these four interrelated technologies become target for absorption: components and computers first, next software, and then networking enabled by the sixth big bang.

These four interrelated technologies shown in Table 7.1 bring new challenges to absorptive capacity: the science dependence of semiconductors, computers, software, and networking is high, demanding domestic investment in educational and scientific institutions. New scientific disciplines are necessary now: solid-state physics, computer sciences. New engineering fields arise: electronics engineering, computer specialists, programmers. Even to buy a computer it is necessary knowledge investments to learn how to operate them.

Table 7.3 summarizes the data on the arrival of these four technologies in our five regions.

In common with the third big bang, the networking technology – basically access to the www – has characteristics of public utility or infrastructure, in all the places it was provided: an infrastructure for the operation of global firms that populate the www.

This section analyses how these technologies spread through these five regions and presents a case study: Taiwan as a producer of semiconductors. This case study

Table 7.3 Year of arrival of each of the four interrelated technologies in India, China, Russia, Sub-Saharan Africa and Latin America

Region	Semi-conductors	Computers	Software	Network (*)
India		1959	1968	2002
China	1956(t) 1962(i) 2001(m)	1958	1974	2000
Russia	1956(t) 1964(i) Mid-1970s(m)	1951	Mid-1950s	1999
Sub-Saharan Africa				
South Africa	1984	Mid-1970s	1969	1997
Nigeria				2004
Mozambique				2008
Latin America				
Mexico		1982		
Argentina		1962		1999
Brazil	Early 1980s(i)	1972	Early 1970s	1998

Source: Semiconductors: (t) transistors, (i) integrated circuits, (m) microprocessor: China: Fuller (2016, p. 17, p. 117), People's Daily (2021); Russia: Miller (2022, p. 36, p. 42), Judy and Clough (1989, p. 314); South Africa (Evertiq, 2021); Brazil (Melo et al., 2001, p. 14, pp. 16–17)
Computers: India: Sharma (2015, p. 20); China: Lu (2000, p. 8); Russia: Judy and Clough (1989, p. 253); South Africa: Leonard (1978, p. 9); Mexico: Nava et al. (2015, p. 7); Argentina: Babini (2006, pp. 197–198); Brazil: Marques (2015b, p. 64).
Software: India: Sharma (2015, p. 45); China: Guo and Sun (1987, p. 114); Russia: Judy (1970, p. 59); South Africa: Software AG South Africa (2023); Brazil: Botelho et al. (2005, p. 104)
Networks: World Bank (2023)
OBS: (*) Networks: Initial year defined as the year when the total of individuals using internet became greater than 1% of the population. The United States achieved that percentage in 1991

uses Taiwan as an economic experiment of technology absorption, and may be compared with the case study of the previous chapter on Saudi Arabia. With no known oil reserves until 1938 in Saudi Arabia and no production of chips until 1969 in Taiwan, in 2018 these products had almost the same weight in their exports: according to the Atlas of Economic Complexity, Saudi Arabia exported $138.6 billion in crude oil and Taiwan exported $138.7 in electronic integrated circuits. How Taiwan achieved this is the subject of the next sub-section – an economic experiment certainly followed with interest by China.

7.5.1 Taiwan as a Case Study: Semiconductors and Lessons for Development

There are comprehensive studies on Taiwan and its development: examples as Wade (1990) and Hou and Gee (1993). This section focuses on a more specific point: how Taiwan developed absorption capacity to become an important player in the semiconductor industry. This focus would help to understand Taiwan as an economic experiment for development of that industry.

Taiwan cannot be understood outside the political and economic framework of a rising East Asian economy, initially around the Japanese post-war catch-up. Freeman (1995, p. 13) presents a scheme that highlights the influence of Japan's experience, capital and investments in the region. Furthermore, the rise of Japan in electronics in general (Chandler, 2005, chapter 3) and in semiconductors specifically (Kimura, 1997)[14] reverberates in Taiwan.

In a broader movement of semiconductor production to East Asia – opened by Fairchild outsourcing to Hong Kong – TI began its production in Taiwan in 1969 (Miller, 2022, p. 65).

However, the key movements took place within Taiwan, articulated with the formation of its national innovation system, in a process that had a strategy for information industries (Hou & Gee, 1993, pp. 396–403): a lesson on one form of construction of absorptive capacity. Since the beginning there was knowledge about what was happening in the leading countries: Mathews and Cho (2000, p. 158) report Y. S. Sun visiting Princeton in 1974 with a perception that "electronics industry is the key for Taiwan future high-tech development".

The creation of government research institutes has a key role in this process. In 1973 the Industrial Technology Research Institute (ITRI) is founded, and in 1974 one division of ITRI is created with the task of "developing the technological

---

[14] Sony acquired the license to produce transistors in 1953 (Chandler, 2005, p. 55), licenses from TI and Fairchild to produce ICs in the 1960s (Kimura, 1997, p. 124), Japan dominated the market for memories in the 1980s, and produced machines for chipmaking (Kimura, 1997, p. 131).

capabilities needed to generate a semiconductor industry": the Electronic Research and Service Organization (ERSO) (Mathews & Cho, 2000, p. 158).[15] In 1979 the Institute for Information Industry (III) was created (Hou & Gee, 1993, p. 396). In 1980 the Hinch/ITRI/Tsinghua Complex is founded (Mathews & Cho, 2000, p. 160).

This group of institutions supported a strong process of technological transfer from developed countries, that combined associations and joint-ventures with multinationals and new firms – spin-offs from those institutes. ERSO developed a mechanism for technology absorption, learning and understanding targeted technologies and then organized its diffusion, that concluded with the formation of a spin-off company (Huo & Gee, 1993, p. 398).

In the 1980s there were six chipmaking firms operating in Taiwan (Huo & Gee, 1993, pp. 397–399), all of them with ERSO as a source of technology (p. 399) – one of them was TSMC, founded in 1987, a joint venture between the ITRI and Philips. TSMC is a key actor for the new foundry/fabless model, assuming a specialized role as foundry (Miller, 2022, pp. 163–164; pp. 166–167).[16]

The outcome of this process is presented in a map by Miller (2022, p. 197) – "East Asia produces" – that shows Taiwan with "41 percent of all processor chips and more than 90 percent of the most advanced chips". This outcome reshaped the international division of labor, with Taiwan, according the Atlas of Economic Complexity, becoming the major exporter of "electronic integrated circuits" – 21.13% of a total $658 billion global exports in 2018.

These policies were part of the general formation of Taiwanese innovation system, one of the sources of an important achievement: the overcoming of underdevelopment (Furtado, 1992, pp. 51–52).

Those achievements were followed in China during the long preparation of its reforms: lessons that could be used for a "coastal development strategy" (Weber, 2021, p. 237). The implications of Taiwanese development in chipmaking for China can also be perceived from the UNCTAD report, that listed the "top 10 contract manufacturers in electronics": there are five firms from Taiwan, all with "major overseas production bases" located in China (UNCTAD, 2011, p. 219).

[15]The influence of the Japanese experience is highlighted by Mathews and Cho (2000, p. 158): "ERSO scoured the world for knowledge of IC fabrication, emulating Japanese methods of study tours and knowledge leverage" and used a "Princeton-based network of advisers".

[16]Mathews and Cho (2000, p. 162) summarize in four stages the "evolution of Taiwanese semiconductor industry": preparation (pre-1976), seeding (1976–1979), technological absorption and propagation (1980–1988), and sustainability (1989–1998). The public sector R&D has an important role in all stages.

7.5.2 Russia: Parity, Widening the Gap, and Destruction

The history of computers in Russia begins between 1948 (Prokhorov, 1999, p. 4)[17] and 1951 (Judy & Clough, 1989, p. 253).[18] Whether it is an independent beginning (Prokhorov, 1999, p. 4) or a copy of Western technology (Sutton, 1973, p. 318; Judy, 1970, p. 63),[19] is still under debate, as summarized by Crowe and Goodman (1994, pp. 11–13).[20]

In 1952, according to Campbell (1976, p. 134), there was parity between the United States' and Soviet computers – a comparison between Soviet BESM-1 and IBM 701.[21] Prokhorov (1999) organizes that history by generations of computers – first generation with valves (between 1948 and 1962); second generation with transistors (between 1962 and 1975); third generation with integrated circuits (between 1970 and 1985).

This history, on the one hand, describes a process of advances in computing: transition for valves to transistors, from transistors to integrated circuits, growing processing speeds and memory capacity (Campbell, 1976, pp. 133–134). However, on the other hand, it is a history of an increasing technological gap: in 1952 there was equivalence, but in 1972 Soviet computers produced then were equivalent to US computers produced in 1965 (Campbell, 1976, pp. 133–134). Hanson (1981, p. 42) includes computers among the industries that had "in the early 1970s a clear and marked lag".

In the late 1960s there is a decision within the USSR to produce computers compatible with IBM (Klimenko, 1999, p. 24). This decision to adopt IBM architecture in Soviet computers meant a recognition of the need to adapt to international standards and dynamics (Graham, 1998, p. 39). But the focus on IBM included a

---

[17] Prokhorov (1999, p. 4) dates his "initial period" of Russian computers in 1948, when "I. S. Brouk and B. I. Rameev received the certificate for the invention of 'The Automated Digital Computers'".

[18] In an earlier work, Judy (1970, p. 53) defined 1950 as the beginning of Russian computers.

[19] Graham (1993, p. 304) in her bibliographical essay lists in the topic "technology" works on "the influence of Western technology". Sutton's three volumes are mentioned, as "a massive work whose author is unwilling to grant independent industrial achievements to the Soviet Union". Graham also mentions Kuchment (1987), an article on the "birth of Soviet microelectronics".

[20] Crowe and Goodman (1994) present the academic roots of Sergei Lebedev – the inventor of the first Soviet computer. Lebedev graduated in the Electrical Engineering Department of the Moscow Higher Technical School in 1928 (p. 4). He worked at the V. I. Lenin All-Union Electric Engineering Institute in the 1930s, together with I. S. Bruk, mentioned by Prokhorov (1999), who since 1936 was interested in analog computing and following V. Bush work at the MIT (Crowe & Goodman, 1994, p. 4). Chapter 5 mentioned how well-connected the Russians were with the global community of electrical engineering in the 1910s – Lebedev had one of its roots in that long-term institutional development in electrical engineering in Russia (see Chap. 5, Sect. 5.3).

[21] For Graham (1998, p. 39), in 1950, "the Soviet Union was at a world level in the development of computers". MESM, its first computer, "was developed totally independently of Western efforts".

weakness too[22]: Judy and Clough (1989, p. 272) shows how a belated beginning to design personal computers might have been a consequence of decision-makers in Russia being "inveterate 'mainframers'" like IBM – an Apple clone was ready in 1983, 30% slower than the original (p. 272).[23]

There was also a lag in the diffusion of computers in the USSR: in the 1960s, "quantitatively the US appears to have about 50 times as many computers installed as does the Soviet Union" (Cave, 1977, p. 397).

In semiconductors, Russia had a long tradition of research, since the early 1930s (Graham, 1993, p. 210). Transistors had been produced in the USSR at least since 1956 (Miller, 2022, p. 36), and it was in 1959 only "two or four years" behind the United States "in quality and quantity of transistors" (p. 36). Over time, this lag increased, as integrated circuits were invented and their production followed the Moore's Law dynamic. Judy and Clough (1989, pp. 314–315) summarize in a table a "sample list of Soviet microprocessors": they show that a K5080 microprocessor, an analog of an Intel 8080, which began to be produced in 1979.[24] In this table, the first microprocessor produced in the USSR is the K536, introduced in the "mid 1970s" (p. 314). There was a production of memory chips, also with a lag (Judy & Clough, 1989, pp. 316–317). Usdin (2005) writes on the contribution of two Americans to the creation of the "Soviet Silicon Valley" – Zelenograd –, a "politically motivated" form of technological transfer, and mentions (p. 316, footnote 26) a report from the CIA (1974) – "Soviet progress in the production of integrated circuits" – that shows a table (p. 11) listing 26 "known integrated circuit plants" – Zelenograd is among the three "major producers".

In software, Judy (1970, p. 59) suggests there were two lines of work: "independent Soviet effort" and "adaptation of Western work in programming languages to Soviet conditions and machines". In the first line Judy mentions that "work was begun in the mid-1950s by A. P. Ershov and A. A. Liapunov in the theory of computer programming", trying to make it a "mathematical discipline" (p. 59). Graham (1993, p. 214), reviewing Soviet Mathematics, evaluates that when it made "great advances in areas with significant potential for applications, such as information theory and computer algorithms, often their work received its most advanced exploitation in other countries" – an example of problems in the interaction between science and technology within the USSR – and another example of assimilation of knowledge generated at the periphery by the center.

The last section of Prokhorov (1999, pp. 12–13) – "Russian computer branch during recent years (1986–1996)" – presents a balance of changes during the transition from a command economy to a new variety of capitalism: "the giants of

[22] As Malerba and Orsenigo (1996, p. 71) evaluate, "[e]stablished mainframes and minicomputer producers perceived demand with a lag with respect to new PC producers". The belated move of IBM to PCs is described by Chandler (2005, pp. 135–139).

[23] Judy and Clough (1989, p. 269) present a table "matching Soviet RIAD computers with IBM counterparts", showing the RIAD computers launched between 1972 and 1987 and the corresponding lag in years – the lag oscillated between 5 and 11 years.

[24] This microprocessor was introduced in the United States in 1974 (Intel, 2018).

the military and industrial field ... had gone out of existence", "a number of cooperative companies appeared during the period 1988–1992" but "essentially nothing from before the early 1990s has survived" (p. 12). In early the 1990s, there was a new scenario with assemblers using foreign parts and "foreign firms entering the Russian marketplace" (p. 12).

This scenario of the early 1990s may be defined by the nature of transition from a command economy to a new variety of capitalism – the shock therapy did not contribute to a reorganization and rearrangement of existing capacities in computer and semiconductors production – and immigration may have been the solution for skilled people in science and technology (Ganguli, 2015).

7.5.3 India: Experimenting with Computers, Discovering Software

Independent India, in 1947, introduced economic planning through its first two Five-Year Plans, for 1951–1956 and 1956–1961. Sarma (1958, p. 211) shows a sectoral distribution of resources in these first plans: in the first, "irrigation and power" get the larger provision (28.1% of the total), and in the second "transport and communication" took the lead (28.9%). Vaidyanathan (1983, pp. 954–955) describes the first plan as "a collation of public investment projects, most of which were already under construction or had been prepared as part of the Postwar Reconstruction Programme" (p. 954), and the second as a "rationale for emphasizing rapid expansion in the domestic production of metals and machinery" (pp. 954–955).

Under these two first Five-Year Plans, initial moves in the electronics and computer technologies were organized. The beginning of a computer industry in India is shaped by two different but combined strands. The first is derived from efforts of an emerging science and technology community in India, specially from two institutions created before Independence: the Indian Institute of Science, in Bangalore – founded in 1909, by J. N. Tata – and the Tata Institute of Fundamental Research (TIFR) – founded in 1945 –, and also from one post-Independence institution, the Electronic Computer Laboratory – created in 1950 (Sharma, 2015). The second is the presence of IBM, "a dominant player in the Indian computing industry from 1950 to 1977" (Sharma, 2015, p. 10).

The first strand will lead to the construction of the first Indian computer in 1959, at the TIFR: using 2700 valves, called TRIFAC (Sharma, 2015, p. 20). TRIFAC inaugurated a line of attempts to build Indian computers, that had benchmarks with the creation of the Electronics Committee in 1963 (p. 41) and of Electronic Corporation of India Limited (ECIL) in 1967. ECIL launched in 1968 a computer modeled after DEC's PDP-8 – TBC-12 –, and in 1969 other two models – TBC-312 and TBC-316 (pp. 43–44). These efforts were in line with the Department of Energy's (DOE) goal of self-reliance in computers (p. 48).

The second strand was the presence of IBM (Sharma, 2015, chapter 3), through the import of its computers for research institutes and universities – important for the formation of local resources to deal with computer programming (Sharma, 2015, pp. 30–32).[25] The presence of IBM had one peculiarity: the import of used computers that were "refurbished and recycled" (p. 58).[26] This form of imports – "marketing of outdated systems" (p. 61) – worked for some time, but the intensity of the progress in computers exposed the limits and problems of this strategy: in 1975 IBM was renting mainframe computers charging $20,000 while there were minicomputers costing $1400 that were "slightly more powerful" (p. 61). Later foreign exchange problems led to a crisis that resulted in IBM leaving India in 1977 (p. 69) – and this movement opened new challenges and opportunities for the computer industry in India (Sharma, 2015, p. 105): developments in software – how to keep the IBM computers working –, and developments in hardware – opportunities for local producers.

Development of Indian hardware firms (Sharma, 2015, pp. 105–127) is illustrated by the cases of DCM Data Group (p. 105), HCL (p. 112), and Wipro ITL (p. 125). There is an important evolution of domestic production of microcomputers using Intel microprocessors (p. 128). But these developments were blocked by internal problems (difficulties with foreign exchange, cuts in public investments) and technological changes abroad (p. 129).

These challenges provoked Indian computer firms to start "searching for deeper foreign collaboration and diversification into software services" (p. 129). This is a form of technological transfer: knowledge accumulated in experiments with hardware and the problems then faced led to new opportunities in software (p. 131).[27] Sharma illustrates this movement towards software presenting the cases of DCI (created in 1972) (p. 132), Infosys (created in 1981), Tata Consulting Services (from 1968) (p. 141), and Softek (created in 1979) (p. 146).[28] Sharma (2015, pp. 151–155) describes the "variety of means" through which "Indians acquired early software development capability": "academic training in India and the United States, interaction with multinational firms operating in India, and linkages with American minicomputer firms and state-funded R&D programs" (pp. 151–152).

In this initial process, India began exporting software, and multinationals learnt about these competencies – "during the decade of 1980–1990, the Indian software industry took shape and exports to the United States and Europe began in a modest

[25] The first IBM-1620 arrived in 1963. The initial training and education on computers and programming used other imported equipment, such as the Russian Urals, in 1958 (Sharma, p. 15), and the US's CDC, in 1964 (p. 26).

[26] In 1974 there were 224 computers in India, 141 were IBM (Sharma, 2015, p. 48).

[27] Earlier, Sharma (2015) noted changes in policies for import of computers – software firms could import computers if they export software – identifying the birth of "Indian software industry in the late 1970s and early 1980s" (p. 52).

[28] Athreye (2005, p. 11) presents a list of the top twenty software exporters from India and the year of their establishment.

manner" (p. 155).[29] In 1991, moment of the sixth big bang, Indian software was ready for a next move: "the transition to offshore" (Sharma, 2015, chapter 7). For this transition a governmental initiative was key: Software Technology Parks – a "game changer" (p. 168).[30] Sharma describes movements in the 1990s of multinationals as IBM, Sun, Oracle, and Microsoft beginning to do business in India (p. 174) – IBM established a research lab at the IIT Campus in July 1997 (p. 191) –, and a "spurt in engineering and design services" (p. 199). This whole process may be summarized as India searching for and finding a new role in the international division of labor (Sharma, 2015, chapter 8). The growth of Indian software industry (after 1989) and exports (after 1993) is presented by Athreye (2005, p. 9). The importance of India as a IT services provider is shown by UNCTAD (2011, p. 223): in a list of "top 15 outsourcing IT-BPO services providers", India has two companies (TCS and Wipro) and hosts "major services centers" of nine other companies.

7.5.4 China: Entry, Reducing the Gap, and Limited Catch Up

The foundation of the People's Republic of China (RPC) is an institutional step forward for absorptive capacity. Sun (2002, p. 478) divides the national innovation system in China during the "pre-reform era" in five phases. In the first phase – "reconstruction and recovery", 1949–1952 – there is the foundation of the Chinese Academy of Sciences and many industrial research institutes.[31] The second phase – the first Five-Year Plan, 1953–1957 – focused on the USSR as a reference for Chinese catch up, a source of a massive technological transfer, therefore also an indirect and a mediated technological transfer from the West.

In this phase, Sun (2002, p. 478) highlights the implementation of the Twelve-Year Plan (1956–1967), "China's first long-run S&T program". This plan, with 12 strategic fields, included transistors, automation and computing techniques among them (p. 478) – military considerations were involved in these choices. Zhang et al. (2006, p. 133) reports that after the approval of this Twelve-Year plan, scientists were organized in four groups, "to develop Computing Technology, Semi-conductor technology, radio electronics, and automatic and long-distance control technology".

[29] Joseph et al. (2020, p. 1200) identify in the 1980s "a shift in policy pendulum from planning to market and from import substitution to export orientation and globalization".

[30] The creation of the STPI was in 5 June 1991 (Sharma, 2015, p. 181), but Sharma stresses that the "rise of Indian software industry... began much earlier" (p. 157).

[31] In 1953 "the first computer research group is set up", led by a researcher from the Institute of Mathematics of the Chinese Academy of Sciences (Zhang et al., 2006, p. 131). Lu (2000, p. 8) mentions the foundation of the Institute of Computing Technology (ICT) "within CAS", "led by a prominent mathematician".

These definitions should be highlighted, because in the first Five-Year plans China was dealing with a backlog of backwardness: a peculiarity of its planning is a combination of initial steps in industrialization with an eye on the emerging computer technologies. Lu (2000, p. 7) stresses that "the development of computer technology had been a priority of the Chinese government ever since the start of the planning system".

The first computer is built by the Institute of Computing Technology (ICT) in 1958, "a copy of the Soviet Mark-3" (Lu, 2000, p. 8), a vacuum tube computer. There is an important institutional change in the early 1960s in relation to the USSR, with implications for internal S&T development (Sun, 2002, pp. 478–479), changes that strengthened more independent developments and encouragement of activities at "provincial and sub-provincial levels".

Guo and Sun (1987, pp. 113–114) list developments in this phase: in 1964–1965 "the first transistorized computers", in 1973 "the first IC computers". Lu (2000, p. 8) reports the first minicomputer, "modelled after Digital's minicomputer Series", in 1974.

After 1971–1972, another important institutional change impacted computer technology: the change of the focus of catch-up process to Western technologies without intermediation. As reported by Heymann (1975, p. 44), there is an exhibition in Beijing (May–June 1974), organized by France, that displayed "data-processing equipment": for Lu (2000, p. 9), this was the first time that "the Chinese saw a microcomputer". In 1977 China produced its first microcomputer prototype – and by 1981 China had produced around 2000 microcomputers (p. 9).

China had also initial experiences with semiconductors, with initial production of transistors in 1956 and integrated circuits in 1965 (Fuller, 2016, p. 117) – Verwey (2019, p. 10) defines a first phase of the Chinese semiconductor policy between 1956 and 1990 – "state-led planning that emphasized indigenous innovation". After 1978, fundamental changes in the chip industry, that within the sixth Five-Year plan "created a 'Computer and Large Scale IC Lead Group' with the intention of modernizing the domestic semiconductor industry" (p. 10). There was an import of "24 secondhand semiconductor manufacturing lines" (p. 10), together in line with other sectors' acquisitions of plants.

In the early 1970s there is the beginning of discussions on the transition from the Maoist model (Weber, 2021), a long and rich process that led to a gradual and dual-track reform (Naughton, 1995, 2007). In this process, there is a combination of reforms for state-owned companies and entry of new firms, initially with strong presence of township and village enterprises (TVEs) (Naughton, 1995, pp. 137–169).

Lu (2000, p. 10–13) shows that since the beginning of the reforms there was a perception of "deficiencies of the old system" (p. 10), "calling for close links between S&T research and economic construction" (p. 11) – in 1985 a reform of the Chinese S&T system is defined, with a new type of firms being created: "Science and Technology (S&T) Enterprise" (p. 11). Among them were spin-offs from universities and research institutes – university-run enterprises were another specificity of the Chinese transition process (Eun et al., 2015, p. 123).[32] One of these firms was Legend, a spin-off from the ICT-CAS, "set up as an institute-run enterprise" (Lu, 2000, p. 65) – a firm renamed as Lenovo in 2003.

The reforms that took place depended on the creation of new firms that transformed the structure of the Chinese economy. The end result is a new variety of capitalism, a state-led form of capitalism, that have a combination of company ownership forms. In the case of semiconductors, for instance, Fuller (2016, chapter 7) describes the institutional diversity as containing domestic (private and state-run firms), hybrid and multinationals. Part of the entry in the semiconductor industry was through global value chains, as shown by UNCTAD: China has overseas production bases for all "top 10 contract manufacturers in electronics" (UNCTAD, 2011, p. 219).

In contrast with the case of USSR, where one feature was the systematic increase in technological gaps, in the case of China there has been a reduction of those gaps, as illustrated by semiconductors: Fuller (2016, p. 122) organizers data on "IC fabrication" showing how China was 16 years behind in 1979 and only 1–2 years behind in 2012. The general outcome, so far, may be one of progress and advances, but within a framework of a limited catch-up (Fuller, 2019; Lee, 2022, chapter 4).[33]

An illustration of changes since the first big bang comes from the initial patents in the post-www economy: according to Greenstein (2015, p. 369), the founders of Google and Baidu filed patents almost simultaneously.[34]

Finally, a look at the Global Fortune 500 shows among them Chinese multinationals such as Lenovo (computers), Tencent and Alibaba (post-www firms), and a look in the current global production of semiconductors shows China producing "15 percent of all chips, mostly low tech" (Miller, 2022).[35] In sum, China did enter in all four technologies discussed in this chapter – and these entries were not reverted by the firms' destruction.

7.5.5 *Sub-Saharan Africa: Superposition of Backwardnesses*

Sub-Saharan Africa illustrates the combination of backwardness, and the diffusion of computer-related processes: Loukou (2016, p. 353) researches the case of Ivory Coast identifying a superposition of an old backwardness – electricity – with a new

[32] Eun et al. (2015, p. 123) report that in 1997 there were 6634 UREs – 2564 high-tech, and 14% of the top Chinese S&T firms were UREs.

[33] According to Verwey (2019), Intel "reports not being aware of any Chinese-headquartered company microprocessors currently sold in the United States".

[34] USPTO 5,920,859 and 6,285,999.

[35] China, with the foundation of SMEE in 2002, has entered the industry of machines for chipmaking (CCS, 2021). The global presence of China in semiconductors is the topic of Miller's part VII: "the Chinese challenge". On recent movements, including failures, of Chinese policy for semiconductors, see Mozur (2021), Zhang and Li (2021) and Yuan (2022).

backwardness – digital.[36] Other colonial legacies impact opportunities for development in Africa: "[e]lectronic and transportation connections between sub-Saharan countries and their former European colonial metropolises are often better and more frequent than direct connections across the continent" (Odedra et al., 1993, p. 25).

Odedra et al. (1993, p. 26) add other prerequisites for the diffusion of information technologies, beyond reliable electricity supply: "a well-functioning telephone network to transmit data, foreign currency to import the technology, and computer-literate personnel". In the region, according to Odedra et al., "[m]ost countries lack the educational and training facilities needed to help people to acquire proper skills... Only a handful of countries such as Nigeria, Malawi and Zimbabwe have universities that offer computer science degrees" (p. 26) – prerequisites for very initial absorptive capacity to buy and operate computers. Odedra (1990) investigates the computers in Kenya, Malawi and Zimbabwe – imports of computers, establishment of centers of data processing using them in governments and large companies, initial services to maintain and repair them. Odedra (1990, pp. 131–134) mentions the beginnings of local capabilities to assemble computers in Kenya (pp. 131–132). Imports of computers may be starting points for software services and industry in different countries, as investigated by Alamdy and Osman (2017) – Sudan –, Soriyan and Heeks (2004) – Nigeria.

South Africa transitioned from apartheid to democracy in the early 1990s. During the 1970s there were international sanctions against apartheid, a specific institutional framework that pressed the apartheid regime to invest in domestic production of diverse sectors, related to a strong defense industry – Nordas (1995, p. 12) mentions the role of defense as one reason for a "remarkably sophisticated technological capacity not expected to be found in a developing country has been built up in production of weapons, fighter aircraft, nuclear energy, computers, electronics and radiation therapy to mention a few".[37] Leonard (1978, p. 9) mentions "the emergence of a local South African computer industry", producing "several minicomputers", by firms such as Messina, Mercedes group, Anker Data Systems and a subsidiary of "the Commercial Systems Division of Computer Automation of the US".[38]

South Africa was, in the early 1990s, overcoming apartheid, and is an exception in the region, as the minerals-energy complex has incentives to introduce computers: "the information technologies community is South Africa ... is embedded in, and contributes to, a 'first world' national infrastructure of tertiary education,

[36]"La fracture numérique vient se superposer à la fracture électrique existante" (Loukou, 2016, p. 353).

[37]The reference for Nordas (1995, p. 12) is L. W. Branscomb (1994): "An analysis of South African Science and Technology Policy".

[38]The emergence of this local production of computers is related to US sanctions against apartheid (1976), as local production would weaken "the effects of US restrictions on computer sales to South Africa" (Leonard, 1978, p. 9). Nordas (1995, p. 21) mentions "pockets of high-technology industries like pharmaceuticals, computers, semiconductors and even aircraft are found" in South Africa.

telecommunications, transportation, and financial and services institutions. World-class indigenous computing capabilities exist in several areas such as banking, the military, and mining" (Goodman, 1994, p. 21). According to Leonard (1978, p. 2) in 1974 apartheid South Africa had more than 1000 computers, with "IBM leading the field".

The end of apartheid in South Africa in 1994 is the final act of African decolonization. A new continental scenario was opened, with lots of challenges for South Africa (Kruss, 2020), a country that may contribute strongly to Sub-Saharan African development (Goodman, 1994, p. 23), including in the information sector.

Although late and slowly, the www is spreading in sub-Saharan Africa – see Table 7.4. This is the first technology of those four presented in Sect. 7.2 that spreads in all countries – given its nature of infrastructure and public utility, as electricity. The spread of www, sometimes using newer technologies such as smart phones, seems to open new opportunities – a topic for further important investigation.

These opportunities and challenges are illustrated by, on the one hand, Sub-Saharan Africa as the region where there is the largest share of the population (15 years and older) using mobile money accounts (UNCTAD, 2019, p. 16), and on the other hand, a region where digital enterprises "are operating under challenging conditions" (UNCTAD, 2019, pp. 117–119).

Among the changes brought by consequences of these two big bangs is the rise in the demand for batteries – for cellphones – that use cobalt, raw material found in Congo (Niarchos, 2021). This new demand impacts that country, an illustration of new technologies demanding other types of raw materials that organize and reorganize the insertion of countries and regions in a changing international division of labor.

7.5.6 Latin America: Initial Entry, Later Exit, and Searching for Niches in the Global Economy

The initial imports of computers in Latin America, during late 1950s and early 1960s, drove the initial investments in training and higher-education formation in computing – this relationship is well-documented in special issues edited by Jacobviks (2006) and Marques (2015a). These educational advances led to other initiatives and may have built the foundation for later development, especially in software.[39]

The larger economies of Latin America have in common attempts to produce computers domestically – at least experimental computers or computer prototypes

[39]The existence of important engineering and scientific resources available in Latin American universities and sometimes not completely used by local firms is a common feature of the region (Dutrénit & Arza, 2015).

Table 7.4 Year arrival of each of the four interrelated technologies, and data on their spread through India, China, Russia, Sub-Saharan Africa, and Latin America

Region	Semi-conductor (initial year)	Total (% global exports) (2018)	Computer (initial year)	Total (% global exports) (2018)	Software (initial year)	Total (% global exports) (2018)	Network (initial year)	Total (individuals using internet – % of population) (2020)
India		0.05	1959	0.06	1968	5.13	2002	43
China	1956(t) 1961 (i) 2001(m)	13.78	1958	49.00	1974	5.09	2000	70
Russia	1956(t) 1962 (i) Mid-1970s(m)	0.01	1951	0.08	Mid-1950s	1.04	1999	85
Sub-Saharan Africa								
South Africa	1984	0	Mid-1970s	0.06	1969	0.16	1997	70
Nigeria		0		0		0.02	2004	36
Mozambique							2008	17
Latin America								
Mexico		0.87	1982	10.33		0.02	1998	72
Argentina		0	1962	0		0.27	1999	86
Brazil	Early 1980s(i)	0.02	1972	0.02	Early 1970s	0.80	1998	81

Source: Global exports (Percentage, %): Atlas Economic Complexity (2023) – electronic integrated circuits, computers, information and communication technologies. Individuals using internet: World Bank (2023)

OBS1- Regarding semiconductors, if "firms are allocated to a country by company headquarter", in 2018, China produces 5%, behind United Sates 45%, South Korea 24%, Japan and European Union 9% each and Taiwan 6% – the rest produces more 2%. (Statista, 2021)

OBS2: Sources for the "initial years", see Table 7.2

were built and operated in universities: in 1962 in Argentina (Babini, 2006, pp. 197–198), in 1982 in Mexico (Nava et al., 2015, p. 7), in 1972 in Brazil (Marques, 2015b, p. 67).

In the case of Brazil, there was a local production of computers during the late 1970s and the 1980s, with a special industrial policy for that purpose – a national policy for informatics, in 1975 (Melo et al., 2001, p. 15). Local firms and subsidiaries of multinationals produced computers and equipment for informatics. Given the peculiarities of the Brazilian banking system (and also, probably, the inflationary dynamics that then prevailed in the economy), the financial sector invested heavily in computer equipment and in computer firms (Cassiolato, 1992).

Furthermore, this national policy for informatics led in the 1980s to the establishment of local firms involved in semiconductors production (Melo et al., 2001, pp. 16–17).

The emergence of a software industry is articulated with its hardware industry (Botelho et al., 2005, p. 104) – in the early 1970s.

Political and institutional changes – the predominance of passive insertion policies in the late 1980s and consequent abrupt market opening – led to the destruction of that participation in the production of computers and semiconductors.[40]

The Brazilian software industry survived and grew between 1980 and 2001 – Botelho et al. (2005, p. 108) show the entry of new firms in this sector, a growth that reflected in Brazilian exports, as Brazil was the sixth global exporter of software (with 1.5%), one position below India (p. 101).

In Mexico, during the early 2000s, a "policy mix" was designed by federal and state governments for manufacturing restructuring and was successful in attracting foreign direct investments in diverse sectors, including computers (Durán, 2019, p. 20) – Table 7.3 shows the participation of Mexico in the exports of computers in 2018, according to the Atlas of Economic Complexity (2023).

The expertise accumulated in all these Latin American experiences, especially the higher education of professionals in areas related to computing sciences, and the consolidation of research groups in universities and research institutes opened up opportunities for advances in software. Botelho et al. (2005) describe the creation of new firms that eventually were acquired by multinationals – an example is Akwan, acquired by Google (UFMG, 2005). There is also the creation of post-www platform firms, such as Mercado Libre, from Argentina (UNCTAD, 2019, p. 110).

However, the post-www economy puts forward a new challenge for the periphery in general: how to avoid becoming "mere providers of raw data to global digital platforms, while having to pay those platforms for the digital intelligence they produce from these data" (UNCTAD, 2019, pp. 99–100).

[40] Wirth et al. (2002, p. 1): "[n]owdays, there are virtually no semiconductor design and manufacturing in Brazil". This is also the diagnostic of ABISEMI (2021): "[b]y 1990 every semiconductor company shut down operations in Brazil and moved them elsewhere". In 2008 the CIETEC was created (ABISEMI, 2021).

7.6 The Spread of These Four Related Technologies

The fifth big bang, in 1971, is the first that impacts a world of independent nations – in 1975 the Portuguese colonies in Africa conclude this process. For the first time, almost all nations could have policies for domestic development – data on GDP per capita show a phase of predominant gap reduction after 1950 (Kruss et al., 2020, pp. 1066–1067).

Independence is an important precondition for improvements in a nation's absorptive capacity, but this improvement faced a more difficult challenge, as the technologies of this big bang demand higher capabilities for learning and absorption – more scientific knowledge, more engineering skills, more capital investment.

The invention of the microprocessor in 1971 is related to three other technologies, as shown in Table 7.1 – these interactions determine a dynamic that affects all those four technologies, changing the configuration of the landscape faced by the periphery in a systematic way. The global nature of this new phase, with cross-border feedbacks, is illustrated by the invention of the microprocessor after a demand coming from Japan, in 1969, then a country concluding its successful catch-up process.

The leading country during those two big bangs – the United States – had at least two domestic policies to answer to changes in the global scenario related to chips: an answer to Japanese rise in the 1980s, with Sematech (Miller, 2022, pp. 105–108), and an answer to Chinese rise in the 2010s, with the Chips Act (The Economist, 2022).[41]

For the periphery, the challenges were a consequence of the intensity of changes in the semiconductor production, following Moore's Law and all the scientific and technological investments to deal with the persistent miniaturization involved – and its impact on the other three related technologies: computers, software and networking.

The combination of independent nations able to implement domestic policies for entry in new technologies and the intensity and increasing sophistication of those four technologies led to peculiarities of this phase: entry in and exit from (firms' destruction) these technologies is one of these peculiarities.

In the case of computers (Tables 7.3 and 7.4), there were attempts in all regions to produced them domestically. The timing is different – Russia, China and India in the 1950s, Latin America in the 1960s, 1970s and 1980s, South Africa in the 1970s. As Table 7.4 shows, Russia, India, South Africa, Brazil and Argentina have produced computers at different times and at different levels, but those industries have not survived: only China and Mexico have relevant exports of computers in 2018.

[41] In the late 1950s there was the "Sputnik moment" (Miller, 2022, p. 19), as answer to Russian initial achievements in the space race. This answer had impacts on the domestic support for semiconductor production.

In the case of semiconductors, there was some production at least in China, Russia, South Africa and Brazil, in different times and at different levels. As of 2018, only in China has a relevant production survived.

Therefore, this movement of entry and exit as a peculiarity of these big bangs. Countries developed the capacity to manufacture computers and semiconductors that were not enough for preserving and updating to cope with a fast-moving industry, and there were domestic failures to keep learning with those advances. The reorganization of the international division of labor erased those local industries. Why? Intensity of changes in the leading countries, limits in the absorptive capacities at the periphery, lack of scale economies necessary to introduce, consolidate and grow these industries. In the case of Russia, both the nature of the economic system before 1986, and the nature of the transition in the late 1980s and early 1990s to a new variety of capitalism, defined the fate of its computer industry. This form of transition may be compared to the other transition that took place after 1971 – China's gradual and dual-track transition – that made room for entry and consolidation in all four technologies presented in Table 7.4. Entry that, by its turn, may be one important factor determining the persistent growth of the Chinese economy after 1971.

This phenomenon – entry and exit in computers and semiconductors – is a peculiarity of this phase: in all previous technological revolutions there was local production of the product that triggered them. In this case, only two countries produce computers and only one country produces chips. The point here is how the international division of labor changed after 1971, reorganizing it until reaching this current shape.

In this reorganization, learning with computers led to development of software that, at least in the case of India, made room for new insertion in the international division of labor – and China which now has an important share of the global software market, as Table 7.4 shows.

These two technological revolutions led to an even more heterogeneous periphery – heterogeneous between regions and within regions –, reorganizing the international division of labor. In special the rise of China, and its new roles in the international division of labor, has important implications for the current reorganization of global capitalism.

References

Abisemi. (2021). *Brazil paves new semiconductor path*. https://www.abisemi.org.br/abisemi/noticia/108/brazil-paves-new-semiconductor-path

Accretech. (2023). *Products in semiconductor production process*. https://www.accretech.jp/english/product/semicon/about.html

ACM. (2016). *Inventor of World Wide Web receives ACM A.M. Turing Award: Sir Tim Berners-Lee designed integrated architecture and technologies that underpin the web*. https://awards.acm.org/about/2016-turing

Alamdy, S., & Osman, R. (2017). Software industry practice in Africa the case of Sudan. In *2017 IEEE 41st annual computer software and applications conference* (pp. 743–748).

Albuquerque, E. M. (2019). Capitalismo pós-www: uma discussão introdutória sobre uma nova fase na economia global. *Cadernos do Desenvolvimento, 14*(24), 131–154.

Alferov, Z. I. (2000). *The double heterostructure: Concept and its application in physics, electronics, and technology – Nobel prize lecture*. Nobel Prize Organization. https://www.nobelprize.org/uploads/2018/06/alferov-lecture.pdf

Amsden, A. (1989). *Asia's next giant: South Korea and late industrialization*. Oxford University.

ASML. (2022). *Responsible supply chain*. https://www.asml.com/en/company/sustainability/responsible-supply-chain

ASML. (2023). *History*. https://www.asml.com/en/company/about-asml/history

Athreye, S. S. (2005). The Indian software industry. In A. Arora & A. Gambardella (Eds.), *From underdogs to tigers: The rise and growth of software industry in Brazil, China, India, Ireland, and Israel* (pp. 7–40). Oxford University Press.

Atlas of Economic Complexity. (2023). https://atlas.cid.harvard.edu/

Babini, N. (2006). Some aspects of the Argentine reception of the computer. In J. Impagliazzo (Ed.), *History of computing and education* (Vol. 2, pp. 193–201). IFIP/Springer.

Bardeen, J. (1947). Surface states and rectification at a metal semi-conductor contact. *Physical Review, 71*(10), 717–727.

Bardeen, John (1956) Semiconductor research leading to the point contact transistor. Nobel Prize Lecture. : . https://www.nobelprize.org/uploads/2018/06/bardeen-lecture.pdf

Botelho, A. J. J., Stefanuto, G., & Veloso, F. (2005). The Brazilian software industry. In A. Arora & A. Gambardella (Eds.), *From underdogs to tigers: The rise and growth of software industry in Brazil, China, India, Ireland, and Israel* (pp. 99–130). Oxford University Press.

Branscomb, L. M. (1994). *An Analysis of South African Science and Technology Policy*. Pretoria: Foundation for Research Development (FRD).

Buzan, B. (2004). *The United States and the Great Powers: world politics in the twentieth-first century*. Cambridge: Polity Press.

Campbell, H. (1976). *Organization of research, development, and production in the soviet computer industry*. Rand Corp. https://archive.org/details/DTIC_ADA037406/mode/2up

Cantwell, J. (2009). Innovation and information technology in the MNE. In A. M. Rugman (Ed.), *The Oxford handbook of international business* (2nd ed., pp. 417–446). Oxford University Press.

Carnota, R. J. (2015). The beginning of computer science in Argentina and the calculus institute, 1957–1970. *IEEE Annals of the History of Computing, 37*(4), 40–52.

Cassiolato, J. E. (1992). *The role of user-producer relations in innovation and diffusion of new technologies: Lessons from Brazil*. DPhil thesis, University of Sussex.

Cave, M. (1977). Computer technology. In R. Amman, J. M. Cooper, & R. W. Davies (Eds.), *The technological level of soviet industry* (pp. 377–406) https://archive.org/details/technologicallev0000unse/page/n5/mode/2up

CCS. (2021, October 18). Chinese chipmakers look inward for equipment suppliers. *CCS Insight*. https://www.ccsinsight.com/blog/chinese-chipmakers-look-inward-for-equipment-suppliers/

CGEE. (2013). *Padrões de desenvolvimento econômico (1950–2008): América Latina, Ásia e Rússia*. Centro de Gestão e Estudos Estratégicos.

Chandler, A., Jr. (2005). *Inventing the electronic century: The epic history of the consumer electronics and computer industries*. The Free Press.

Chuma, H. (2006). Increasing complexity and limits of organization in the microlithography industry: Implications for science-based industries. *Research Policy, 35*(3), 394–411.

CIA. (1974). *Soviet progress in the production of integrated circuits*. Available at https://www.zelenograd.ru/f/11405_1.pdf

Clark, D. (2022, July 4). The tech cold war's 'most complicated machine' that's out of China's reach. *The New York Times*. https://www.nytimes.com/2021/07/04/technology/tech-cold-war-chips.html

CNBC. (2021). *Google reportedly plans to put its own chips in Chromebook laptops from 2023*. https://www.cnbc.com/2021/09/01/google-reportedly-plants-to-use-own-chips-in-chromebooks-from-2023-.html

CNBC. (2022). *ASML is the only company making the $200 million machines needed to print every advanced microchip*. Here's an inside look. https://www.cnbc.com/2022/03/23/inside-asml-the-company-advanced-chipmakers-use-for-euv-lithography.html

Crowe, G. D., & Goodman, S. E. (1994). S. A. Lebedev and the birth of Soviet computing. *IEEE Annals of the History of Computing, 16*(1), 4–24.

Drèze, J., & Sen, A. (2002). *India: Development and participation*. Oxford University.

Drèze, J., & Sen, A. (2013). *An uncertain glory: India and its contradictions*. Penguin.

Durán, C. (2019). Globalization and the scrambling process of catching up in Mexico. *Seoul Journal of Economics, 32*(1), 83–106.

Dutrénit, G., & Arza, V. (2015). Features of interactions between public research organizations and industry in Latin America: The perspective of researchers and firms. In E. Albuquerque, W. Suzigan, G. Kruss, & K. Lee (Eds.), *Developing National Systems of innovation: University-Industry interaction in Global South* (pp. 93–119). Edward Elgar Publishing/Idrc.

Eun, J.-H., Wang, Y., & Wu, G. (2015). China's university-industry links in transition. In E. Albuquerque, W. Suzigan, G. Kruss, & K. Lee (Eds.), *Developing National Systems of innovation: University-Industry interaction in Global South* (pp. 120–142). Edward Elgar Publishing/IDRC.

Evertiq. (2021). *Semiconductor fab is inaugurated in the African continent*. https://evertiq.com/design/49931

Freeman, C. (1987). *Technology policy and economic performance: Lessons from Japan*. Pinter Publishers.

Freeman, C. (1995). The "National system of innovation" in historical perspective. *Cambridge Journal of Economics, 19*(1), 5–24.

Freeman, C., & Louçã, F. (2001). *As time goes by: From the industrial revolutions and to the information revolution*. Oxford University.

Fuller, D. B. (2016). *Paper tigers, hidden dragons: Firms and the political economy of China's technological development*. Oxford University Press.

Fuller, D. B. (2019). Growth, upgrading, and limited catch-up in China's semiconductor industry. In L. Brandt & T. Rawski (Eds.), *Policy, regulation and innovation in China's electricity and telecom industries* (pp. 262–303). Cambridge University Press. https://doi.org/10.1017/9781108645997.007

Furtado, C. (1986). *Teoria e política do desenvolvimento econômico* (2ª ed.). Nova Cultural.

Furtado, C. (1987). Underdevelopment: To conform or to reform. In G. Meier (Ed.), *Pioneers of development* (Second series) (pp. 203–227). Oxford University/World Bank.

Furtado, C. (1992). *Brasil: a construção interrompida*. Paz e Terra.

Ganguli, I. (2015). Immigration and ideas: What did Russian scientists "bring" to the United States? *Journal of Labor Economics, 33*(S1), S257–S288.

Goodman, S. E. (1994). Computing in South Africa: An end to "apartness"? *Communications of ACM, 37*(2), 21–25.

Graham, L. R. (1993). *Science in Russia and the Soviet Union: A short history*. Cambridge University Press.

Graham, L. R. (1998). *What have we learned about science and technology from the Russian experience?* Stanford University Press.

Greenstein, S. (2015). *How the internet became commercial: Innovation, privatization and the birth of a new network*. Princeton University Press.

Guo, P., & Sun, Q. (1987). General review of computer technology and application in China. *Computers in Industry, 8*, 113–117.

Hanson, P. (1981). *Trade & technology in Soviet-Western relations*. The Macmillan Press.

Heymann, H., Jr. (1975). *China's approach to technology acquisition: Part III: Summary observations*. RAND.

Hou, C.-M., & Gee, S. (1993). National systems supporting advance in industry: The case of Taiwan. In R. R. Nelson (Ed.), *National innovation systems: A comparative analysis* (pp. 384–413). Oxford University.

Hymer, S. (1970). The efficiency (contradictions) of multinational corporations. *American Economic Review, 60*(2), 441–448.

Intel. (2018). *Intel at 50: the 8080 microprocessor.* https://newsroom.intel.com/articles/intel-50-8080-microprocessor/

Jacobviks, P. M. (2006). The first decade of computer science in Argentina. In J. Impagliazzo (Ed.), *History of computing and education* (Vol. 2, pp. 181–191). IFIP/Springer.

Joffe, J. (1945). Schottky's theories of dry rectifiers. *Electrical Communication, 22*(3), 217–225.

Joseph, K. J., Kakarlapudi, K. K., & Joseph, A. (2020). Deindustrialization and innovation under globalization: An analysis of India's catch up in manufacturing. *Nova Economia, 30*(Especial), 1199–1224.

Judy, R. W. (1970). The case of computer technology. In S. Wasowski (Ed.), *East-West trade and the technological gap: A political and economic appraisal* (pp. 43–72). Praeger Publishers. https://archive.org/details/eastwesttradetec0000unse/

Judy, R. W., & Clough, R. W. (1989). Soviet computers in the 1980s: A review of the hardware. *Advances in Computing, 29*, 251–330.

Kilby, J. S. (2000). *Turning potential into realities: The invention of the integrated circuit – Nobel prize lecture.* Nobel Prize Organization. https://www.nobelprize.org/uploads/2018/06/kilby-lecture.pdf

Kimura, Y. (1997). Technological innovation and competition in the Japanese semiconductor industry. In A. Goto & H. Odagiri (Eds.), *Innovation in Japan* (pp. 121–158). Oxford University Press.

Klimenko, S. V. (1999). Computer science in Russia: A personal view. *IEEE Annals of the History of Computing, 21*(3), 16–30.

Kruss, G. (2020). Catching up, falling behind: The need to build upgrading coalitions for innovation and inclusive development in South Africa. *Nova Economia, 30*(Especial), 1115–1144.

Kruss, G., Lee, K., Joseph, K. J., & Albuquerque, E. M. (2020). Breaking middle income traps in a post Covid-19 World: An introduction to the special issue. *Nova Economia, 30*(Especial), 1063–1088.

Kuchment, M. (1987). Active technology transfer and the development of Soviet microelectronics. In C. Perrry & R. Pfaltzgraff Jr. (Eds.), *Selling the rope to hang capitalism? The debate on West-East trade & technology transfer* (pp. 60–69). Pergamon-Brassey's International Defense Publishers. https://archive.org/details/sellingropetohan0000unse/page/n9/mode/2up

Lee, K. (2022). *China's technological leapfrogging and economic catch up.* Oxford University Press.

Leonard, R. (1978). *Computers in South Africa: A survey of US firms.* The Africa Fund.

Loukou, A. F. (2016). Le développement des technologies de l'information et de la communication en Côte d'Ivoire face aux contraintes d'énergie électrique. In A. Beltran, L. Laborie, P. Lanthier, & S. Le Gallic (Eds.), *Electric Worlds/Mondes électriques: Creations, circulations, tensions, transitions (19th–21st C.)* (pp. 343–363). https://www.jstor.org/stable/j.ctv9hj6hk

Lu, Q. (2000). *China's leap into the information age: Innovation and organization in the computer industry.* Oxford University Press.

Machado, G. T. M. (2017). *Redes globais de inovação e as metamorfoses de uma empresa multinacional – o caso da IBM.* FACE-UFMG (Trabalho de conclusão do curso de Ciências Econômicas).

Maddison, A. (2010). *Historical statistics of the world economy – 1-2008 AD.* Groningen Growth and Development Centre. http://www.ggdc.net/maddison/Historical_Statistics/horizontal-file_02-2010.xls

Malerba, F., & Orsenigo, L. (1996). The dynamics and evolution of industries. *Industrial and Corporate Change, 5*(1), 51–87.

Mandel, E. (1989). *Beyond perestroika.* Verso. (1991).

Marques, I. C. (2015a). History of computing in Latin America – Introduction. *IEEE Annals of the History of Computing, 37*(4), 10–12.

Marques, I. C. (2015b). Brazil's computer market reserve: Democracy, authoritarianism, and ruptures. *IEEE Annals of the History of Computing, 37*(4), 64–75.

Mathews, J. A., & Cho, D.-S. (2000). *Tiger technology: The creation of a semiconductor industry in East Asia*. Cambridge University Press.

Melo, P. R., Rios, E. C., & Gutierrez, R. M. (2001). Componentes eletrônicos: perspectivas para o Brasil. *Bndes Setorial, 13*, 3–64. https://web.bndes.gov.br/bib/jspui/handle/1408/2725

Miller, C. (2022). *Chip War: The fight for world's most critical technology*. Scribner.

Mowery, D. C. (1999). The computer software industry. In D. C. Mowery & R. R. Nelson (Eds.), *Sources of industrial leadership: Studies of seven industries* (pp. 133–168). Cambridge University Press.

Mowery, D. C., & Rosenberg, N. (1993). The U.S. national innovation system. In R. R. Nelson (Ed.), *National innovation systems: A comparative analysis* (pp. 29–75). Oxford University.

Mozur, P. (2021, July 19). The failure of China's microchip giant tests Beijing's tech ambitions. *The New York Times*. https://www.nytimes.com/2021/07/19/technology/china-microchips-tsinghua-unigroup.html

Naughton, B. (1995). *Growing out of the plan: Chinese economic reform, 1978–1993*. Cambridge University Press.

Naughton, B. (2007). *The Chinese economy: Transitions and growth*. The MIT Press.

Nava, J. D., Acosta-Guadarrama, J. C., Rosas, R. M. V., Ramos, V. H. S., César, N. P., Rebollar, L. Q., & Pérez, R. D. (2015). A brief history of computing in Mexico. *IEEE Annals of the History of Computing, 37*(4), 76–86.

Niarchos, N. (2021, May 31). The dark side of Congo's cobalt rush. *The New Yorker*. https://www.newyorker.com/magazine/2021/05/31/the-dark-side-of-congos-cobalt-rush

Nobel Prize Committee. (2023). *The Nobel Prize in physics 1956 – Summary*. https://www.nobelprize.org/prizes/physics/1956/summary/

Nordas, H. K. (1995). *South Africa manufacturing industries: Catching up or falling behind*. Chr. Michelsen Institute. (WP 1995: 2).

Odagiri, H., & Goto, A. (1993). The Japanese system of innovation: Past, present and future. In R. Nelson (Ed.), *National innovation systems: A comparative analysis* (pp. 76–114). Oxford University.

Odedra, M. R. (1990). *The transfer of information technology to developing countries: Case studies from Kenya, Zambia, and Zimbabwe*. London School of Economics and Political Science (Dissertation for the degree of Doctor of Philosophy).

Odedra, M., Lawrie, M., Bennett, M., & Goodman, S. E. (1993). Sub-Saharan Africa: A technological desert. *Communications of ACM, 36*(2), 25–29.

Panitch, L., & Gindin, S. (2012). *The making of global capitalism: The political economy of American empire*. Verso.

People's Daily. (2021). *China's first CPU chip developed*. http://www.china.org.cn/english/2001/Jul/15994.htm

Perez, C. (2010). Technological revolutions and techno-economic paradigms. *Cambridge Journal of Economics, 34*(1), 185–202.

Prates, B. P. (2022). *Revoluções tecnológicas e o catch up da China na era digital*. Belo Horizonte.

Prohkorov, S. P. (1999). Computers in Russia: Science, education and industry. *IEEE Annals of the History of Computing, 21*(3), 4–15.

Pugh, E. W. (1995). *Building IBM: Shaping and industry and its technology*. The Mit Press.

Reid, T. R. (2001). *The Chip: How two Americans invented the microchip and launched a revolution* (Revised ed.). Random House Trade Paperbacks.

Sarma, N. A. (1958). Economic development in India: The first and second five year plans. *IMF Staff Papers, 6*(2), 180–238.

Semiconductor Industry Association. (2022, February 14). *Global semiconductor sales, units shipped reach all-time highs in 2021 as industry ramps up production amid shortage*. https://www.semiconductors.org/global-semiconductor-sales-units-shipped-reach-all-time-highs-in-2021-as-industry-ramps-up-production-amid-shortage/

Sharma, D. C. (2015). *The outsourcer: The story of India's IT revolution*. The MIT Press.
Shockley, W. (1950). *Electrons and holes in semiconductors*. D. Van Nostrand Company, Inc.
Shockley, W. (1956). *Transistor technology evokes new physics* (Nobel Prize Lecture). Nobel Prize Organization. https://www.nobelprize.org/uploads/2018/06/shockley-lecture.pdf
Software AG South Africa. (2023). *Get to know Software AG South Africa*. https://www.softwareag.com/en_corporate/company/offices/south-africa/overview.html
Soriyan, H. A., & Heeks, R. (2004). *A profile of Nigeria's software industry* (Working paper series 21). Institute for Development Policy and Development.
Srnicek, N. (2017). *Platform capitalism*. Polity Press.
Statista. (2021). *Share of the global semiconductor industry by country from 2018 to 2020*. https://www.statista.com/statistics/510374/worldwide-semiconductor-market-share-by-country/
Sun, Y. (2002). China's National Innovation System in transition. *Eurasian Geography and Economics, 43*(6), 476–492.
Sutton, A. C. (1973). *Western technology and Soviet economic development – 1945 to 1960*. Hoover Institution Press/Stanford University. https://archive.org/details/Sutton%2D%2DWestern-Technology-1945-1965
The Economist. (2018, June 30). *Special report – Fixing the internet*. https://www.economist.com/special-report/2018/06/28/how-to-fix-what-has-gone-wrong-with-the-internet
The Economist. (2020, February 29). *How ASML became Chipmaking's biggest monopoly*. https://www.economist.com/business/2020/02/29/how-asml-became-chipmakings-biggest-monopoly
The Economist. (2022, July 29). *America takes on China with a giant microchip bill*. https://www.economist.com/united-states/2022/07/29/america-takes-on-china-with-a-giant-microchips-bill
The Information. (2021). *Amazon steps up silicon ambitions with new networking chip*. https://www.theinformation.com/articles/amazon-steps-up-silicon-ambitions-with-new-networking-chip
UFMG. (2005, July 20). *Google compra empresa mineira de buscas na internet*. https://www.ufmg.br/online/arquivos/001902.shtml
UNCTAD. (2011). *World investment report 2011 – Non-equity modes of international production and development*. UNCTAD.
UNCTAD. (2013). *World investment report 2013 – Global value chains: Investment and trade for development*. UNCTAD.
UNCTAD. (2019). *Digital economy report 2019*. UNCTAD.
Usdin, S. F. (2005). *Engineering communism: How two Americans spied for Stalin and founded the Soviet Silicon Valley*. Yale University Press.
Vaidyanathan, A. (1983). The Indian economy since independence. In Kumar (Ed.), *The Cambridge History of India, volume 2 – c. 1789-c. 1970* (pp. 947–996). Cambridge University Press.
Verwey, J. (2019, July). Chinese semiconductor industrial policy: Past and present. *Journal of International Commerce and Economics*. https://www.usitc.gov/publications/332/journals/chinese_semiconductor_industrial_policy_past_and_present_jice_july_2019.pdf
Wade, R. (1990). *Governing the market: Economy theory and the role of government in East Asian industrialization*. Princeton University.
Weber, I. (2021). *How China escaped shock therapy: The market reform debate*. Routledge.
Wirth, G. I., Bampi, S., Dewes, M., Santos Filho, N., Valente, D., Gomez, A. T., & Azevedo, D. (2002). *Challenges for semiconductor manufacturing in Brazil*. https://www.lsi.usp.br/~patrick/sbmicro/papers/P237_8WNBAD.pdf
World Bank. (2021). *Data for better lives: World development report 2021*. World Bank.
World Bank. (2023). *World Bank indicators*. https://data.worldbank.org/indicator
Yuan, L. (2022, August 29). Xi Jinping's vision for tech self-reliance in China runs into reality. *The New York Times*. https://www.nytimes.com/2022/08/29/technology/china-semiconductors-technology.html
Zhang, R., & Li, C. (2021). With money, and waste, China fights for chip independence. *The New York Times*, 24 December 2020. https://www.nytimes.com/2020/12/24/technology/china-semiconductors.html
Zhang, B., Zhang, Z., & Yao, F. (2006). Technology transfer from the Soviet Union to People's Republic of China, 1949–1966. *Comparative Technology Transfer and Society, 4*(2), 105–171.

Part III
Revisiting the Theoretical Framework

Chapter 8
The Interplay Between Expansionary and Assimilatory Forces

8.1 Introducion

The tentative framework presented in Part I suggested a combined operation of expansionary forces emanating from the center and assimilatory forces emerging from the periphery.

An investigation on some elements of the interplay between these two forces in each of six big bangs is organized in Part II. The literature reviewed, and the data presented in Part II are evidence of how the theoretical contributions of Kondratiev, Furtado, and Cohen and Levinthal may underly interpretations of technological revolutions and their impacts on the periphery.

The processes described in Part II contributed to a better understanding of the operation of and interplay between expansionary and assimilatory forces. Thus, the objective of this chapter – in Part III of this book – is to revisit the theoretical framework presented in Part I in order to explore related insights from a broader historical point of view, elaborating on the content of Part II.

Each chapter in Part II showed how expansionary forces triggered by big bangs reached our five peripheric regions and how assimilatory forces contributed to the arrival and spread of each technological revolution. A starting point for the analyses of Part III is the concluding section of Chaps. 3, 4, 5, 6 and 7: the arrival year of each technological revolution and data on their initial spread through each region. Table 8.1, organizes information from Tables 3.3, 4.2, 5.3, 6.3 and 7.4.

Table 8.1 summarizes the initial operation expansionary and assimilatory forces in the six technological revolutions. This initial and condensed systematization of the successive technological revolutions reaching the periphery might contribute to improvement of our understanding of the combined operation of expansionary and assimilatory forces as drivers of global spread of big bangs.

What can we learn from Table 8.1 and from the discussions of Part II? A first look at Table 8.1 suggests two phenomena. First, comparing its first line (the arrival of textile mechanization) and the sixth line (the arrival of www), there is a picture of

E. da Motta e Albuquerque, *Technological Revolutions and the Periphery*, Contributions to Economics, https://doi.org/10.1007/978-3-031-43436-5_8

Table 8.1 Arrival year and statistics of initial spread of each technological revolution at peripheric countries/regions

"Big bang", technological revolution	India	China	Russia	Sub-Saharan Africa	Latin America	Spread at the leading country
1771 – (United Kingdom) Mechanization textiles	1856	1889	1793	1925 (Nigeria)	1834 (Brazil)	United Kingdom
	5,800,000 spindles in 1909	800,000 spindles in 1909	8,076,000 spindles in 1909	–	1,000,000 spindles in 1909	53,312,000 spindles in 1909
1826 – (United Kingdom) Railways, steam engines	1853	1876	1837	1860 (South Africa)	1854 (Brazil)	United States
	61,957 km in 1920	11,283 km in 1920	71,600 km in 1920	16,266 km in 1920	28,535 km in 1920	654,309 km in 1920
1882 – (United States) Electricity	1899	1882	1886	1882 (South Africa)	1883 (Brazil)	United States
	1,200 million kwh in 1937	3,930 million kwh in 1937	36,400 million kwh in 1937	5,336 million kwh in 1937	2,030 million kwh in 1937	146,476 million kwh in 1937
1908 – (United States) Automobile, comb. Engines	1926 (a) 1954	1955	1901	1924 (a) (South Africa)	1920 (a) 1958	United States
	72,000 units in 1965	40,000 units in 1965	814,000 units in 1965	173,000 units (a) in 1965	185,000 units in 1965	11,058,000 units in 1965
1971 – (United States) Microprocessor		1956(t) 1962 (i) 2001(m) 5% global production in 2018	1956 (t) 1964 (i) Mid-1970s(m)	1984 (South Afica)	Early 1980s (Brazil)	United States 45% global production in 2018
1991 – (CERN, Europe) world wide web	2002	2000	1999	1997 (South Afr.)	1998	United States
	in 2020, 43% internet access of population	in 2020, 70% internet access of population	in 2020, 85% internet access of population	in 2020, 70% internet access of population	in 2020, 81% internet access of population	in 2020, 91% internet access of population

Source: Big bangs: Perez (2010, p. 190), except for www. Arrival years and initial spread through the five regions: see references in Part II and Tables 3.3, 4.2, 5.3, 6.3 and 7.4. Author's elaboration

acceleration of the arrival time. Second, a look at the arrival dates of the first and second big bangs in India and China shows a different order vis-à-vis the leading country. These two empirical data may be consequences of how expansionary and assimilatory forces operate and interact, as addressed in this chapter.

By definition, expansionary forces come first: the initial movement is innovation, a culmination of previous and long invention, learning and innovation processes. Expansionary forces trigger global transformations, starting at the leading country. Within the leading country that innovation should have a significant domestic diffusion – is there a threshold? – before going abroad. This time lag is also a time for improvements in the original innovation, in general to enable new changes that will be incorporated when the diffusion starts to take place at the periphery: a much more sophisticated and economically efficient product will be the goal of absorption. As Table 8.1 summarizes, the expansionary forces operate at different speeds, defining different arrival dates for different regions.

Assimilatory forces operate, by definition, after a time lag. The duration of this lag depends both on the nature of the technology – Cohen and Levinthal's "ease of learning" – and the strength of absorptive capacity previously accumulated. The initial impact of "pure" expansionary forces may provoke the initial organization of assimilatory forces – unintended consequences. As the assimilatory forces develop – rudiments of innovation systems at the periphery that may grow stronger, with increasing absorptive and innovative capacities -, new technologies may reach peripheric regions through local initiatives: assimilatory forces act before the impact of expansionary forces. In this case, the time lags inherent to the isolated operation of expansionary forces may be long enough for domestic initiatives to identify, learn and assimilate a given technology.

These developments of expansionary and assimilatory forces provoke feedbacks between them, an important interplay that deserves further investigation. This interplay is multifaceted, as both expansionary forces and assimilatory forces change over time, from one technological revolution to the next.

8.2 Arrival of Technological Revolutions at the Periphery

The periphery does not replicate even the initial order of each technology. Therefore, the dynamics at the periphery cannot be explained only by the expansionary forces – unlike the cosmological big bang, the propagation of the technological big bangs follows different speeds across the world, reaching different regions at different times. Also unlike the cosmological big bang, in the capitalist economic dynamic it is not a single and unique event. On the contrary, there is a succession of big bangs, that may even overlap. The dynamic of propagation of these big bangs is very peculiar, with newer big bangs sometimes arriving in certain regions later than more recent big bangs.

The cases of India and China illustrate these different speeds of spread of technologies from the center to the periphery. As Table 8.1 shows, railways arrived earlier than textile mechanization in both regions. Probably because, on the one hand, the motivation of pure expansionary forces to spread railways was stronger given the role of that innovation in consolidating and improving an existing international division of labor – access to their hinterlands. On the other hand, both assimilatory forces and expansionary forces related to the spread of cotton mechanization demanded more time to mature – at the center, developments in the machine-making industrial sector, at the periphery, initial domestic wealth accumulation and learning to enable the acquisition of machines. It should be noted that this difference in the arrival order of technologies at the periphery is related to an interplay between expansionary and assimilatory forces.

Different arrival dates show that the pure expansionary forces do not guarantee an instant propagation, or even any propagation at all, of technologies across all world regions. These features may be explained by the very basic microeconomics of innovation that articulates profits with innovation, with the profits being related to temporary monopoly of given technologies (Schumpeter, 1911, chapter 2). This microeconomics of innovation is reinforced by domestic policies of leading countries – exports' ban of selected products, patents, regulations related to defense, etc. – that, at least temporarily, restrain the technological diffusion while demanding stronger absorptive capacities from peripheric innovation systems.

Table 8.1 shows, beyond those different arrival dates, different intensities of diffusion of these new technologies. There is an articulation between the late arrival and the slow diffusion compared to the leading center(s). There might be a relationship between the arrival time and the intensity later diffusion: it may take time for local processes to begin and consolidate domestically.

At the periphery there is another peculiarity related to the arrival order of technological revolutions: the delayed and limited diffusion of one previous technology may retard and restrain the diffusion of a subsequent new technology. This phenomenon is illustrated by the effects of limited electrification, either in countries or in specific regions within countries, on the diffusion of access to computers and to the internet.

These comments after Table 8.1 suggest that the process of arrival and diffusion of technological revolutions across the periphery is asymmetric and adds elements of turbulence to the global dynamic of capitalism.

8.3 The Sensitivity of Assimilatory Forces to Political Institutions

The formation and development of political institutions are determinants of absorption capacity of backward countries, therefore, determinants of initial steps of assimilatory forces.

In Part II, much evidence of this relationship came from the consequences of political independence of countries to their assimilatory forces. The colonial rule may be seen as a condition in which the expansionary forces operate almost alone, thus political independence brings changes that enable countries to invest in local skills/capacities to identify foreign knowledge that can be useful for their development. The creation of local institutions – firms, universities, research institutes – on the one hand depends on the country's capacity to fund them, on the other hand those institutions are loci for technological absorption. Political independence puts forward new challenges for countries, especially the definition of development priorities and the design of policies to implement them.

Military events and military considerations are also important triggers of domestic initiatives, sometimes as political eye-openers events – indications of relative backwardness and its consequences on political sovereignty of countries/regions –, sometimes as stimulus for governments to produce key inputs for armies and navies.[1]

Part II also shows that political independence is a necessary but not a sufficient condition for the strengthening of assimilatory forces. Independent countries with institutions that matched old economic realities may need to transform institutions to answer new challenges, among them the perturbations triggered by the big bangs.

These initial relationships between political institutions at the periphery and assimilatory forces may be summarized by the idea of the sensitivity of assimilatory forces to these institutions. Political institutions shape assimilatory forces. Small changes in political institutions may improve assimilatory forces: political reforms, domestic political changes within a specific political framework may establish new channels for technology absorption.

Political institutions are, by their turn, sensitive to global economic and technological change: an increasing economic and technological gap vis-à-vis leading regions may be a strong motivation for the fermentation of domestic initiative for political reform.

These very general comments on the relationship between political institutions and assimilatory forces can be systematically formulated in terms of innovation systems: at the periphery, innovation systems are formed and develop depending on domestic political decisions and institutions. The formation of an integrated national market – one of the sources of selection mechanisms that constitute the very basic microeconomics of innovation –, basic infrastructure, educational and research institutions, the establishment of organized international relations, all these institutions depend on domestic and local political initiatives. The formation of a limited, immature innovation system is a politically dependent process. And, an innovation system is the consolidation of assimilatory capacities. Incomplete or immature innovation system are able, at the most, to achieve an incomplete catch up process – none of the five countries discussed in this book was able, so far, to overcome underdevelopment or the middle-income level.

The dynamic framework built according to Kondratiev's elaboration – the succession of technological revolutions emanating from the center – may be reinterpreted here as a dynamic framework that over time puts forward new

[1] The broad relationship between war and formation of modern nation states is elaborated by Tilly (1993, especially chapter 3, pp. 123–156).

challenges to political institutions at the periphery. Political changes may become prerequisites for strengthening and renewal of assimilatory forces at the periphery: political arrangements that matched one set of technologies may not be able to deal with new big bangs. There is a dynamic of matching and mismatching of institutions, alignment, misalignment and realignment of technologies and institutions. This dynamic demand political action.[2] Lock-ins in old political arrangements may even lead to regime collapses. These collapses are, by their turn, lessons for existing regimes to engage in political transformations in time.

Over time, the overlapping of big bangs at the center, forms a systemically growing portfolio of available technologies. This portfolio includes an increasing range of technologies that are candidates for assimilation at the periphery. As this portfolio grows, the decisions and choices to be made at the periphery become more complicated – investment decisions and investment processes demand more sophisticated policy-making institutions and learning processes. Again, institutions successful in previous absorption processes may become obsolete and institutional mismatching may appear.

8.4 Expansionary Forces Change Over Time

Expansionary forces emanating from the leading region were not able to spread technological revolutions across the world. Their operation did not organize replicas of the leading region in all continents. The propagation of new technologies to the rest of the world is not a smooth teaching process.

As Part II shows, expansionary forces may reach the periphery in different speeds, times, and forms. The first impact on the periphery may not – and usually it is not – the arrival of the innovation as a whole, but only the product that resulted from the whole process that led to the innovation. As shown in various chapters in Part II, it is not unusual for there to be rules against the spread of key machines of technological revolutions towards peripheric regions. The preservation of the monopoly of production of each technological revolution at the center is an empirical regularity: improvements and further innovations with the original technology are part of a dynamic that renews the monopoly of the center over these technologies – a dynamic process that is behind other structural changes that may take place over time, with the periphery producing the consumer good while the center produces the capital good, sequentially updated. The initial operation of expansionary forces is the search for markets to sell the innovative product. The arrival of that product, and not of its production process, triggers a chain of events that will transform the peripheric economy – unintentionally.

[2] Kruss et al. (2015) present a framework of this dynamic and apply it to Sub-Saharan Africa.

Expansionary forces, as suggested by Kondratiev, may reach new regions searching for raw materials and in this process include these new regions in the global economy as producers of that input. Again, this inclusion may trigger a chain of events that will transform the newly included region, which may look for new roles in the international division of labor.

The drivers of expansionary forces, as shown in Part II, change over time. In a very schematic way, each technological revolution may be related to a different driver.

In the first big bang, the initial driver was exports of goods – United Kingdom replaced India as the major global exporter of cotton textiles, mechanized-produced cotton textiles. Later, exports of textile machinery changed the nature of operation of those expansionary forces, but that change depended on an important change at the periphery: an initial local wealth and knowledge accumulation sufficient to import these machines – an outcome of interplay between expansionary and assimilatory forces.

In the second big bang, the expansion of railways at the periphery is related to foreign investments from the United Kingdom, derived from previous capital accumulation after the initial steps of the industrial revolution. Foreign investments from United Kingdom were a convenient form of expansionary forces given the motivation to improve an existing international division of labor – the revolution in transport and communication made room for integration of hinterlands in the global economy.

The third big bang had early forms of multinational companies beginning the spread of electrification. A more science-based technology, a more capital-intensive innovation, and a challenging public utility nature of these new investments demanded new forms of diffusion from the center. A world more integrated by the railways (and steamships) prepared conditions for this initial operation of multinationals.

The fourth big bang had more mature forms of multinational companies as drivers of expansionary forces. These expansionary forces took different forms, initially selling cars, searching for oil, and building roads globally. These different forms of expansion further sophisticated the international division of labor, with subsidiaries of multinational companies operating in countries that specialized as oil producers.

The fifth and the sixth big bangs are related to new developments and international operations of multinational companies that turned more and more into organizers of international production of more complex goods. These international operations were within the multinational and outside it in a growing network with other firms, coordinated by the multinational. Sophisticated global value chains orchestrated by leading multinational companies involve more fragmented international division of labor, enabled by the revolution in information and communication. These international connections may also be an indication of other structural changes taking place in global capitalism that becomes more and more a truly international system – mainly economically speaking.

8.5 Assimilatory Forces Change Over Time

The theoretical concept that underlies assimilatory forces is Cohen and Levinthal's absorption capacity. As suggested in Part I, their seminal concept may be extended to be used for nations and regions, as Cohen and Levinthal (1989, p. 128) suggest. The institutional arrangements that support the absorptive capacity of nations and regions are innovation systems.

As discussed in Sect. 8.3, political institutions and their development are, at the periphery, prerequisites for initial steps for building assimilatory forces. The very first steps for absorption are awareness and a capacity to identify and recognize external knowledge. As seen in Part II, this awareness is neither automatic nor spontaneous: domestic initiative and initial learning are necessary for this very initial step – without that awareness, no absorption capacity is possible. That is why in Appendix 1, Chapter 1, a new variable was proposed: the variable α (awareness of new technologies abroad), that precedes γ (absorptive capacity): when $\alpha =$ zero, no absorption can occur.

The awareness of an external knowledge available abroad may come from different sources: individuals travelling abroad, potential entrepreneurs creating new firms, educational institutions. The awareness may also come from political and military events that alert people and existing institutions that there is something important that is not known by them. Independent of its source, when awareness appears ($\alpha > 0$) a key threshold for the formation of assimilatory forces is overcome.

This comment on a very initial step – and a fundamental step – for the formation of assimilatory forces is an introduction of their necessary changes over time. Awareness triggers changes for the building of absorptive capacity (investments in firms, travels, equipment acquisition, knowledge development by technical and scientific personnel, necessary infrastructure, etc) that take some time to be completed and to become able to introduce a new technology. This time interval is one source of the lag in the technological diffusion, seen from the periphery.

Assimilatory forces at the periphery need to change following the differences in the nature of technologies related to succeeding big bangs. As seen in Part II, there is a systematic increase in the scientific content of each successive technological revolution – affecting the variable β of Cohen and Levinthal formulation, that expresses "the complexity of knowledge to be assimilated". As β changes after each big bang – see topic A.2 in Appendix 1, Chapter 1 – the assimilatory forces need to be updated to be able to learn, understand, and introduce the newer technology at the periphery.

This necessary dynamic in the assimilatory forces imposed by the succession of technological revolutions at the center may be investigated through the history of innovation systems at the periphery. The formation of domestic firms and universities – and the interactions between them – are evidence of local institutions that might identify, understand, and assimilate foreign technologies. This dynamic is not simple, because institutions (firms, universities and their interactions) that were successful for one technology may not be adequate for the next technology.

Therefore, new institutions – new firms, new university's courses – need to be developed, dependent on political and economic reforms, new industrial and technological policies. These dynamic demands on changes in assimilatory forces make room for lock-ins that underscore traps like the underdevelopment trap (Furtado, 1992, pp. 37–59) or the middle-income trap (Lee, 2013).

Over time, the succession of technological revolutions and their overlapping present more complicated choices to peripheric regions, given the growth of the technological portfolio available at the center. The question to be answered by economic planning of firms, sectors and governments includes which should be the sector(s)/industry(ies) targeted for entry.

The overlapping of different technologies means that the last technological revolution affects all previous technologies, changing the nature of productive processes – illustrations of these changes are found in the production of textiles that was affected by the introduction of steam-engines, electricity, and computers. These changes affect assimilatory forces not only because the last technology has new sources, but also because it increases the complexity of previous and sometimes already assimilated technologies – that may be destroyed by new forms of production.[3]

Even within each technological revolution there are different demands for assimilatory forces: to buy – to import – machines that produce goods related to one big bang is a process less demanding than the domestic production of these machines – a process less common, as the development of capital goods industries at the periphery is limited and incomplete.

8.6 The Multifaceted Interplay Between Expansionary and Assimilatory Forces

After the short discussions on expansionary and assimilatory forces that focused on their isolated operations, there are hints that their operation impacts each other. Each of these two forces introduce changes in economies that will affect, by chain of events, the rest of the economy. In these processes, expansionary forces affect assimilatory forces, and vice-versa.

Before the big bang, the leading center assimilate foreign knowledge that feeds its key innovation. This knowledge may come from the periphery. Chapter 3 illustrates this showing the Western and British learning with India's textiles and techniques before the first big bang. Chapter 7 presents knowledge on semiconductor properties

[3]This might mean that Cohen and Levinthal's β is not static, and the suggested adaptation (β_n in Appendix 1, topic A.2, where n is the technological revolution) needs one more specification, to include a time lag in that technology. The subscript of β would be n (t), with the possibility that $\beta_{n\ (t)} < \beta_{n\ (t\ +\ 1)}$.

produced by Russian physicists flowing to the Bell Labs before the fifth big bang. Thus, there is assimilation before expansion.

The big bang starts the process unleashing the expansionary forces. One of their first impacts may provoke a spark that begins the formation of assimilatory forces. This could be included among multifarious impacts caused by expansionary forces, triggering a series of events. Expansionary forces may provoke unintentional strictly economic reactions as they open new business opportunities for local agents (merchants, would-be entrepreneurs): an illustration of this type of impact may be the implementation of railways that shows a demand for rails – and iron/steel and iron-ore -, a demand that could be met by local production, leading to the creation of new firms, representing a step forward in absorptive capacity. Expansionary forces, sometimes operating using military support – as in the opening of markets for British goods in China, in the 1840s and 1860s (Darwin, 2009, p. 56) – trigger political reactions – another type of chain of events – that organize initial steps of learning processes – travel abroad to understand a specific technology, foundation of educational institutions, establishment of industrial enterprises after governmental initiatives. Sometimes to expand, in processes with complete initiative from the center, there is the need to develop some absorptive capacity – train local personnel to deal with that foreign technology – that may later be a source for subsequent unfolding of local capabilities.

The operation of assimilatory forces, on the other hand, may provoke changes in the mechanisms of expansionary forces, starting feedback processes that may generate a specific path. The transition from imports of a consumer good to its local production depends on advances in the assimilatory forces: the capacity to identify capital goods – machines – to be imported, the capacity to accumulate resources or to create financial operations to pay for these imports, the capacity to operate the machines after their installation. Thus, advances in assimilatory forces may reconfigure the expansionary forces, strengthening the move from exports of consumer goods to exports of capital goods. This new form of operation of expansionary forces – exports of capital goods -, by its turn, initiates a new round of challenges and opportunities for assimilatory forces that sometimes may be able to take a new step: to locally produce at least some of the machines previously imported. For this step in the assimilatory forces, learning processes derived from the operation of local production that demands skills to operate, maintain, and repair those machines, and might lead to competence to produce them. Once local production of machines starts – a consequence of advances in assimilatory forces – expansionary forces at the center may react, improving the production of these machines, reorganizing their international division of labor, innovating in the direction of more sophisticated equipment.

Developments in assimilatory forces impact expansionary forces as they open room for new mechanisms for the arrival and use of new technologies from the center: contracts for technological transfer need a previous accumulation of domestic knowledge and a previous process of institutional formation – local firms with minimal absorptive capacity must be formed to enable such transfer mechanisms.

Different forms of expansionary forces provoke and/or demand different configurations of assimilatory forces. The changes of expansionary forces summarized in Sect. 8.4 – from exports of goods to the operation of multinational companies – change potential impacts that may lead to new forms of technological absorption. For example: a subsidiary of a multinational company once installed in a peripheric region may provoke changes that lead to the formation of new local firms to supply some inputs for its local production process. Multinational companies operating in peripheric regions may after a while learn about available skills and change their employment practices, hiring local personnel, thus activating a new type of local learning. This new type of learning may lead to either a new position of that subsidiary within its international networks or to a spin-off process that may form new firms to populate local networks around the subsidiary.

As the sophistication of the coordinating mechanisms increases, the improvement of assimilatory forces – new firms, new skills, new capacities of local universities – may make space for a new international division of labor within the multinational: local capacities distributed through peripheric regions may be incorporated by them as they become "global economic systems" (Cantwell, 2009). This process may be present also in the formation and evolution of global value chains orchestrated by leading multinationals, as they discover potential roles for firms from different regions in these networks – improvements in their absorptive capacities may change those roles, possibly upgrading them.

The sophistication of new technologies developed at the center increases the demand on assimilatory forces at the periphery, and these assimilatory forces should develop to create new forms of technology transfer: acquisition of firms at the center by firms headquartered at the periphery. This type of technology transfer requires highly sophisticated advances of firms at the periphery that involve, among other aspects, the identification of new knowledge, awareness of limitations of other forms of learning, and accumulation of financial resources to buy a firm abroad. In sum, it refers to the ability of a firm at the periphery to become multinational driven by learning motives.[4]

The opposite movement may also take place: a firm at the periphery may become target of a multinational firm headquartered at the center and its acquisition becomes a form of entry or diversification.

Both movements – foreign acquisitions by firms at the center or at the periphery – contribute to changes in international knowledge flows, being one of the drivers of the internationalization of innovation systems (Britto et al., 2013, 2021). This internationalization is a structural change in the global economy with new routes for the interplay between expansionary and assimilatory forces – both forces have new channels to operate, learn and be influenced by each other.

---

[4]This form of learning – acquisition of firms at the center – may be listed as a sophisticated type of international contract, that begins with travels abroad to understand specific technologies, involves intermediate steps as studying abroad, hiring foreign personnel, buying machines, signing contracts of technological transfer, and buying turn-key plants. Each of those different forms of learning demands different levels of absorptive capacity.

As assimilatory forces improve at the periphery – innovation systems become more sophisticated, especially with local universities graduating more people with higher qualifications -, international movements of scientists and engineers intensify. Emigration of people educated at the periphery is at the root of the phenomenon of brain drain – people from the periphery strengthening innovation systems at the center. Over time, further increases in assimilatory forces may open a reverse flow, bringing talented people back to their original regions – the phenomenon of brain gain. The emergence of a global innovation system may create other routes for those interactions – scientists from a peripheric region working at the center are located in nodes or hubs of this global system, a position that contributes to strengthen international flows from the periphery (Ribeiro et al., 2018).

However, this interplay is not automatic nor guaranteed, as shown by the phenomenon of obsolete competencies at the periphery. This phenomenon is based on a successful initial assimilation of a new technology, that may create a lock-in following that successful entry. As shown in Part II, technological advances follow each new product or process – Rosenberg's "improvement upon improvement" – that should be followed by the periphery. If continuous improvements do not take place at the peripheric region, that successful assimilation becomes obsolete and can be destroyed by the new forms of expansionary forces.

In sum, assimilation forces, as they develop and strengthen, press expansionary forces to be reconfigured. Expansionary forces, by their turn, as they change put up new challenges to existing assimilatory forces that must readapt to survive and take advantage of new opportunities. These movements, combined movements with many potential feedbacks and ramifications, are illustrated by a series of concrete cases presented in Part II.

8.7 Islands of Technological Absorption

An initial outcome of the interplay between expansionary and assimilatory forces at the periphery may be the formation of a localized nucleus of technological absorption – mainly local firms but also educational and research institutions. This nucleus, or these nuclei, may be seen as island(s) in an ocean of traditional or relatively backward forms of production.

Part II shows that the arrival of new technologies at the periphery takes time – there is always a time lag – and that the initial spread of these technologies is slower than its diffusion at the leading region(s). Thus, the existence and importance of these islands within peripheric regions.

These nuclei of initial absorption, although circumscribed, are important because they are the source of a new dynamic at the periphery. Their inception creates local sources of perturbations that reverberate across that economy. These islands, once formed, trigger chains of events that launch the transformation of local economies.[5]

The arrival of new technologies at the periphery and the consolidation of the initial nuclei of technological absorption trigger chains of events that does not necessarily or immediately destroy traditional forms of production, but rather reconfigure them. Traditional and/or established producers may use new goods to reorganize their production – an illustration is Indian handcraft textiles using yarns of mechanized production.

Provisional effects of those chains of events are the initial structural transition of traditional economies – the tributary modes of production of India and China in the late eighteenth century – towards a capitalist dynamic. The specific forms of combination between the change provoked by those islands on the rest of the local economy shape new economic formations that become new varieties of (peripheric) capitalism.

How far does the local repercussions of those movements go, how broad is the chain of events – as they may include more or fewer sectors in those initial islands – defines the dimension of the dissipation effects presented in Part II. The stronger the assimilatory forces, the longer the chain of events transforming local economies, the larger the domestic backward and forward linkages enabled by the arrival of a new technology. The weaker the assimilatory forces, the more isolated the island of technological absorption, the larger the dissipation effects – or the larger the imports of goods related to that new technology.

However, while the chain of events provoked by the initial nuclei of technological absorption is taking place, a new technology at the center provokes a new perturbation that demands new absorption efforts. An ongoing chain of events is disturbed by a change abroad that may trigger another local chain of events – evidence of overlapping of different technologies at the periphery.

The new absorption effort may have as its starting point either the initial nucleus inherited from previous assimilation or any new institution – firm, university, etc. – created during the events triggered by the previous technology. On the one hand, the new technology does not impact the same society and economy, but rather a society and an economy transformed by the combined effect of expansionary and assimilatory forces. The new technology impacts an amalgam that did not exist in the previous shock. On the other hand, that amalgam has new capacity to understand, to identify, and to begin an absorption process – pick up the process of adapting absorptive capacity to the new features of the more recent technology. These new features may involve the amount of the capital demanded, the complexity of knowledge,[6] the new characteristics of expansionary forces.

---

[5] These islands and their impact transform the peripheric region creating, at the end of a certain time-span, amalgams of new and traditional formations (Trotsky, 1930, chapter 2).

[6] How the complexity of knowledge – Cohen and Levinthal's β – imposes new demands to assimilatory forces can be summarized by the need of different university disciplines after each big bang: basic mechanic knowledge to buy and operate textile machines, engineering schools for railway building and metallurgic skills for iron/steel processing, electrical engineers, mechanical and chemical engineers to deal with cars and refining processes, electronic engineers and computer sciences, for the last two big bangs.

Sometimes this process of local technology upgrading – improvements in the absorption capacity to assimilate new and more complex technologies – may not be enough to deal with new products and processes. Innovation systems that were successful in absorbing some products and processes of one technological revolution may not be able to assimilate he next. Or, in terms of industrial policies, the policies that built firms and institutions that installed local production of technologies of one technological revolution do not match the challenges of newer ones (Suzigan, 2017). These phenomena are very common in countries within the middle-income trap. The extreme case of this problem is the appearance of technologies that are beyond the reach of innovation systems at the periphery – the kind of technologies that are unable to be assimilated. Countries or regions may only have sufficient absorptive capacity for products and processes of older technological revolutions. These phenomena open up an important issue for the formulation of industrial policies and for the development of innovation systems: which technologies can be targets for assimilation?

8.8 Superposition and Overlapping of Different Technological Revolutions

Part I – Chap. 2 – presented reasons for adopting the pragmatic simplification and stylization of six technological revolutions to organize the investigations of Part II. After the discussions presented in Part II, this section revisits these six technological revolutions and how they spread across the periphery to conjecture on how those processes have a more turbulent behavior: thus, the investigation on superposition and overlapping.

Superposition and overlapping were mentioned in Part II and the two previous sections may be read as part of this investigation: the interplay between expansionary and assimilatory forces is a source of overlapping between different technological revolutions, and islands of technological absorption at the periphery may be a materialization of these superpositions.

8.8.1 At the Center

As there is a time lag for the arrival at the periphery of a given innovation that triggers a technological revolution, during that time lag changes may occur in that product or process – improvement upon improvement that is a prerequisite for a broader diffusion of radical innovation (Rosenberg, 1996). As an empirical regularity, the innovation that arrives at the periphery never was the exact version that Perez chose as the big bang of each technological revolution. Therefore, the version of the new product or process that arrives at a peripheric region is already a transformed and/or renewed version that incorporates various improvements.

Revisiting Kondratiev's original elaboration, there was always a long list of interrelated inventions/innovations around the beginning of each long cycle. Probably Kondratiev believed that a single major innovation – even the most important innovation of each long cycle – depended on other related innovations. This interrelation might have inspired Slutsky's 1927 work on superposition of cycles in his classic paper on "cyclic processes" (Slutsky, 1937).[7]

Slutsky (1937, p. 107) identifies waves of different duration – "long waves", "shorter cycles", and "very short waves" – as "a fact begging for explanation" (p. 107), suggesting the hypothesis of "superposition of regular waves" (p. 107). That paper dealt with cycles generated by "random causes". Would that work be only a first exercise on the subject of superposition of cycles to be later investigated with causes related to Kondratiev's structural determinants of long cycles? Could those random causes be replaced by technological causes as sources of cyclic processes – superposed cyclic processes?

This line of theoretical elaboration can be supported by Rosenberg's (1998, p. 180) identification of a superposition between innovations in automobiles and in chemistry – without the huge progress in the production of gasoline, strongly dependent on the emerging chemical engineering, the automobiles with combustion engines could not have matched the big growth in demand during the 1920s.[8]

Part II presents evidence on how overlapping and superposition between different technologies take place as soon as the innovations identified as big bangs by Perez (2010, p. 190) are implemented. But there is also superposition between technologies of different big bangs. Each new technological revolution impacts products and processes of all preceding big bangs – older technologies are not immune to newer technologies, they are transformed by the more recent innovations. This is illustrated by machines for textiles – initially driven by hydraulic sources, then by steam-power, then by electricity, and today using integrated circuits.[9]

8.8.2 At the Periphery

The superposition of different technological revolutions at the center puts forward new challenges to the periphery, as a belated entry in a previous big bang will necessarily demand new absorptive capacities, transformed by the last technological revolution. This process may transform into learning of obsolete competencies

[7]The intellectual interactions between Kondratiev and Slutsky are presented in Franco et al. (2022). Barnett (1998, p. 93) explains the differences in the versions published by Slutsky in 1927 and 1937.

[8]Ribeiro et al. (2017b) find hints of superposition of different cycles for the United States economy.

[9]According to the Atlas of Economic Complexity (2023), the third more complex product in their ranking is a machine related to textiles: "Machines to extrude, draw, cut manmade textile fibres" (HS 1992 code: 8444, PCI = 2.25).

(Pavitt, 1997) for absorption of a previous technological revolution: machines to produce the consumer goods of a previous big bang now incorporate new inventions that increase the complexity of these capital goods.[10]

However, if a country/region at the periphery invests successfully in assimilating the knowledge related to the new technological revolution, it will become easier to achieve entry not only in the newer technology but also in older technologies that incorporate these changes.

At the periphery the superposition of technologies may involve a broader time span, as traditional technologies – handcraft, older methods – may use newer ones: handcraft production using machine-produced inputs, rural workers using sickles after being hired through cellphones, etc.

Part II shows how in our five peripheric regions the spread of each technological revolution was, at most, limited. Thus, as newer technological revolutions start at the leading region in peripheric areas the previous innovation has not completed its diffusion – sometimes there may be only a very limited initial diffusion, sometimes no diffusion at all. Their different level of incomplete spread of previous technologies shapes a very specific form of overlapping at the periphery: the superposition of backwardnesses. This superposition of backwardnesses creates problems for diffusion of newer technologies, as these may need resources and/or infrastructures inherited from previous phases.

This superposition of backwardnesses at the periphery – a phenomenon that has different gradients, different levels – faces a superposition of technological revolutions at the center – a portfolio of all available technologies, with older technologies transformed by the impact of newer big bangs. This asymmetric coexistence shapes the framework within which industrial and technological policies at the periphery must be designed – the first question should be what is assimilable, what sectors are within reach of the feasible existing or potential absorptive capacity of a given country/region.

8.9 Heterogeneity at the Periphery

The different interplay between expansionary and assimilatory forces shapes different socio-economic structures in different countries/regions: contemporary different varieties of capitalism at the periphery – a important topic for understanding current global capitalism.

Heterogeneity at the periphery, therefore, has long-standing historical roots. Part II shows how each technological revolution, with its specific interplay between expansionary and assimilatory forces, impacted differently the different socio-

[10]With reference to Cohen and Levinthal's (1989, pp. 571–572) formulation adapted to deal with countries and successive technological revolutions – see Appendix 1, Chapter 1 – the variable β would behave as mentioned in Sect. 8.5, opening the possibility that $\beta_{n\,(t)} < \beta_{n\,(t\,+\,1)}$.

economic formations that existed at the start of each phase. These different impacts led to different chains of events, and different processes of transformation of each country/region.

Table 8.2 summarizes the economic transformations in our five regions/countries during six technological revolutions, providing a global and synthetic overview of the differentiation of economic systems at the periphery.[11]

First, each phase – each technological revolution – has different impacts leading to different forms. The first technological revolution triggered different processes of transition in different pre-capitalist societies, with different political organizations and nations. The second technological revolution shows the sizeable differences between the initial nuclei of local capitalist accumulation, and the routes that transmitted the initial shocks of the first two big bangs. The third technological revolution witnessed the emergence of a non-capitalist economy, an economic system that by its turn impacted, through a myriad of channels, the rest of the world – even the center of capitalist dynamics. The fourth technological revolution contains an expansion of non-capitalist economies – different economic systems, that changed over time in different phases. These non-capitalist economies added heterogeneity to the global economy, and their transition back to capitalism – different transitions from different non-capitalist economies – contributed to the current reconfiguration of global capitalism introducing new varieties of capitalism (King & Szelényi, 2005). These socio-economic differences – varieties of peripheric capitalism – are related to differences in economic and technological specializations of these countries and regions.

The end result, a provisional end result of the interplay between ever-changing expansionary and assimilatory forces, is the last line of Table 8.2.

8.10 Further Evidence on Capitalism as a Complex System?

The multifaceted outcome of the interplay between expansionary and assimilatory forces over time may contribute to investigations of the dynamic of global capitalism, leading to a fruitful dialogue between evolutionary economies and complex systems.[12]

First, because each isolated impact of expansionary forces triggers a chain of events, with both unintended and intended consequences, that initiates changes in the impacted economies – a multitude of different feedback mechanisms, fractal-like processes, and other phenomena investigated under the research agenda of complex systems.

[11]Table 8.2 organizes information presented in Tables 3.3, 4.2, 5.3, 6.3, and 7.4.

[12]Capitalism as a complex system at the leading country has been investigated and discussed from various approaches in economics. Ribeiro et al. (2017a, b) are two exercises on this topic, that includes a short review of those other approaches.

Table 8.2 Political organization and institutional change in India, China, Russia, Latin America and Sub-Saharan Africa – selected events around each TR phase

Long wave – TR	India	China	Russia	Sub-Saharan Africa	Latin America	Timing
1750 – *Before* the Industrial Revolution	Tributary MoP. Local kingdoms and princely states. Localized British colonial presence. Caste system	Tributary MoP. Ching´s imperial state	Forced modernization under Peter, the Great. Serfdom. Tributary MoP (?)	Slave mode of production, fragmented political organization. Colonial presence	Spanish and Portuguese (with slavery) colonies	c 1750
1771 – (United Kindgom) Mechanization textiles	British colony. Caste system	Defeat in the Opium War, Treaty-port cities	Feudalism/serfdom	Broader colonial presence	Independent (Brazil with slavery) and fragmented states	c. 1850
1826 – (United Kindgom) Railways, steam eng.	British colony. Post-1857 administration from British Monarchy. Foundation of INC (1885).	Ching´s imperial state in crisis. Self-strengthening movement.	Abolition of serfdom in 1861 Czarist state	Post-Berlin Conference (1885) colonialism.	Ind. and fragmented states. Slavery abolished (Cuba 1886, Brazil 1888)	c. 1890
1882 – (United States) Electricity	Strengthening of the Indian National Congress	Treaty-port cities, areas under Japanese occupation. Republic after 1911	End of Czarism. A non-capitalist economy. “War communism”. NEP. Stalinist model	Consolidated colonialism.	Independent and fragmented states	c. 1937
1908 – (United States) Automobile	Independence in 1947 First five-year plans (1951-1961). Import substitution industrialization	Foundation of PRC (1949). First five-year plan. Catch-up: USSR as reference	Stalinist model. Limited and incomplete catch up concluded	Beginning of the end of the colonial period	Beginning of import substitution industrialization	c. 1950
1971 – (United States) Microprocessor	Third and fourth five-year plans	Great step ahead. Crisis. Cultural Revolution. Catch-up: USA as reference	Long stagnation in Soviet Union	Consolidation of the movement for independent African nations	Independent and fragmented states. Import substitution industrialization	c. 1971

1991 – (CERN, Europe) world wide web	Reforms. End of political hegemony of the INC	End of Maoism. Transition: dual-track. New VoC. Catch-up: USA as reference	Final crisis of the Stalinism. Gorbachev. Transition: shock therapy. New VoC	Consolidation of independent and fragmented nations. Crisis of apartheid	Independent and fragmented states. End of import substitution industrialization	c. 1991
2011 – ????	A new peripheric VoC	Middle-income country. State-led VoC	Post-shock therapy VoC. Crisis. State-led VoC	Post-apartheid South Africa. Five different types of economies	Independent and fragmented states A Latin American VoC	c. 2011

Source: Big bangs: Perez (2010, p. 190), except for www. Arrival years and initial spread through the five regions: see references in Part II and Tables 3.1, 5.1, 6.1 and 7.2. Author's elaboration

Second, because specific feedback cycles between expansionary and assimilatory forces create different and unforeseen dynamics that shape and reshape economies.

Third, since technological revolutions are generated and spread globally, in uneven processes as shown in Part II, they create new layers, new structures and new hierarchies in the global economy. As these integrated processes take place, these old and new layers reshape the economic dynamics because new levels of aggregation mean new emergent properties (Ribeiro, 2022).

Fourth, because the different nuclei of capitalist accumulation and political initiatives from innovation systems at the periphery contribute also to a structural change – the emergence of a global innovation system.[13] This structural change, in turn, creates new channels both for expansionary and assimilatory forces, changing and strengthening them. Given the strength of their national systems of innovation countries at the center benefit from this global innovation system as they can assimilate knowledge from the rest of the world, including the contemporary periphery.

Fifth, these new institutions at the periphery – firms, universities, innovation systems – and the growth of their economies,[14] are among factors that create a new phenomenon: the impact of the periphery on the center – the boomerang effect (Marques, 2014). This new phenomenon should be integrated into an analysis of the international conjuncture. Changes at the periphery, consequences of the interplay between expansionary and assimilatory forces, are new sources of perturbations that affect the center – triggering a type of "infinity reciprocity" that Simmel (1907, p. 56) suggested in another context.

A final question deals with how the dynamics at the center and at the periphery might be combined. There might be a dynamic of the global system, with enough evidence of its self-organization – a key feature of complex systems. Ribeiro et al. (2017a, b) present evidence on the self-organized dynamic of capitalism in the United States, while Cimini et al. (2020) present evidence on the lack of this dynamic for peripheric countries in Latin America and India. The self-organized nature of the capitalist system at the center has also evidence for the United Kingdom, a feature that begins in the late eighteenth century (Melo, 2023). A conjecture would suggest that the periphery helps to organize the capitalist system at the center – cotton imports during UK's industrial revolution, global oil production for US postwar hegemony. Thus, an interesting research question – to investigate how a system that seems to be self-organized as a whole (global capitalism, as it has a dynamic defined by its leading center) may have parts that do not show this nature (peripheric regions without self-organized dynamic)?

[13]This structural change can be related to a new layer in this complex system, with new hierarchies (Britto et al., 2021).

[14]According to the World Bank (2023), since 2012 the aggregate GDP (PPP, 2017 international $) of low- and middle-income countries has overtaken the aggregate GDP of high-income countries (Marques, 2014).

References

Atlas of Economic Complexity. (2023). https://atlas.cid.harvard.edu/

Barnett, V. (1998). *Kondratiev and the dynamics of economic development: Long cycles and industrial growth in historical context*. Macmillan Press Ltd.

Britto, G., Camargo, O. S., Kruss, G., & Albuquerque, E. (2013). Global interactions between firms and universities. *Innovation and Development, 3*, 71–87.

Britto, J. N. P., Ribeiro, L. C., & Albuquerque, E. M. (2021). Global systems of innovation: Introductory notes on a new layer and a new hierarchy in innovation systems. *Innovation and Development, 11*(2–3), 259–279.

Cantwell, J. (2009). Innovation and information technology in the MNE. In: Rugman, A. M. (ed.), *The Oxford Handbook of International Business*. Oxford University Press: Oxford, Second Edition, pp. 417–446.

Cimini, F., Britto, J. N. P., & Ribeiro, L. C. (2020). Complexity systems and middle-income trap: The long-term roots of Latin America underdevelopment. *Nova Economia, 30*, 1225–1256.

Cohen, W., & Levinthal, D. (1989). Innovation and learning: The two faces of R&D. *The Economic Journal, 99*(397), 569–596.

Darwin, J. (2009). *The empire project: The rise and fall of the British world-system, 1830–1970*. Cambridge University Press.

Franco, M. P. V., Ribeiro, L. C., & Albuquerque, E. M. (2022). Beyond random causes: Harmonic analysis of business cycles at the Moscow Conjuncture Institute. *Journal of the History of Economic Thought, 44*(3), 456–476. https://doi.org/10.1017/S1053837221000092

Furtado, C. (1992). *Brasil: a construção interrompida*. São Paulo/Rio de Janeiro: Paz e Terra.

King, L. P., & Szelényi, I. (2005). Post-communist economic systems. In N. Smelser & R. Swedberg (Eds.), *The handbook of economic sociology* (2nd ed., pp. 205–229). Princeton University Press/Russel Sage Foundation.

Kruss, G., Adeoti, J. O., & Nabudere, D. (2015). Bracing for change: Making universities and firms partners for innovation in Sub-Saharan Africa. In E. Albuquerque, W. Suzigan, G. Kruss, & K. Lee (Eds.), *Developing national systems of innovation: University-industry interaction in global South* (pp. 31–54). Edward Elgar Publishing/IDRC.

Lee, K. (2013). *Schumpeterian analysis of economic catch up: knowledge, path-creation, and the middleincome trap*. Cambridge: Cambridge University Press.

Marques, S. F. (2014). *Mudanças na Clivagem Centro-Periferia e o Efeito Bumerangue: o impacto da periferia na reconfiguração sistêmica do capitalismo no século XXI*. Cedeplar-UFMG. (Tese de Doutorado).

Melo, B. C. (2023). *Estudo empírico de séries de preços com instrumental de sistemas complexos (Capítulo 3 da tese A economia como sistema complexo e o mercado como propriedade emergente: em busca de sinais de complexidade nos preços do trigo desde o séc. XIII)*. Cedeplar-UFMG.

Pavitt, K. (1997). Transforming centrally planned systems of science and technology: The problem of obsolete competencies. In D. A. Dyer (Ed.), *The technology of transition: Science and technology policies for transition countries* (pp. 43–60). Central European University Press.

Perez, C. (2010). Technological revolutions and techno-economic paradigms. *Cambridge Journal of Economics, 34*(1), 185–202.

Ribeiro, L. C. (2022). Sistemas complexos, economia e Covid-19. In E. M. Aluquerque, F. G. Jayme Jr., & G. Britto (Eds.), *Crise, pandemia e alternativas* (pp. 165–191). Cedeplar-UFMG.

Ribeiro, L. C., Deus, L. G., Loureiro, P. M., & Albuquerque, E. M. (2017a). Profits and fractal properties: Notes on Marx, countertendencies and simulation models. *Review of Political Economy, 29*(2), 282–306. Available at https://doi.org/10.1080/09538259.2016.1265823

Ribeiro, L. C., Deus, L. G., Loureiro, P. M., & Albuquerque, E. M. (2017b). A network model for the complex behavior of the rate of profit: Exploring a simulation model with overlapping technological revolutions. *Structural Change and Economic Dynamics, 43*, 51–61. Available at https://doi.org/10.1016/j.strueco.2017.07.001

Ribeiro, L. C., Rapini, M. S., Silva, L. A., & Albuquerque, E. (2018). Growth patterns of the network of international collaboration in science. *Scientometrics, 114*, 159–179.
Rosenberg, N. (1996). Uncertainty and technical change. In R. Landau, T. Taylor, & G. Wright (Eds.), *The mosaic of economic growth* (pp. 334–353). Stanford University.
Rosenberg, N. (1998). Chemical engineering as a general purpose technology. In E. Helpman (Ed.), *General purpose technologies and economic growth* (pp. 167–192). The MIT Press.
Schumpeter, J. A. (1911). *A teoria do desenvolvimento econômico*. Nova Cultural, 1985.
Simmel, G. (1907). *The philosophy of money* (3rd ed.). Routledge. (2004).
Slutsky, E. E. (1937). The summation of random causes as the source of cyclic processes. *Econometrica, 5*(2), 105–146.
Suzigan, W. (2017) Elementos essenciais da política industrial. In: Albuquerque, E. M. (org) *Metamorfoses do capitalismo e processos de catch-up*. Belo Horizonte: Editora da UFMG, pp. 253–267.
Tilly, C. (1993). *Coerção, capital e estados europeus*. Edusp. (1996).
Trotsky, L. (1930). *A história da revolução russa* (Vol. 1). Paz e Terra. (1978).
World Bank. (2023) *World Bank indicators*. https://data.worldbank.org/indicator

Chapter 9
Conclusion: An Agenda for Global Reform

The first technological revolution started a global geopolitical change – "an astonishing reversal" – with the United Kingdom becoming the leading cotton textile producer and the Indian subcontinent transformed in part of the periphery. The expansionary forces emanating from the "initial nucleus of industrialization" (Furtado, 1987) defined a new international division of labor. The www, the more recent technological revolution – and new technologies fermenting today – is the scenario for a "second reversal", in the opposite direction: increasingly powerful assimilatory forces organized at a heterogeneous periphery have changed the international division of labor to a point that it impacts the current reconfiguration of global capitalism.

From 1771 to 2023 the interplay between expansionary and assimilatory forces involved a multifaceted global scenario with many contradictions. On the one hand, institutions such as a global innovation system emerged, requiring more coordination and interaction among countries and regions. On the other hand, inequality increased among and within nations – reflecting more unevenness (Piketty, 2013).

The current reconfiguration of global capitalism presents, at the same time, opportunities and challenges. Those challenges – old and new – may present opportunities, especially the new potential created by the emergence of a global innovation system. This contradictory scenario, this contrast between new potential and new problems, suggest the need to elaborate, collectively and democratically, an agenda for global reform.

The interplay between expansionary and assimilatory forces presented in this book is behind the three big challenges faced by all societies, at the center and at the periphery.

First, this interplay led to successive reconfigurations of global capitalism – metamorphoses of capitalism -, changing the international division of labor. The current reconfiguration, based on a heterogeneous periphery, presents a growth of nuclei of capital accumulation dispersed throughout the five regions discussed in this

E. da Motta e Albuquerque, *Technological Revolutions and the Periphery*,
Contributions to Economics, https://doi.org/10.1007/978-3-031-43436-5_9

book. One of the main characteristics of today's capitalism is the boomerang effect (Marques, 2014), with the periphery impacting the center. A new geopolitical landscape is in formation, with new sources of international tensions and armed conflicts – previous geopolitical transformations involved wars in their making (Arrighi, 1994). This can be interpreted as an old challenge – how these broad geopolitical changes can unfold without wars, especially wars between the largest economies. This challenge includes one topic in an agenda for global reform: disarmament. A good starting point for disarmament could be a revival of discussions about peace dividend (Brzoska, 2007), that was on the agenda during the final moments of a big geopolitical change, the end of the Cold War.

Second, previous technological revolutions, especially the second – stemming from the appearance of the steam-engine – and the fourth – attributable to the rise of the combustion engine – led to an exponential growth of fossil fuels – respectively coal and oil -, with consequences related to global warming (Nobel Prize Committee, 2021, p. 6). Global warming is an international challenge that cannot be solved by countries acting in an isolated manner. Policies to contain global warming have proposals generated by international commissions – as the United Nations' International Panel on Climate Change (IPCC) – that highlight the importance of international R&D.

Third, as the interplay between expansionary and assimilatory forces led to a more interconnected world yet, also a world that aggressively transformed the natural environment around us, an unintended consequence is the systematic emergence of new infectious diseases, with strong potential of cross-country diffusion. Covid-19 is just a terrible most recent example of this problem (Cazzolla Gatti et al., 2021).

These three challenges interact with the emerging global system of innovation, although in different ways.

International tension, armed conflicts and wars – as the war in Ukraine now – may weaken international knowledge flows, and block further increase in international collaboration in science and technology. These impacts on international flow and collaboration weaken the process of formation of a global innovation system. Thus, one key point for an agenda for international reform is disarmament. This point is not an easy one, given the strong entrenchment of military reasons in the dynamic of modern capitalism, both in the center and in the periphery. Over time, both expansionary and assimilatory forces, as Part II shows in many different contexts, are related to military investments and actions. Innovations and economic policies of different nations had military motivations and military impacts. This entrenchment, this economic embeddedness of military investments in the structure of governments expenditures has survived the end of wars and big geopolitical changes, as the end of the Cold War. Consequently, this structural feature of contemporary capitalism leads to a total of US$ 2113 billion spent yearly in arms – data for 2021 (SIPRI, 2022). This might be evaluated as a great waste of scarce resources available for humankind to confront current global challenges.

Global warming is a challenge to be met by a provision of global public goods that can be produced by an emerging global innovation system (Franco et al., 2022, pp. 8–9). As global warming demands global actions, global investments and global R&D, the emergence of a global innovation system is a welcome structural change – this might be an institution necessary to match that challenge. Energy transition from fossil fuels, for example, demands much international research and international coordinated action.

The challenge of emerging infectious diseases (Brooks et al., 2019) is related to global warming, as it demands a new relationship with the environment. Thus, policies that deal with global warming will have positive impact on the risk of new emerging infectious diseases – precautionary action (Franco et al., 2022, pp. 2–3). But, to face emerging infectious diseases more global initiatives and global coordination would be necessary – an important editorial in *Science* (Berkley, 2020, p. 1407) suggested a big science approach to deal with Covid-19, with various international initiatives. The uneven and unbalanced distribution of resources for vaccine development, production, and distribution existing in early 2020 was a problem – this need is to be solved for a better management of next epidemics. These issues may be addressed with a more coordinated effort through the links that shape the emerging global innovation system.

If the global innovation system is related to the three challenges put forward to humankind now, it also has a relationship with another key contemporary problem: an international institutional mismatch. The interplay between expansionary and assimilatory forces built this increasingly interconnected world, an increasingly internationalized economy. However, there is a lack of international coordinating mechanisms and institutions to match that level of internationalization. Different agencies and entities from different spheres of action are demanding more international coordination. The Bank of International Settlements (BIS) evaluates globalization and reiterates the need for "international cooperation" (BIS, 2017, pp. 112–114). This institutional mismatch may be identified by the behavior of one Central Bank – the United States Federal Reserve Bank – that during the Covid-19 crisis had an international action, "as a global lender of last resort has been further cemented" (BIS, 2020, p. 48). The World Health Organization (WHO, 2020), during the Covid-19 pandemics tried to organize international fora to strengthen society's response to that challenge. The Intergovernmental Panel on Climate Change (IPCC, 2022) has been arguing for growing collaboration in multifarious dimensions to face the challenge of climate change.

So far, the emergence of a global innovation system has been a product of the interplay between expansionary and assimilatory forces. Is it possible to have a more organized and coordinated intervention to strengthen its formation? If yes, this intervention would be in line with other initiatives for more international coordination. In the case of the global innovation system, it could be funded by a reallocation of current arms expenditures – selected institutions of a global innovation system could be the target of these new investments.

As discussed elsewhere (Britto et al., 2021), a global innovation system is a new layer in innovation systems, a new layer that creates a new hierarchy that rearranges the role of other layers: the national, the sectoral, the regional and the local have new roles in this new international arrangement. These different layers were created at the periphery as part of the dynamic of assimilatory forces, institutional building to improve absorptive capacity, as illustrated in Part II across different technological revolutions. These national and local innovation systems have over time had peculiar interactions with expansionary forces, in an interplay discussed in Part III. The understanding of this interplay might help to design specific interventions to take advantage of the diversity of national systems to strengthen international knowledge flows that shape the global layer of innovation systems.

Heterogeneity, as it is linked to unevenness and inequality, is a problem. But diversity and different national specializations within a global system can be a strong point, an advantage. A better distribution of scientific and technological resources, starting from available innovation systems, is a necessary step in the agenda for reform.

New forms of interaction between expansionary and assimilatory forces could be investigated and discussed. As presented in Part III, there are various feedbacks between these forces, that may suggest lines for further elaboration.

Changes in expansionary forces would affect assimilatory forces, on the one hand: an international reform related to intellectual property rights could improve the diffusion of new technologies, especially for a potential contribution for assimilatory forces. A reform in intellectual property rights, dealing with the negative consequences of excessive monopoly power for patent owners (Boldrin & Levine, 2008),[1] may facilitate absorption and strengthen assimilatory forces.[2]

Changes in assimilatory forces, that would feedback expansionary forces, could be international reforms leading to disarmament. Global disarmament would have a positive impact on poorer countries' investments as they could avoid waste with arms expenditures reallocating them to focus on development policies with peaceful goals. This new framework could impact the center with further disarmament and further commitment with an agenda searching for new technologies for energy transition and management of emerging diseases.

The emergence of a global innovation system might have been one major unintended consequence of the interplay between expansionary and assimilatory forces. Now, this emerging new layer in innovation systems can be transformed into a channel that starts a new form of interaction between those two forces, articulating them to build from human diversity a more innovative and shared world.

---

[1] Arrow (2010, p. 47) cites Boldrin and Levine (2008).

[2] This reform would affect the variable θ in equation 1 from Cohen and Levinthal (1989, p. 571) – see Appendix in Chap. 2. If $\theta =$ zero, the absorption becomes more difficult. This situation would happen with strong patent protection of a specific innovation.

References

Arrighi, G. (1994). *O longo século XX: dinheiro, poder e as origens do nosso tempo*. Contraponto/Unesp (1996).

Arrow, K. J. (2010). The economics of inventive activity over fifty years. In J. Lerner & S. Stern (Eds.), *The rate and direction of inventive activity revisited* (pp. 43–48). University of Chicago Press.

Bank for International Settlements. (2017). *87th annual report*. BIS. (www.bis.org)

Bank for International Settlements. (2020). *90th annual report*. BIS. (www.bis.org)

Berkley, S. (2020). Covid-19 needs a big science approach – Editorial. *Science, 367*(6485), 1407. https://doi.org/10.1126/science.abb8654

Boldrin, M., & Levine, D. K. (2008). *Against intellectual monopoly*. Cambridge University Press.

Britto, J. N. P., Ribeiro, L. C., & Albuquerque, E. M. (2021). Global systems of innovation: Introductory notes on a new layer and a new hierarchy in innovation systems. *Innovation and Development, 11*(2–3), 259–279.

Brooks, D. R., Hoberg, E. P., & Boeger, W. A. (2019). *The Stockholm paradigm: Climate change and emerging diseases*. The University of Chicago Press.

Brzoska, M. (2007). Success and failure in defense conversion in the "long decade of disarmament". In T. Sandler & K. Hartley (Eds.), *Handbook of defense economics: Defense in a globalized world* (pp. 1177–1209). North Holland.

Cazzolla Gatti, R., Menéndez, L. P., Laciny, A., Bobadilla Rodríguez, H., Bravo Morante, G., Carmen, E., Dorninger, C., Fabris, F., Grunstra, N. D. S., Schnorr, S. L., Stuhlträger, J., Villanueva Hernandez, L. A., Jakab, M., Sarto-Jackson, I., & Caniglia, G. (2021). Diversity lost: COVID-19 as a phenomenon of the total environment. *Science of the Total Environment, 756*, 144014. https://doi.org/10.1016/j.scitotenv.2020.144014

Cohen, W., & Levinthal, D. (1989, September). Innovation and learning: The two faces of R&D. *The Economic Journal, 99*(397), 569–596.

Franco, M. P. V., Molnar, O., Dorninger, C., Laciny, A., Treven, M., Weger, J., Albuquerque, E. M., Gatti, R. C., Hernandez, A. V., Jakab, M., Marizzi, C., Menendez, L. P., Poliseli, L., Rodriguez, H. B., & Caniglia, G. (2022). Diversity regained: Precautionary approaches to COVID-19 as a phenomenon of the total environment. *Science of the Total Environment, 825*, 1–14. https://doi.org/10.1016/j.scitotenv.2022.154029

Furtado, C. (1987). Underdevelopment: To conform or to reform. In G. Meier (Ed.), *Pioneers of development* (Second series) (pp. 203–227). Oxford University/World Bank.

Intergovernmental Panel on Climate Change. (2022). *Climate change 2022: Impacts, adaptation and vulnerability*. Cambridge University Press. https://report.ipcc.ch/ar6/wg2/IPCC_AR6_WGII_FullReport.pdf

Marques, S. F. (2014). *Mudanças na Clivagem Centro-Periferia e o Efeito Bumerangue: o impacto da periferia na reconfiguração sistêmica do capitalismo no século XXI*. Cedeplar-UFMG. (Tese de Doutorado).

Nobel Prize Committee. (2021). *The Nobel prize in physics 2021 – Popular science background*. The Royal Swedish Academy of Sciences. https://www.nobelprize.org/uploads/2021/10/popular-physicsprize2021-2.pdf

Piketty, T. (2013). *Capital in the twenty-first century*. The Belknap Press of Harvard University Press (2014).

SIPRI. (2022). *Trends in world military expenditure, 2021*. SIPRI. https://www.sipri.org/sites/default/files/2022-04/fs_2204_milex_2021_0.pdf

World Health Organization. (2020). *Global research on coronavirus disease (COVID-19)*. https://www.who.int/emergencies/diseases/novel-coronavirus-2019/global-research-on-novel-coronavirus-2019-ncov

MIX
Papier aus verantwortungsvollen Quellen
Paper from responsible sources
FSC® C105338

If you have any concerns about our products,
you can contact us on
ProductSafety@springernature.com

In case Publisher is established outside the EU,
the EU authorized representative is:
Springer Nature Customer Service Center GmbH
Europaplatz 3, 69115 Heidelberg, Germany

Printed by Libri Plureos GmbH
in Hamburg, Germany